המסורה

The ArtScroll History Series®

Rabbis Nosson Scherman / Meir Zlotowitz
General Editors

Adapted by
Rabbi Hersh Goldwurm

from Dr. Eliezer Ebner's translation of
Yekutiel Friedner's
"Divrei Y'mei HaBayit HaSheini"

Published by
Mesorah Publications, ltd

in conjunction with
HILLEL PRESS / *Jerusalem*

History of the Jewish People

THE SECOND TEMPLE ERA

FIRST EDITION
First Impression . . . November, 1982
Second Impression . . . August, 1983
Third Impression . . . September, 1986
Fourth Impression . . . February, 1988

Published and Distributed by
MESORAH PUBLICATIONS, Ltd.
Brooklyn, New York 11223

Distributed in Israel by
MESORAH MAFITZIM / J. GROSSMAN
Rechov Harav Uziel 117
Jerusalem, Israel

Distributed in Europe by
J. LEHMANN HEBREW BOOKSELLERS
20 Cambridge Terrace
Gateshead, Tyne and Wear
England NE8 1RP

THE ARTSCROLL HISTORY SERIES®
HISTORY OF THE JEWISH PEOPLE / The Second Temple Era
© Copyright 1982, by MESORAH PUBLICATIONS, Ltd.
1969 Coney Island Avenue / Brooklyn, N.Y. 11223 / (718) 339-1700

ILLUSTRATION CREDITS:
Most photographs appearing in this volume are by courtesy of the Israel Government Printing Office, Jerusalem.
Grateful acknowledgment is hereby also made to the Keter Publishing House Archives
and to the following sources:
Bank of Israel Collection, Jerusalem / *Bibliotheque Publique*, Dijon / H. Bieberkraut, Jerusalem
N. Garo, Jerusalem / David Harris, Jerusalem / Israel Dept. of Antiquities, Jerusalem
Israel Museum, Jerusalem / Bessin Collection, Jerusalem / Shrine of the Book, Jerusalem
J.B. Pritchard, *The Ancient Near East* (Supplementary Texts), Princeton, 1979
Zeev Radovan, Jerusalem / Vatican Library, Rome / Y. Yadin, Jerusalem

ISBN
0-89906-454-X (hard cover)
0-89906-455-8 (paperback)

Typography by CompuScribe at ArtScroll Studios, Ltd., Brooklyn, NY
1969 Coney Island Avenue / Brooklyn, N.Y. 11223 / (718) 339-1700

Printed in the United States of America by
EDISON LITHOGRAPHING AND PRINTING CORP.

Table of Contents

Preface

It is scarcely believable, but true, that the story of the People of the Book has been woefully ill-told, particularly in English. Only in recent times have Jews produced professional historians, and in the great majority of cases they have plied their craft with the tools of their profession, using acknowledged sources and accepted methods, and following the traditions and prejudices of the ancient Greek and Roman writers to whom Judea represented an enemy, a vassal state, and an unacceptable religion and culture. The result is that historians have seen ancient Israel from the outside looking in. They have understood it — and portrayed it — as a plaything of the Greek and Macedonian kingdoms, a hapless victim of triumphant Rome and a benighted foe of emergent Christianity. There has been a remarkable and regrettable paucity of historical writing that dealt with Israel as it saw *itself* and as it interpreted its *own* mission, successes and failures. It is as though the history of the United States had been written by Indians, Englishmen, Germans, and Russians — but never by Americans.

Obviously, there must be many gaps in any history of ancient times, because the sort of contemporary sources we take for granted today simply did not exist in ancient times. Even the dating systems from Creation or relative to the Common Era were not in use then. Consequently, we often lack firm identification even of reigning monarchs, and there are frequent discrepancies regarding dates, places, and happenings. Not surprisingly, given the dependent state of Judea during the period described in this book, the Jewish version of events has been given little credence. The written histories of the time were by Greeks and Romans; the accounts of their victims have either not survived or been disregarded. Truth is always a victim in such a state of affairs. Even contemporary times illustrate amply well that to the winner usually belong not only the spoils, but the privilege and power to define the "truth" as it will be read and accepted by future generations.

In this sense, little Judea was the victim not only of the superpowers of its day, but of the chroniclers of the period. Tragically, the Jewish nation has had little more influence on the authorship of its own history than the Sioux Indian nation has had on that of American history.

We are particularly gratified, therefore, to make available to teachers, students, and the general public this volume on the history of the Second Temple era. It is based on Yekutiel's Friedner's *Divrei Yemei HaBayis HaSheni,* which has become a standard text in the Israeli school system. Friedner's research concentrated on traditional Jewish sources and incorporated other material that does not do violence to this primary focus. In this edition, Friedner's work has been considerably augmented by the noted scholar and historian, Rabbi Hersh Goldwurm.

Clearly this relatively short volume does not pretend to be exhaustive; on the other hand, so little is known about the period that no authentically Jewish book could pretend to chronicle the times like a modern newspaper. Nevertheless, this book — and those that will follow it — is an important contribution to Jewish students of all ages. It is our hope that it will help launch a greater awareness and appreciation of the past, and encourage others to do further research in the field.

Transliteration, Names, and Dates

In this book, the transliteration follows the method used throughout the ArtScroll Series: Ashkenazic consonants and Sephardic vowels. For example, we use *Beis HaMikdash,* rather than *Bet HaMikdash* or *Beis HaMikdosh.*

In the case of names, we are faced with the dilemma of Hebrew names, Biblical or otherwise, that are Anglicized in such a way that they may be unrecognizable to the reader or student of Hebrew literature (for example, Shlomo/Solomon). On the other side of the coin are non-Jewish figures whose Hebraicized names are much different from the names one encounters in general reading (for example, Darius/Daryavesh). We have adopted the following course: in the case of Hebrew names that are familiar from Scripture or the Talmud, but whose Anglicized names are much different, we use the Hebrew name, but the first time it appears, it is followed by the Anglicized name in italics. For example, Chizkiyahu [Hezekiah]. In the case of non-Jewish names, we follow the opposite course: Darius [Daryavesh].

Generally we have used the name "Judea" to refer to the area inhabited by the Jewish people during the Second Temple era. We have done this because the territory given to the returnees, as well as that controlled by Jews through most of the period of this book, was a relatively small province with Jerusalem at its center. It was not the much larger area "from Dan to Beer Sheba" that is implied by the name *Eretz Yisrael.*

In the matter of dates, we have used the familiar system of BCE (Before the Common Era) and CE (Common Era), and given the year from creation in parentheses. For example, 538 BCE (3223) and 70 CE (3830). The apparent downgrading of the Hebrew year from creation was done with some misgiving, obviously. However, since we consider it important to relate the events of Jewish history to those in the world around Judea, the use of the more familiar dating seems advisable. This is especially true of the forthcoming volumes of this History Series. Clearly, the average reader would see no special significance in a mention of the year 5536, but its secular equivalent, 1776, immediately gives the reader a perspective of the world in that year.

In connection with the dating of Jewish history, we call the reader's attention to the two important appendices and the chronology table at the end of this volume.

Acknowledgments

We are grateful to Rabbi Dr. Eliezer Ebner, the noted scholar and educator, who translated the work from Hebrew, and we express our thanks to Uri Kaploun who edited the initial draft of the translation.

Rabbi Hersh Goldwurm placed the stamp of his brilliance and erudition on this book as he has on so many other ArtScroll volumes.

We are humbly grateful to Maran Harav Yaakov Kaminecki for his guidance in many delicate questions of fact and approach.

In planning this publication we benefited from the guidance and constructive suggestions of such leading scholars and educators as Rabbis Asher L. Ehrenreich, Joseph Elias, Avi Greenberg, Joel Kramer, Michoel Levi, Moshe Possick, Shlomo Teichman; Mrs. Miriam Cohen, Mrs. Devorah Greenberg, Mrs. Buna Shulman, and others. We hope the finished product adequately reflects their kindness and sagacity.

Finally we express our gratitude to our colleagues, Reb Sheah Brander, whose graphic skill makes the book a thing of beauty; Rabbi Avie Gold, for his perceptive reading and criticism; and the entire staff of Mesorah Publications Ltd., and Hillel Press for their yeoman efforts in the production of the book.

Rosh Chodesh Kislev, 5743 / November, 1982

Rabbis Nosson Scherman / Meir Zlotowitz   Meir Holder
Mesorah Publications   *Hillel Press*

The End of the First Temple Era

Theme of Jewish History

Since the time of Avraham *Avinu* [the Patriarch Abraham], the Jewish mission had been a spiritual one. Its prophets and leaders had constantly drummed into the people's national consciousness that Israel's national success depended on its spiritual and moral strength. The historical accounts of the early books of the Prophets recount how spiritual downfall resulted in foreign invasion and overlordship; repentance and spiritual renewal were followed by military triumph and political independence.

This concept is the thread that runs through the history of the Jewish people from the time it left Egypt throughout the 890 years until the First Temple was destroyed and the people were exiled. And this concept is important for a proper understanding of both the Biblical narrative and the Jewish people's view of itself throughout its later history.

In a sense, similar phenomena occur frequently in the history of countries, institutions, movements — even of families. People organize themselves to carry out an ideal. The result is that the new body — whether a government or some other sort of organization — is

devoted to carrying out an ideal. All activities are judged by how well they

The seated figure painted on this pottery sherd found in Jerusalem and dating back to c. 600 BCE is believed by archaeologists to represent one of the kings of Judah.

contribute to the common cause. In a family, for example, as long as each of its members strives to achieve the goal of the entire unit — spiritual, economic, health, or whatever else it may be — the chances are good that there will be love, cooperation, mutual respect, and even success. But as time goes by, individual members of the family may begin to turn selfish or lazy, or look for new personal goals. When that happens, the result is usually strife and disruption. On a much larger scale, such easing of dedication has caused the failure of corporations and the decline of nations.

When the signs of such decay first begin to set in, they are rarely recognizable. Only the historians, usually generations later, can sift the evidence and point to the first symptoms of breakdown. They will seldom agree completely on exactly when and where the slide began, but they can show us how it progressed. Library shelves are filled with learned works tracing the "decline and fall" of nations and industrial empires. It is axiomatic, when history is understood in this manner, that the unit under study has ceased to exist as a vigorous, thriving, aggressive entity long before its final collapse. When its vitality is gone, it is only a matter of time before its destruction, just as the breakdown of the human brain, heart, or lungs are inevitably followed by the death of the body.

When we understand the mission of the Jewish people as the Torah and the nation itself defined it, we realize that the destruction of the First Commonwealth of Israel in its land began long before the physical conquest of Jerusalem and the dispersal of the people. Once the people began to fall from the high moral standards demanded of it, inner rot began to set in. Once the spiritual justification for Israel's independence began to be undermined, it was only a matter of time before the end.

Menashe's Reign — The Turning Point

The final turning point came in 533 BCE (3228 from Creation). Until then, the people could still be expected to reverse their course and return to the level that had made them great in the reigns of David, Shlomo [Solomon] and Chizkiyahu [Hezekiah]. But in that year, Menashe [Manasseh] became king of Judea, and he began a chain of events that made it virtually impossible for the eventual tragedy to be averted.

With the ascension of Menashe to the throne of Jerusalem, the sun began to set upon the era of the First Temple. For one hundred and ten more years, until the Babylonian conquest in the year 423 BCE (3338),[1] some semblance of independence would continue. But more and more, the soul of the Jewish people would crumble, eroded by the cancerous evil of the idol worship, which Menashe planted among them during his long, fifty-five year reign

1. This date is taken from *Seder Olam* (which, with the Talmud, is the most authoritative source of Jewish chronology) as are the other dates cited in the Prologue and in ch. 1-3 of this book. However, as explained in the appendix "Year of the Destruction," the Jewish calendar currently in use adds one year to the Talmudic chronology. Thus, *Seder Olam's* date of 3338 for the Destruction, would be called 3339 under the current calendar. [This does *not* mean, of course, that there is any disagreement over when the respective events *happened*. As the appendix explains, the difference involves only from when we count the year 1.] Nevertheless, in the first part of this book, we have retained the dates of *Seder Olam* simply because they are so familiar that it

[533-478 BCE (3228-3283)]. In the end, the physical destruction of the Land and Temple would be little more than the outward completion of the inner decay to which the nation had gradually succumbed.

Menashe's father, Chizkiyahu, had carried his people to a glorious peak of spiritual attainment. He had been a "Prince of Peace" and had come very close to becoming the Messiah. In his Divinely inspired vision, however, he saw that he would give birth to a son whose destructive wickedness would go beyond anything that had been known before —

and this knowledge was the sorrow of his life.

His worst fears were confirmed. Although Menashe eventually repented, his wickedness was so destructive of the moral fiber of the people, that the fate of Jerusalem was sealed. The Land would be laid waste and the Temple would be destroyed, because of the "anger which Menashe had angered Him."

Menashe's fifty-five years were followed by the two-year reign of his son Amon, whose wickedness exceeded even that of his father.

Yoshiyahu — Vain Hope

Just as a flame flickers most brightly just before it dies, hope shone once more in Jerusalem. Amon's son, Yoshiyahu [Josiah], who reigned 476-445 BCE (3285-3316), rejected the heritage of evil which had come to him from his father and grandfather. With unprecedented energy Yoshiyahu set about to forge a renewed covenant between G-d and people and to cleanse the land of the idolatrous filth by which it had been inundated.

Yoshiyahu died at the hands of the Egyptian king, Pharaoh Nechoh. Had he lived, the final holocaust might have been averted; as it was, his life was extinguished before his task was completed. Outwardly the people followed his lead, but their souls remained sick and their allegiance belonged to the familiar idols in whom Menashe and Amon had taught them to seek comfort.

For another twenty-two years, the agony was to draw out. Yoshiyahu's son, Yehoachaz [Jehoahaz], reigned for only three months in 445 BCE (3316). The Pharaoh who had killed Yoshiyahu deposed Yehoachaz and placed his brother Yohoyakim [Jehoiakim] on the throne.

The eleven turbulent years, 445-434 BCE (3316-3327), of Yehoyakim's rule witnessed the beginnings of the power struggle between the ascending might of Babylon and its firmly entrenched archenemy, Egypt. After becoming a tributary of Nebuchadnezzar of Babylon, Yehoyakim eventually died an ignominious death while a captive in Babylonian hands.

In 434 BCE (3327), his son Yehoyachin [Jehoiachin] succeeded to the throne, but reigned for only three months. He was taken to Babylon with the first great wave

would have been confusing for us to change them. This is especially true for the date of the Destruction of the First Temple, which many people have memorized as 3338. For this reason, we have not tampered with these familiar dates. A well-known memory device has been used for this date: the word שָׁלַח, "He sent away," i.e., G-d sent away the Jewish nation; the word שָׁלַח has the numerical value of 338.

Nebuchadnezzar's capture of Jerusalem and destruction of the First Beis HaMikdash (see II Kings 24:10ff) is described in this tablet of the Babylonian Chronicle.

final eleven years, 434-423 BCE (3327-3338), of Israel's travail. Yirmeyahu [Jeremiah] was the prophet in Jerusalem, exhorting the people until the very end to turn once more to G-d.

His message fell upon deaf ears. Israel's future lay not with the pitiful remnant which was left in Jerusalem, but with the vibrant exile community which was about to be established in Babylon.

Yechezkel [Ezekiel] would be prophet, guide, and mentor to this emerging community. Upon them, he would erect his fabulous visions of the glorious future which would be built upon the ruins of their tragic history.

In the ninth year of Tzidkiyahu's reign, Nebuchadnezzar besieged Jerusalem. In the eleventh year of his reign, hunger overpowered the city and its fortifications were breached. Tzidkiyahu fled but was taken captive and brought to Nebuchadnezzar who ordered that he be forced to witness the slaughter of his children and then be blinded. The Temple, the royal palace, and the entire city were burned down by the Babylonian conquerors, and the city wall was destroyed. The remnant of the people were exiled by Nebuzaradan, the Babylonian commander. The vessels and copper pillars of the Temple were looted, and the leaders of the people executed in Rivlah by order of Nebuchadnezzar.

of exiles. These exiles were the elite of Jerusalem's people, including the great scholars and leaders of the period, including such men as Mordechai, Daniel and Yechezkel [Ezekiel] who were to shape Israel's future.

Only the "lowly people of the Land" remained. Over them, Yehoyachin's uncle, Tzidkiyahu [Zedekiah], would reign for the

The Exile Begins

In addition to the burning of the Temple, the Babylonians conquered the whole land, devastating its cities and villages. Even the Jews who survived the catastrophe were not allowed to remain in their homeland. Caravans of tortured and humiliated Jews were led in iron chains into exile in Babylonia, their captors having left only a small number of the poorer inhabitants behind.

The Babylonians did not want to exile Yirmeyahu together with the rest of the people, but he refused to remain a free man while his brothers were led away in chains as slaves. He searched for them on all the roads that led to Babylonia, until he came upon one road marked with traces of blood. Then he knew — this was the road on which his brothers had been taken into exile.

He looked closely at the ground and when he discerned traces left by the feet of small children he stooped low and kissed them. Reaching the captives, he embraced them and wept aloud, and they, too, wept with him. He moaned, "Woe to you, my brothers and my people, for this happened to you because you did not listen to the words of my prophecy."

So deep was his love for his brothers that he took one of their iron chains and put it around his neck. In this way he hoped to show how he identified with them in their suffering.

As Yirmeyahu and the captives reached the border of the Holy Land on their way to Babylonia, G-d appeared to him and commanded him to return to Judea. G-d assured him that He Himself would accompany the exiles to Babylonia and be for them a "Small Sanctuary." Upon hearing this, the Prophet took leave of his brothers and returned to Jerusalem.

Even after they arrived at their destination their suffering was not over. Many of them died because they drank the unsanitary waters of the Euphrates river. Nebuchadnezzar, the Babylonian king, continued to humiliate the captive Jews: when he noticed their erect posture, he forced them to stoop.

The *Psalms* reflect vividly both their misery and their proud reaction to it. We read: "By the rivers of Babylon we sat and wept as we recalled Zion." When the king saw the Levites on the shore of the Euphrates, carrying the musical instruments they had used in the Holy Temple in remembrance of their past glory, he commanded them: "Sing for us a song of Zion!" But the Levites took their lyres and hung them on the branches of the willow trees. Then they put their right thumbs into their mouths and mutilated them with their teeth. "How can we now play?" they asked. Their answer really meant: "How can we sing the song of G-d on foreign soil?" They then took this solemn oath:

If I forget you, O Jerusalem, let my right hand forget its skill. Let my tongue adhere to my palate if I fail to recall you, if I fail to elevate Jerusalem above my foremost joy (Psalms 137).

Gedaliah is Assassinated

A minority of the survivors were allowed to remain in their land under the leadership of Gedaliah ben Achikam [Ahikam]. When this became known, Jews who had escaped from the horrors of the war into neighboring countries — Edom, Moab, and Ammon — gradually returned to their towns and homesteads in Judea.

The neighbors of Israel were still not satisfied with the extent of the Jewish defeat; nothing but complete annihilation would do. Baalis, King of Ammon, induced Yishmael [Ishmael] ben Nesanyah [Nethaniah] to assassinate Gedaliah. Yishmael, one of the princes of Judea, envied Gedaliah's royal appointment as governor of Judea; this jealousy so blinded him that he agreed to carry out the designs of the Ammonite king.

Gedaliah's friends, particularly Yochanan [Johanan] ben Kareach [Kareah], tried to warn him against Yishmael, but to no avail. Gedaliah refused to listen to evil gossip. Yishmael and his followers arrived in Mitzpah, where Gedaliah lived. They acted as if they were friends, and Gedaliah invited them to his table. Suddenly, in the middle of the meal, they sprang up and fell upon Gedaliah and his people, killing them all. He had been governor of Judea for only fifty-two days.

The murder of Gedaliah ben Achikam extinguished the last spark of hope for a renewal of Jewish life in the Holy Land. Now the destruction became complete. Within seven years, the land turned into a barren desert. For fifty-two years all living creatures shunned it, as Yirmeyhau had foretold:

> Upon the mountains I shall weep and lament and to the desert oasis shall I carry mourning. Because they have become deserted by men, and the lowing of the cattle is no longer heard; even the birds of the sky and the cattle all wandered away (Jeremiah 9:9).

The day Gedaliah ben Achikam was killed has been likened to the day when the Temple was destroyed because it caused the end of a Jewish settlement in Eretz Yisrael for many years. The prophets declared that the anniversary of the tragedy should be a day of fasting. Since that time our people have four days of fasting and repentance related to the destruction of the Holy Temple:

— The tenth day of Teves, marking the beginning of the siege of Jerusalem;

— the seventeenth day of Tammuz, marking the breaching of the city's walls [actually, the walls were breached on the ninth of Tammuz in the year of the first Destruction; nevertheless, since the walls were breached on the seventeenth during the second Destruction, that day was proclaimed as the permanent fast day];

— the ninth day of Av is the anniversary of the burning of both Temples; and

— the fast of Gedaliah, on the third day of Tishrei, is the memorial to the murder of the righteous governor and the final devastation of Judea.

Those who survived the bloody war following Yishmael's assassination of Gedaliah sought to escape to Egypt. They were afraid that the Babylonians would seek revenge on them for the murder of the governor they had appointed. They went down to Egypt, and even forced Yirmeyahu and his disciple, Baruch ben Neriah, to go with them.

For seven years they lived in the Egyptian exile. In the eighth year the Babylonian king, Nebuchadnezzar, sent his army against Egypt. They laid waste to the country and brought ruination to the Judean remnant who had settled there. Only a few people succeeded in escaping the sword. Among them were Yirmeyahu and Baruch, who now went to join their brothers in Babylonia.

1

The Babylonian Exile

Rabban Yochanan ben Zakkai said: "Why was Israel exiled to Babylonia and not to another land? Because the household of their patriarch Abraham came from there" (Tosefta, Bava Kama 7:2).

The Jewish Community in Babylonia

The Holy Temple in Jerusalem had been destroyed and Jewish independence had been ended by the Babylonian army of King Nebuchadnezzar. Not since the brutal years of slavery in Egypt had Israel's destiny been so bleak. But the blackest clouds of the Destruction had a silver lining. As the Talmudic sages describe it, "G-d had poured out His wrath on wood and stones," but spared the nation. The people were exiled to Babylonia, a good land, where they rallied from their sufferings and where they repented. Despite the initial humiliation of the exile, they were gradually able to build their lives anew in this alien environment, which in time proved to be the crucible in which they were to be cleansed.

The Babylonian rulers allowed the exiles to conduct their lives with much independence. They no longer looked upon the Jews as objects of persecution, as they did at the time of the destruction of Jerusalem and during the forced march into exile.

The expected difficulties of adjustment in a new country were tolerable as well. To begin with, the Jews did not find it hard to learn the native language, Aramaic, as it closely resembled Hebrew. Furthermore, upon their arrival they were helped by their fellow Jews who had come to Babylonia before the Destruction, which took place in 423 BCE (3338). The earlier exiles had established themselves and were able to comfort the newcomers and make it easier for them to adapt to their new and strange environment.

Eleven years before the Destruction, in the time of King Yehoyachin, Nebuchadnezzar exiled some 10,000 Jews — the sages and righteous men of the nation, the elite of the people. Among these exiles were the youths whom Nebuchadnezzar had brought to Babylonia. They included Daniel, Chananiah [Hananiah], Mishael and Azariah, who later became the instruments of great miracles through which G-d displayed His power among the nations.

The earlier exiles did not believe that their banishment would last for very long. They expected every day to return to their homeland, to go up to Jerusalem and the Holy Temple. But the Prophet Yirmeyahu sent them a message, saying that their exile was a decree from Heaven which they had to accept:

> Build houses and settle down, plant gardens and eat their fruit. Marry women and bear sons and daughters, and take wives for your sons and give your daughters to husbands, so that they may bear sons and daughters; increase there and do not become less. Seek the welfare of the city to which I have exiled you and pray to Hashem for her, because through her peace you will have peace (Jeremiah 29:5-7).

Accordingly, the Jews in Babylonia settled in towns along the Euphrates River, built their houses at a distance from the gentiles, and worked for their livelihood.

"I have been for them a small sanctuary in the countries where they came" (Ezekiel 11:16)

Living in a land of idolaters, how could they maintain their lives as Jews? How could they serve G-d, they asked themselves, when they could no longer offer sacrifices in the Holy Temple in Jerusalem, the place chosen by G-d for the presence of His spirit?

They received the answer to these troubling questions from the sages and prophets in their midst. Their spiritual guides told them that they must establish "Small Sanctuaries" — houses of Torah study and synagogues for prayer. Thus, in the course of time, Babylonia became a

spiritual center for the entire people.

Jewish life flourished there throughout the period of the Second Temple and for hundreds of years thereafter, until that center, too, was destroyed. It produced the giants who established and laid the foundation for the study of the Torah for all coming generations, ensuring by their life-work that the Torah would not be forgotten from Israel. Two such men are Ezra the Scribe, who "restored the crown of Torah to its former glory" at the beginning of the Second Temple era, and Hillel the *Nasi* (leader or prince) who lived near its close.

There was, however, a serious threat. Living in a flourishing civilization that boasted mighty cities teeming with trade and commerce, and impressive pagan temples and monuments, would not the Jews succumb to their environment and assimilate in it? This did not happen because now that they could observe their idolatrous neighbors at close range, the Jews realized how inferior and corrupt the Babylonian lifestyle was. They rejected it and kept their distance from it.

Predictably, there were some Jews who veered toward assimilation. They argued that by allowing the Temple to be destroyed, G-d had rejected His people. Despairing of the future, they sought to separate themselves from their fellow Jews and become like the gentiles around them. These men the Prophet Yechezkei addressed as follows:

"What enters your thoughts — it shall not be! What you say: 'Let us be like the nations, like the families of the lands, to serve wood and stone.' As I live," the words of Hashem/Elokim, "with a strong hand and an outstretched arm and an outpoured fury will I rule over you" (Ezekiel 20:32-33).

As the people turned their hearts to G-d in *teshuvah* (repentance), the prophet roused in them a spirit of hope. He brought them this divine assurance:

"As I live," the words of Hashem/Elokim, "I do not desire the death of the wicked one, but the wicked one's return from his way that he will live. Repent from your evil ways; why should you die, O family of Israel?" (Ezekiel 33:11).

Daniel and his Friends

Daniel, Chananiah, Mishael and Azariah had been exiled to Babylonia eleven years before the Destruction of the Temple. Together with the sons of princes, they were selected to serve King Nebuchadnezzar in person. Daniel was only fifteen years old when he was put to a severe test. The king had commanded that these youthful but promising attendants be served the same food and wine that graced only the royal table. Daniel and his friends refused to taste these delicacies; they would not soil their souls with forbidden food. G-d caused the chief cook to take a liking to them, and instead of the regular meals, he gave them various beans and water. After ten days of such a diet, they looked healthier than the non-Jewish attendants who ate the choicest food. In wisdom, too, they rose tenfold above all the sages of the kingdom. Before long, therefore, the king appointed them officials in his court.

During this period G-d had made

Nebuchadnezzar great and powerful, giving him dominion over many kingdoms. When Nebuchadnezzar had reached the peak of his glory, G-d subdued before him the Kingdom of Yehudah, but the year after the conquest of *Eretz Yisrael,* Nebuchadnezzar began to worry about the future of his mighty empire.

Then he had a dream in which G-d revealed to him the end of his kingdom and the sequence of historical eras until the coming of *Mashiach* [the Messiah].

In his dream-vision, Nebuchadnezzar saw a huge and fearsome statue. Its head was of gold, its chest and arms of silver, its thighs of copper, its legs of iron, and its feet and toes were partly of iron and partly of earthenware. Suddenly a small stone rolled, as if by itself, towards the statue and hit it, whereupon the colossus broke up, its fragments flying in all directions. The small stone then grew into a mighty mountain — and the king awoke from his sleep.

Deeply disturbed, he tried to recall the frightening dream, but to no avail. As his distress grew, he summoned all his wise men and commanded them to reveal to him both the dream and its meaning. If they failed to do so, they would die. The Babylonian sages were perplexed and terrified. How could they be expected to interpret a dream that the king could not even remember?

Daniel and his friends, too, were subject to the command and the threat. He prayed fervently, and G-d granted his plea in a dream by revealing to him both the king's dream and its meaning.

Daniel appeared before Nebuchadnezzar and revealed to him the dream and its interpretation. The golden head represented Nebuchadnezzar himself, who, by the will of G-d, ruled over all the known kingdoms. The silver chest and arms symbolized Persia and Media, which, although of lesser power, would replace Babylonia. The copper thighs represented Greece, the third and weaker empire, copper being inferior to silver and gold. The iron legs were a symbol of the harsh rule of the fourth empire, Rome, the successor to Greece. It was likened to iron because it would be harsh and cruel to those it conquered. The feet, partly of iron and partly of clay, represented the two kingdoms that would rise from the ruins of Rome. One was the Christian kingdom of Edom, the so-called Holy Roman Empire, and the other, the Moslem kingdom of Ishmael. The toes (again of iron and clay) indicated the many countries that would come from the break-up of these large empires. As to the small stone, it was the symbol of the King *Mashiach,* who would overthrow these kingdoms and rule in their place.

Well pleased with Daniel's words, Nebuchadnezzar elevated him to high honors. But at the same time, disturbed by the above prophecy that *Mashiach* would rule at the End of Days, he thought of a plan calculated to hurt the Jews. He erected a large statue in the Valley of Dura and commanded all the peoples under his rule — including representatives of the Jews — to bow down before it. When the king was told that Chananiah, Mishael, and Azariah refused to obey this command, he had them cast into a burning furnace. But G-d sent an angel to protect His holy servants: the fire had no power over them. The king, who was present to witness their punishment, was stunned. He had them released, and they were completely unharmed! To this day we refer to this miracle when we pray: "May He Who answered Chananiah, Mishael and Azariah inside the burning furnace answer us."

The Valley of Dura was the scene of yet another miracle. G-d sent the Prophet Yechezkel to a part of the valley that was filled with bones. They were the remains of members of the tribe of Ephraim, who had left Egypt thirty years before the appointed time of Israel's liberation. G-d told Yechezkel to address the withered bones in prophecy. Suddenly there was movement among them — bone came to bone; flesh, muscles and skin formed around them; within them life began to stir, and they rose on their feet; they were now an exceedingly great army. Yechezkel brought the message of this vision to the dispirited exiles, telling them that just as dry bones could come to life, so G-d

Artist's conception of the floor plan of the future Temple as envisioned by Yechezkel. From ArtScroll Ezekiel, volume 3.

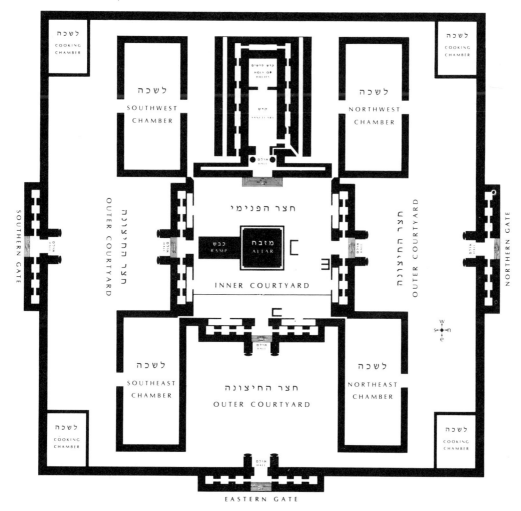

would breathe new life into the exiled nation of Israel. It would leave the pit of exile and return to its homeland.

> And He said to me, "Son of man, these bones — they are the whole family of Israel. Behold! they say, 'Our bones have dried and our hope is lost. We are doomed.' Therefore, prophesy and say to them: 'Thus says Hashem/Elokim: Behold! I ' open your graves and raise you up from your graves, O My people, and I shall bring you to the soil of Israel. Then you shall know that I am Hashem' " (Ezekiel 37:11-13).

"When the wicked perish there is joy" *(Proverbs 11:10)*

In 397 BCE (3364), twenty-six years after the Destruction of the Temple, Nebuchadnezzar died, and was succeeded by Evil-merodach. The death of Nebuchadnezzar caused rejoicing among the Jews. For the two Judean kings Yehoyachin and Tzidkiyahu it meant the end of their imprisonment. Although the blind Tzidkiyahu died soon after he was released and told of the death of his cruel captor, Yehoyachin lived on for many years and became an honored guest at the court of the new king, Evil-merodach. While Yehoyachin was still in prison, a son, She'altiel, had been born to him. She'altiel was the father of Zerubavel [Zerubbabel] who was to become the leader of those Jews who returned from the Babylonian exile to their homeland, after the proclamation of the future King Cyrus [Koresh].

The reign of Evil-merodach lasted twenty-three years. He was followed by Belshazzar who, unlike his predecessor, persecuted the Jews under his rule. But Belshazzar was the last of the Babylonian kings. Nebuchadnezzar's ominous dream, as interpreted by Daniel, was now unfolding, and the days of the mighty empire were numbered.

King Darius [Daryavesh] of Media and King Cyrus of Persia joined forces in a campaign that conquered Assyria, Elam, Armenia, Asia Minor, and all of Babylonia except for the capital city, Babylon. The triumphant armies closed in on Babylon in a siege of the highly fortified metropolis that lasted many days. Then, on the night of Passover, the armies withdrew temporarily from their positions near the walls of the city. Confident that the retreat meant his city was saved, Belshazzar thanked his gods profusely for this victory, at the same time contemptuously abusing the G-d of Israel. In his arrogance he ordered his servants to bring the holy vessels that his grandfather had looted from the Temple in Jerusalem. The king called for a drinking orgy and the golden Temple vessels were filled with wine. But as soon as he and his guests raised the vessels to their lips, a hand was seen writing Hebrew letters against the wall of the chamber. The meaning of these letters baffled all of the king's scholars.

Belshazzar was bewildered and frightened. He summoned his advisers and scholars, but no one could understand the handwriting on the wall. Finally, the queen came in and exclaimed that since the days of Nebuchadnezzar, it was known that the wisest of all of the sages in the empire was Daniel. He would surely solve the mystery. She was right. He came and looked at the strange letters which read, "מְנֵא מְנֵא תְּקֵל וּפַרְסִין, MENEI MENEI TEKEIL UFARSIN," but were not readily recognizable because they were written in coded form. According to one opinion the letters were written as five rows of three letters, each read top to bottom rather than across.

מ	מ	תּ	ו	ס
נ	נ	ק	פ	י
א	א	ל	ר	ו

Belshazzar offered Daniel great honors and a third of the kingdom if he could solve the riddle. The Jewish leader refused all the rewards, but agreed to interpret the writing. "MENEI — G-d has *counted* your kingship and terminated it; TEKEIL — You were *weighed* in the scales of judgment and found wanting; UFARSIN — Your kingship is *broken up* and given to Media and Persia" (Daniel 5:26-28).

That same night the armies of these two powers under Darius and Cyrus broke into the city. Belshazzar was assassinated by his own servants (according to some accounts he was killed by the invading soldiers), and Darius the Mede, the older of the two conquerors, succeeded him as emperor.

In the Persian-Median kingdom, too, Daniel was appointed to a high office in the royal court. This brought upon him the envy of the other high dignitaries, who sought a way of harming him. Approaching the king they prevailed upon him to issue a decree that during the next thirty days no one was allowed to pray

according to his own religion. In Daniel's house there was a window that faced Jerusalem, so that when praying he could direct himself toward the site where the Holy Temple had once stood. Disregarding the king's decree he continued to pray there three times a day to the G-d of his fathers.

His enemies had expected this to happen and asked the king to have Daniel cast into the lions' den — surely a suitable punishment for disobedience to the king's command. Though he loved Daniel, the king had no choice but to comply. But G-d was with Daniel: the lions did not touch him. When the king saw this great miracle he had Daniel released and commanded instead that his enemies be thrown to the lions. Moreover, he issued an epistle throughout the kingdom, exhorting his subjects to worship the G-d of Daniel.

After a rule of one year, Darius the Mede was followed on the throne by Cyrus of Persia. This was the same king of whom the Prophet Yeshayahu [Isaiah] had predicted some two hundred years before, that G-d would subdue many nations under him, and that he would enable the exiles to return to their own Land: "So said Hashem to His anointed, to Cyrus … 'For the sake of Jacob, My servant and Israel, My chosen … He shall build My city and he shall free My captives'" (Isaiah 45:1,4,13). When Cyrus ascended the throne, the predicted seventy years beginning with the exile of the captive youths had passed. The time had come for the realization of Yeshayahu's prophecy.

2

The Aliyah of Zerubavel and the Building of the Second Temple

If she is a wall, we will build upon her a citadel of silver. But if she is a door, we will guard her with a cedar panel (Song of Songs 8:9).

If you had made yourselves like a wall and you had all returned in the days of Ezra, you would have been like silver that is not subject to decay. But now that you have returned only like doors [i.e., you returned in part, like a double-door, half of which opens while the other half remains shut], you are like cedar wood which does decay (Yoma 9b).

The Proclamation of Cyrus

In the course of the Babylonian exile, the enemies of Israel were in possession of the Land — the Cuthites in Samaria [Shomron], the Edomites in the Negev, the Ammonites in the eastern part of the country, and the people of Tyre in the coastal region. Only in the Land of Yehudah, particularly in and around Jerusalem, no gentiles settled and the soil remained desolate. This is what the Torah had foretold: "Your land will be desolate and your cities devastated. Then the soil will recompense for the unkept rest-years and lie uncultivated, while you are away in the lands of your enemies" (Leviticus 26:33,34). Yet even here a blessing lay hidden, for G-d had promised that as long as His people were absent from their land, the soil would remain barren and not yield its fruit to others who wished to possess it.

Now the time had come to revive the desolate hills and valleys of Judea.* The exiles would soon return to the homesteads of their families, rebuild the

---

* For the sake of simplicity, we will use the term "Judea" to describe the portion of *Eretz Yisrael* occupied by those who returned from Babylonia. It would be more accurate to call it Judah [Yehudah], since that is the name actually used by the settlers. "Judah," as used in Scriptures, refers to the territory of the tribes of Judah and Benjamin, which had Jerusalem as its capital and center. After the Ten Tribes seceded from the kingdom of Rechavam [Rehoboam] son of Shlomo [Solomon], the name *Eretz Yisrael* could not be used to refer to the land of Judah and Benjamin, since their territory was only a fraction of the entire land.

The name "Judea" is of Roman origin, and was not applied to the land until the Roman conquest, several centuries after the events of this chapter. However, since Judea is the familiar and commonly used name for this part of *Eretz Yisrael,* it is used in this book.

ruins of their houses, and begin to cultivate their soil, praying to G-d that He should send them the blessings of heaven and earth.

In the first year of his rule, 371 BCE (3390), King Cyrus issued the following proclamation throughout his empire:

> Hashem, G-d of Heaven, has given me all the kingdoms of earth, and He has commanded me to build Him a Temple in Jerusalem, which is in Yehudah. Anyone among you from His entire people — may His G-d be with him — let him go up to Jerusalem, which is in Yehudah; let him build the Temple of Hashem, G-d of Israel — He is the G-d! — which is in Jerusalem (Ezra 1:2-3).

The prophecy of Yeshayahu [Isaiah] concerning the seventy years of exile thus became a reality.

The leaders of the people — Zerubavel ben She'altiel, who was a descendant of King David; Yehoshua [Joshua] ben Yehotzadak [Jehozadok], the High Priest; Nechemiah [Nehemiah]; Mordechai; and the Prophets, Chaggai [Haggai], Zechariah and Malachi — called upon the Jewish people throughout Babylonia and urged them to respond to the king's proclamation. Rejoicing at the fulfillment of a prophecy, 42,360 people, attended by 7,337 servants, answered their leaders' call. The Jews set out on the road that led from Babylonian captivity to freedom in their own country. Those who remained behind helped them generously with gold, silver, cattle, and other property. Additionally, Cyrus returned the holy vessels which the Babylonians had taken from the Holy Temple before they destroyed it. He even dispatched troops to protect them from marauders on the way. And as the Jews walked they were accompanied by more than two hundred singers who sang in exultation: "Let us arise and go up to Zion, to Hashem our G-d" (Jeremiah 31:5).

This was a time of divine favor for our people. Had we been worthy of it and taken full advantage of this opportunity, and had the Jews returned with Zerubavel, that generation would have witnessed the Final Redemption, and the Second Temple would never have been destroyed.

Reinstitution of the Sacrificial Service

The first task of the returnees was to realize their hope of many years — the renewal of the sacrifices in Jerusalem. The prophets who had returned with them taught that it was permissible to erect a temporary altar even before the Temple was rebuilt. Accordingly, in the month of Tishrei they all went up in pilgrimage to Jerusalem, an altar was erected, and the sacrifices were offered once again.

In a spirit of joy and awe they then proceeded to build the Holy Temple itself. Yehoshua and Zerubavel appointed the Levites to supervise the work, while questions of halachah which arose in the course of construction were decided by the Sages of the Sanhedrin, among whom were many prophets.

Excited crowds gathered to witness the laying of the foundation for the Holy Temple. It was one of the supreme moments in their lives. At long last they had lived to see with their own eyes the erection of that building for which they had prayed, dreamed, and hoped. Most of the people rejoiced and celebrated, but the very old men wept, for they still remembered the First Temple in all its glory. They knew that the Divine Presence would not rest in the same full measure on this House as It had rested on the first one.

The Cuthites who lived in the mountains of Samaria were angered when they saw that the Jews had come back to Judea to rebuild their houses and their Temple. Spitefully, the Cuthites decided to interfere with the construction. First they pretended to be friends and came with the request that they be allowed to take part in the building of the Temple. But the Jewish leaders rejected their offer and told them: "It is not proper for you and us to build a Temple for our G-d." As this tactic failed, the Cuthites decided on a different method. They sent a message to King Cyrus of Persia in which they accused the Jews of conspiring to rebel against him. Unfortunately the king believed their malicious charge and ordered that the building of the Temple be stopped.

Persia Rules Far and Wide

The extent of the Persian Empire under Cyrus was enormous, ranging from India in the east to Lydia (in present-day Turkey) on the eastern coast of the Aegean Sea. Altogether, 120 countries were tributary to his government. He established local law and order and maintained a fine network of roads for quick and efficient communications throughout his far-flung empire.

Many and varied peoples, each with its own language and culture, inhabited this vast kingdom. Cyrus allowed each people to speak its own language and live its own way of life, and the kings who succeeded him likewise followed this policy. As *Megillas Esther* tells us about King Ahasuerus [Achashveirosh]:

> And he sent messages to all the countries of the king, to each country in its own script, and to each nation in its own language … (Esther 1:22).

This event occurred only two years after the death of Cyrus. Only in one aspect did the transfer of power from Babylonia to Persia-Media result in a major change — in religion. The collapse of their kingdom caused the Babylonians to doubt the power of their own idols, which had proven to be helpless when their followers needed them most. After the Persian conquest, therefore, most Babylonians accepted the religion of the victors.

This religion was based on the teachings of Zoroaster (also known as Zarathustra). It is not known exactly when he lived, but his influence shaped the religious life of the Medians long before their overthrow of Babylonia. He convinced his countrymen to turn away from idols of stone and wood, but he did not preach a belief in One deity. The Zoroastrian belief held that there are two powers that are constantly engaged in a struggle for supremacy, one power being personified by the idol for good and the other by the idol for evil. According to this belief man is obliged to do good deeds in order to assist the idol for good to vanquish the idol for evil. In direct opposition to this view stand the words of the Prophet Yeshayahu — that One G-d created the world: He created both light and darkness, good and evil.

Since the Zoroastrians considered fire

the symbol of the idol of goodness, their cult was known as the "Religion of Fire." Since they considered the earth to be holy, they did not bury their dead in the ground, but rather burned the corpses, or discarded them where they would be devoured by scavenging animals and birds of prey.

The Miracle and Lesson of Purim

A short time after the death of Cyrus, Ahasuerus ascended the throne of Persia. The story of the great danger his reign brought the Jews and the miracle that saved them is told in *Megillas Esther*.

King Ahasuerus gave a 180-day banquet for the aristocracy of his entire kingdom, and then he ordered a second feast, this time for the residents of Shushan, to last seven days. His intention was that the Jews would be tempted to join in the festivities and drink forbidden wine, eat forbidden food, and commit other sins. Then, he thought, their G-d would no longer protect them and he could do to them as he pleased. Our Sages explain that because many Jews attended his banquet and succumbed to temptation, they deserved to forfeit their lives. The king appointed Haman as his prime minister and that notorious Amalekite issued a decree that every Jewish man, woman, and child should be murdered.

However, G-d prepared the remedy in advance. Before the king had published Haman's evil decree against the Jews, Esther was brought to the royal palace and crowned queen in place of Vashti. Her cousin Mordechai, a member of the *Anshei Knesses HaGedolah*, the Men of the Great Assembly, was stationed at the gate of the palace. Mordechai and Esther, two Jewish leaders who were raised to high office at the king's court, were messengers of

Two Purim scenes — Haman leading Mordechai on horseback through the streets of Shushan (Esther 6:11); and Ahasuerus and Esther receiving the report of those slain (Esther 9:11). The artist was obviously familiar with the Midrash, for he represents the king as seated on the throne of King Shlomo, the steps of which are guarded by various birds and animals. This panel is one of many murals in the synagogue completed in the year 244-245 CE in the city of Dura-Europos on the Euphrates, and discovered in an excellent state of preservation in 1932.

The Aramaic inscription with the letters יהד spells Yehud, the name used for Judea when it was a province of the Persian Empire in the fourth century BCE. The bird shown on this silver coin is a falcon.

clear that Mordechai's stubbornness was the cause of Haman's anger:

> When Haman saw that Mordechai did not bow down nor prostrate himself before him, then Haman was filled with rage. However, it seemed contemptible to him to lay hands on Mordechai alone ... So Haman sought to destroy all the Jews ... the people of Mordechai (Esther 3:5-6).

However, the Sages teach that the true cause for Haman's decree was that the Jews participated in the king's feast — in defiance of Mordechai's warnings and pleadings. At the time, nearly all the Jews thought that Mordechai was responsible for the danger that threatened them, but it was only when they recognized their sin and repented that the miracle of Purim took place.

To look for true and underlying reasons rather than superficial and direct causes is one of the great lessons to be learned from the Megillah. This approach must be applied to all subsequent historical events. For beginning in the period of Esther the ways of G-d in the affairs of men were no longer as open and perceivable as they were in the times of the Patriarchs and the prophets. It is for us to detect and discover the hidden ways of G-d in history.

Divine Providence. They roused their fellow Jews to fasting, prayer, and wholehearted teshuvah; the decree was abolished; and those critical days were transformed — "from anguish to rejoicing and from mourning to a festival" (Esther 9:22).

Megillas Esther was written with Divine inspiration. Aside from its historical narrative, it teaches us that the real causes of historical events are often far different from the ones that seem to be "obvious." As Megillas Esther tells the story, it seemed

Building of the Second Temple

Eighteen years had passed since Yehoshua and Zerubavel had returned to Jerusalem — but the Temple had not yet been built. Those were difficult years for our people. In Persia there had been Haman's threat of extermination, and in Judea the new settlers struggled unsuccessfully to support themselves. A picture of their economic hardships emerges

clearly from the words of the Prophet Chaggai:

> You have sown, but reap little; you eat, but you are not sated; you drink, but you cannot get drunk; you dress, but are not kept warm; and he who earns money, earns for a purse with a hole (Chaggai 1:6).

Chaggai did not stop there. He told the

people why they were suffering so, *because of My House which is in ruins* (1:9).

This state of affairs came to an end exactly seventy years after the First Temple was destroyed. The time to complete the building of the Second Temple had come. The prophets aroused the people to renew the work without waiting for royal permission. In the words of the Prophet:

"Now be strong, Zerubavel;" says Hashem, "and be strong, Yehoshua ben Yehotzadak, the High Priest; and be strong, all the people of the land ... because I am with you" (Chaggai 2:4).

Thus encouraged, the people renewed the holy work in 353 BCE (3408). Again the resentful and envious neighbors tried to interfere, but Persia was ruled now by the son of Esther and Ahasuerus, Darius the Persian, a benevolent ruler, who did not listen to the slander of the enemies of Judea. On the contrary, he lent assistance to the builders. He sent them materials for the building and oil and salt for the sacrifices, and exempted the *Kohanim* and Levites from paying taxes.

Within four years, on the third of Adar in the sixth year of the reign of Darius the Persian, the building was completed: the Holy Temple stood once more on its original site. Joy and jubilation electrified the people as they gathered to celebrate the dedication of the Sanctuary. One prayer filled all hearts as they watched the sacred service of the *Kohanim* and heard the almost-forgotten songs of the Levites:

May the pleasantness of Hashem, our G-d, be upon us — may He establish our handiwork for us; our handiwork may He establish (Psalms 90:17).

3

Ezra and Nechemiah

You offer defiled sacrifices upon My altar yet you say: "With what have we defiled You?" ... If you offer a blind animal, is nothing wrong? Or if you offer a lame or a sick sacrifice, is nothing wrong? Bring such an offering to your governor, if you please! Will he show you favor? Will he be gracious to you? ... (Malachi 1:7,8)

Disappointment Awaits Ezra

Ezra the Scribe came to Jerusalem only after the Temple was built. As long as his teacher, Baruch ben Neriah, was alive, Ezra stayed with him in Babylonia and studied Torah under him. But now that his mentor had died and the community in Zion needed a leader who could guide them, he no longer hesitated. On the first of Nissan, in the seventh year of the reign of Darius the Persian, Ezra left Babylonia, and on the first of Av, four months later, he arrived in Jerusalem.

1,496 men chose to come to Jerusalem, but there was not a single Levite among them. Since their presence was necessary in the Temple service, Ezra persuaded thirty-eight Levites with their 220 servants to join him. But because no Levites came voluntarily, Ezra punished them for their reluctance. Until that time, the *maaser*-tithe could be given only to the Levites, but Ezra permitted the Israelites to give it to the *Kohanim* as well.

The Persian king appointed Ezra as the chief judge over the Jews, and authorized him to enforce his decisions. He also removed all restrictions on the numbers of Jews who were permitted to go to *Eretz Yisrael*, and allowed the remaining Babylonian Jews to contribute freely for the maintenance of the Temple and the sacrifices. Despite the honor and kindness that the king showed him, Ezra did not ask for a military escort to guard him on the journey because he did not want the king to believe that G-d's protection would not suffice.

When Ezra arrived in Jerusalem he quickly discovered the truth of the many reports that he had heard concerning the disappointing spiritual level of the local Jews. True, the physical construction of the Temple was completed — but the spiritual structure of the people was not. Many did not live according to the Torah and the Commandments; there were many breaches in their spiritual defenses; and the study of the Torah was nearly forgotten in Israel.

Difficult living conditions were no doubt much to blame for the sorry state of affairs. Twenty-three years had passed since the arrival of the first Jews. During that time they had suffered many trials and tribulations. The land was desolate, and only after great exertion were they able to rebuild their ruined communities. Many obstacles were placed in their path by their antagonistic neighbors, who resented the Jewish Return, just as they had succeeded in interrupting the building of the *Beis HaMikdash* itself.

Another reason for the poor spiritual level in *Eretz Yisrael* was that the earlier returnees were cut off from their fellow Jews who had stayed behind in Babylonia, the land whose synagogues and houses of study represented the spiritual center of the entire people. Moreover, after the initial *aliyah* [immigration] the Persian king forbade further emigration. Without contact with Babylonia or reinforcements from new immigrants, the settlers in *Eretz Yisrael* were unable to cope with the many problems facing them. Assimilation became so widespread that even leading Jews intermarried with their gentile neighbors. Even some of Yehoshua the High Priest's sons married gentile women.

When Ezra came face to face with this dismal picture he ripped his garments and tore out his hair in anguish. Then he summoned all the men of Judah and Benjamin to Jerusalem, threatening those who would not come with the confiscation of their property. On the twentieth of Kislev they assembled near the *Beis HaMikdash*. Ezra fasted and wept. He spoke of the people's sinful ways and begged G-d to forgive them. So great was Ezra's impact on the people that they all promised to divorce their foreign wives. All that winter, until the first of Nissan, the Sanhedrin [Supreme Court] in Jerusalem and the various local courts occupied themselves with establishing the family purity of the returnees. Since many Jews had married foreign women, and such marriages were invalid, the courts investigated all families in order to determine which women were non-Jewish and could not remain with their Jewish husbands.

Seeing that the lack of Torah sages and teachers was the cause of Israel's downfall, Ezra promptly sent scholars to the different communities, with instructions to teach the Torah to the people and encourage its observance. These men were known as *Sofrim* [סוֹפְרִים], or Scribes. But not only did they write the scrolls of the Torah, they also "counted" [סָפְרוּ] the exact number of all its letters, so that nothing could be added or subtracted from it in the future. This was very important because each letter (and even the little points on the top of many letters) is the source of many laws.

Among the measures taken by Ezra for the reconstruction of Jewish life in the Holy Land were some which promoted harmony between man and wife, and the prevention of mixed marriages. Ezra also performed the special service of the "Red Cow" [פָּרָה אֲדֻמָּה], the ashes of which were used in the ritual cleansing process described in the Torah. It was only the second such cow that had been found since the time of Moshe *Rabbeinu* [Moses, our teacher] in the desert. It was important for Ezra to do this so that the people could cleanse themselves of ritual contamination [טוּמְאָה] before going to the Temple.

Nechemiah Builds the Walls

Ezra accomplished many major improvements in the life of the people, but even he was unable to eradicate all that was wrong. There were still Jews who refused to divorce their foreign wives, while others were negligent in the laws of the sacrifices and of the Sabbath, and in the required tithes (terumah and maaser) that had to be given to the Kohanim and Levites.

But Divine Providence provided him with an assistant, Nechemiah, who was one of the foremost officials of King Darius [the Persian]. While in Babylonia he had been told that the walls of Jerusalem were still in ruins. He therefore approached the king and asked permission to go to Jerusalem in order to fortify it both materially and spiritually. Understanding Nechemiah's sorrow over the ruin of the Holy City, the king not only granted his request, but appointed him governor over the Land of the Jews, giving him broad authority. Accordingly, in the twentieth year of Darius, and thirteen years after Ezra's return, Nechemiah arrived in Eretz Yisrael.

Reluctant at first to publicize his arrival, Nechemiah and his retinue entered Jerusalem secretly. For three nights he surveyed the ruined walls and devised a plan for their reconstruction. He then assembled the people and called to them: "Let us go and build the walls of Jerusalem and no longer be an object of scorn" (Nechemiah 2:17).

Since all the people took part in the erection of the wall, it took only fifty-two days to complete. The enemies of Judah and Benjamin tried to interfere with the work and even planned armed attacks on the builders. But Nechemiah was prepared. He stationed armed defenders on all sides and distributed swords even to the builders:

> From that day on, half of my men were working and the other half were holding the spears, the shields, the bows and the coats of mail ... As for those who built the wall and those who carried the loads, one hand was doing the work, while the other held a weapon (Nechemiah 4:10-11).

When the city wall was completed, with its gates and other defense requirements, the people dedicated it with great joy and ceremony. They walked around it in solemn procession with thanksgiving offerings of bread carried by the Kohanim and Levites, according to the procedure for sanctifying the city or any new extensions to it.

Strictly speaking, according to the halachic view of the Rambam, it was not necessary to sanctify the city because the holiness of Jerusalem was never interrupted, even when the First Temple was destroyed. The city of Jerusalem became holy because Hashem's Presence rested upon it, and His Presence can never be destroyed. The ceremony of sanctification was performed nonetheless, in commemoration of the original procedure. Unlike Jerusalem, the sanctity of the rest of Eretz Yisrael did end when Nebuchadnezzar conquered the Land. The original holiness of the Land resulted from Israel's conquest of it; once the Jews lost possession, their conquest was nullified and the Land lost its holiness. This holiness was renewed wherever the returning Jews settled it, and it was made permanent.

The erection of the wall strengthened

the city and raised the morale of its inhabitants. From then on their enemies could no longer exploit the weakness of an open city to plot against the Jews. As to fortifying the spiritual structure of the people, Ezra, Nechemiah, and the Men of the Great Assembly now turned their attention to this task.

Borders of the Land which were sanctified forever by the returnees from the Babylonian Exile (according to Rabbi Yechiel Michel Tukachinsky).

"Land occupied by those who came from Egypt became sanctified, but its sanctity lasted only until the expulsion from the land. Because the first sanctity rested on conquest, it had no permanent validity But when the Jews returned from their exile and settled part of the land, they sanctified it with a renewed sanctity that endures forever, for that time and the future" (Rambam: Laws of Terumah, 1:5).

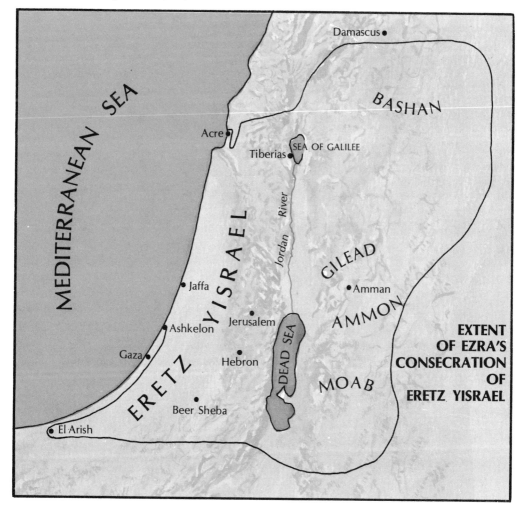

4

Anshei Knesses HaGedolah —
The Men of the Great Assembly

R' Yehoshua ben Levi said, "Why are they called the Men of the Great Assembly? — Because they restored the crown to its former glory. Moses had come and addressed 'The great, mighty and awesome G-d.' Yirmeyahu came and said: 'Foreigners are croaking in His Sanctuary! Where is His awesomeness?' So he omitted 'awesome.' Daniel came and said: 'Foreigners are enslaving His sons! Where is His might?' So he omitted 'mighty.' Then came the Men of the Great Assembly and said: 'On the contrary, this is His might — that He can restrain His will and tolerate the wicked. And this is His awesomeness — for if not for Him, how could one nation survive among all the nations?' " (Yoma 69b).

The New Leadership

The *aliyah* [immigration] from Babylonia and completion of Jerusalem's walls were no substitute for the lack of an organized religious authority that could provide a framework for the people's new national life. The lack of such a religious authority was felt particularly in the period of the Second Temple, because now the Divine Presence did not manifest itself to the degree that it did in the time of the First Temple. Prophecy, too, continued to flourish for only the first forty years of the Second Temple period. With the death of Malachi it came to an end.

The society's need for national spiritual leadership was met by the creation of a body called the *Knesses HaGedolah*, or Great Assembly. Its central role in Jewish history is evident in the Mishnah:

> *Moshe received the Torah at Sinai and handed it on to Yehoshua; Yehoshua to the Elders; and the Elders to the Prophets. The Prophets handed it on to the Men of the Great Assembly (Avos 1:1).*

Essentially the Great Assembly was the Great Sanhedrin, the supreme legal and religious authority of the nation. Among them were many prophets, including Chaggai, Zechariah, Malachi, Daniel, Chananiah, Mishael, Azariah, Ezra, Nechemiah, Mordechai, and Zerubavel. Altogether, 120 sages were members of the Great Assembly, although not all 120 were members at the same time or lived in the same place. Together they took steps that would enable them to transmit the Torah in its entirety to the coming generations.

The Men of the Great Assembly asked all the people to convene on Rosh Hashanah in front of the Water Gate of Jerusalem's wall. There Ezra read and other sages explained the words of the Torah to the assembled Jews. Only then did the people realize how far they had gone astray. When they heard the passage about Rosh Hashanah, and realized that it was the Day of Judgment, they were overcome with tears of remorse. But Nechemiah encouraged them by saying:

> Do not mourn and do not weep! ... Go, eat choice food and drink sweet beverages, and send gifts of food to him who has nothing prepared for himself — because this day is holy to our L-rd (Nechemiah 8:9-10).

His words raised their spirits. They went home and celebrated the Days of Awe and the festival of Sukkos in a spirit of inspiration and joy. After the festival, on the twenty-fourth of Tishrei, they gathered again, this time for a day of fasting and prayer, and under solemn oath committed themselves to live up to all the commandments of G-d. Their decision was recorded in a special scroll signed by all the leaders, some eighty-four names; it was called the Bris Amanah [Covenant of Trust].

The Sages have compared the undertaking recorded in this Covenant to no less a moment than the Receiving of the Torah on Mount Sinai — except that then G-d had raised the mountain over the heads of the Children of Israel; that is, at Sinai they had felt compelled to accept the Torah on account of the many miracles they had witnessed. But the supernatural way of life was to be no more. Henceforth there was to be a concealment of Providence [הַסְתָּרַת פָּנִים]. This time, therefore, they reaffirmed their acceptance of the Torah out of their own free will. In fact the Jews of this era had already done so in the days of Ahasuerus. These are the words of the Talmud:

> It is written, "And they stood at the foot of the mountain" (Exodus 19:17). Said Rav Avdimi ... This teaches us that G-d lifted the mountain over their heads like a barrel and said to them: "If you will accept the Torah — well and good, but if not, here shall be your grave." ... Said Rava: Even so, they accepted it again in the days of Ahasuerus, as it is written: "The Jews confirmed and undertook" (Esther 9:27) — that is, they

Mount of Olives photographed in June 1967, with the pyramid-topped tomb of the prophet Zechariah, a member of the Anshei Knesses HaGedolah, flanked by rockhewn burial chambers overlooking the Kidron Valley. The one at left is the mausoleum of the Bnei Cheizir family (see Nechemiah 10:21).

confirmed what they had already accepted (Shabbos 88a).

In this holy convocation and covenant the people committed themselves to observe in particular the laws they had previously neglected — not to assimilate with the gentiles, to bring the gifts for the priesthood to the Temple, to observe the Sabbath in all its details, and to keep the laws of Shemittah, the Seventh (Sabbatical) Year.

When the Men of the Great Assembly saw that this was a moment of divine favor, they beseeched G-d to abolish the evil inclination [יֵצֶר הָרָע] in the heart of man, for because of it the First Temple had been destroyed and the people led into exile. He accepted their prayer and abolished the evil inclination towards idolatry. Since that time, unlike the surrounding nations, our people no longer worshiped idols.

Strengthening Torah Study and Observance

The Men of the Great Assembly undertook many activities to strengthen the spiritual lifestyle of the people. These activities formed the sacred spiritual legacy that the last generation of prophets left to all future generations that would not be privileged to see and hear the spirit of prophecy. From their time to ours, we live according to their heritage, and so will it continue until the coming of Mashiach, when G-d will again bestow the spirit of prophecy upon us.

The most important asset that the Men of the Great Assembly transmitted was the Oral Law [תּוֹרָה שֶׁבְּעַל פֶּה], which had originally been given to Moshe at Sinai. For all laws and Rabbinic commandments, they composed a text that was to be handed down and explained from teacher to student. This teaching later became the basis of the Mishnah. Likewise, to give the prayers a clear framework, they established the wording of the Shemoneh Esrei, Eighteen Blessings, as well as the blessings before and after the reading of the Shema, and the various blessings recited over food and when performing a mitzvah. They also ordained that the sanctification of the Sabbath be pronounced at the day's beginning [Kiddush] and end [Havdalah] by a blessing over a cup of wine, in addition to its sanctification in the course of the prayers.

They translated the books of the Tanach [Bible] into the Aramaic vernacular as an authoritative interpretation of each verse of the sacred text. This they divided into twenty-four books, corresponding to the twenty-four rotating groups (mishmaros) of Kohanim serving in the Temple. Then they sealed the Tanach, meaning that only these were declared holy books to which nothing could be added and from which nothing could be subtracted. The Five Books of the Chumash were written by Moshe Rabbeinu at the dictation of G-d; eight books were written by the Prophets by the inspiration of prophecy (the twelve books of the so-called Minor Prophets are counted as one book); and the eleven books of the Writings (Kesuvim) were written by Divine Inspiration, Ruach HaKodesh (the books of Ezra and Nechemiah are also counted as one).

The concern of the Anshei Knesses HaGedolah for the welfare of the community and the pursuit of Torah study is clear from their instructions to their

The Twenty-four Biblical Books

THE PENTATEUCH (תּוֹרָה)
1. Genesis (בְּרֵאשִׁית)
2. Exodus (שְׁמוֹת)
3. Leviticus (וַיִּקְרָא)
4. Numbers (בְּמִדְבָּר)
5. Deuteronomy (דְּבָרִים)

THE PROPHETS (נְבִיאִים)
6. Joshua (יְהוֹשֻׁעַ)
7. Judges (שׁוֹפְטִים)
8. Samuel (שְׁמוּאֵל)
9. Kings (מְלָכִים)
10. Isaiah (יְשַׁעְיָהוּ)
11. Jeremiah (יִרְמְיָה)
12. Ezekiel (יְחֶזְקֵאל)
13. The Twelve (תְּרֵי עָשָׂר)

THE HAGIOGRAPHA (כְּתוּבִים)
14. Psalms (תְּהִלִּים)
15. Proverbs (מִשְׁלֵי)
16. Job (אִיּוֹב)
17. Song of Songs (שִׁיר הַשִּׁירִים)
18. Ruth (רוּת)
19. Lamentations (אֵיכָה)
20. Ecclesiastes (קֹהֶלֶת)
21. Esther (אֶסְתֵּר)
22. Daniel (דָּנִיֵּאל)
23. Ezra/Nehemiah (עֶזְרָא/נְחֶמְיָה)
24. Chronicles (דִּבְרֵי הַיָּמִים)

disciples: "Be deliberate in judgment; raise many students; and make a fence around the Torah" (*Avos* 1:1).

Here we have three major teachings:

(a) Judges must be cautious and not render decisions without careful consideration;

(b) every scholar is obligated to teach as many pupils as possible, so as to spread the knowledge of Torah in Israel;

(c) it is necessary to make a "fence" around the Torah, that is, decrees should be enacted to prevent violations of the Torah's laws. One must protect the law itself, just as one constructs a fence around one's property to prevent any damage. The Torah, for example, forbade working on the Sabbath; these Sages added a "fence" with a prohibition against handling any tool usually used for forbidden work, lest one come to use it.

Ordinances Concerning the Torah and Court Sessions

Many ordinances adopted during the period of the Great Assembly are attributed to Ezra. He ordained that on Mondays and Thursdays, when the villagers would come to town for market day, at least ten verses of the Torah should be read publicly, with three men called to do the reading. This ordinance was based on one dating back to Moshe *Rabbeinu* himself. On the basis of the verse, "And they went three days in the wilderness and found no water" (*Exodus* 15:22), Moshe and his fellow prophets ordained that the Torah should be read on the Sabbath, Monday, and Thursday, so that no three-day period may pass without the reading of the Torah; consequently, we do not remain for more than three days without its "living waters." But Moshe decreed only that one man read three verses or that three men read one verse each.

Ezra also arranged that judges should sit in court on these busy market days, so that they would be available to decide any legal claims or answer halachic inquiries.

Our Sages teach: "Ezra was worthy of having the Torah given through him, had not Moshe *Rabbeinu* preceded him" (*Sanhedrin* 21b). Nevertheless, Ezra was privileged to reintroduce the writing of Torah scrolls in *ksav Ashuri* [אֲשׁוּרִי], ["Assyrian" or "praiseworthy" script], the same script in which the Torah was originally written by Moshe *Rabbeinu*.

The Two Tablets of the Ten Commandments and the Torah scrolls written in the days of Moshe Rabbeinu used this sacred script. For secular purposes, a different

The aleph-beis in "ksav Ashuri" (the bold square letters used for writing Torah scrolls) and in an ancient script that some scholars identify as "ksav Ivri."

script, *ksav Ivri,* was used. However, as the years passed and Israel began to sin, G-d caused the *Ashuri* script to become forgotten.

The fateful words written by the hand of an angel on the wall of Belshazzar's palace were written in *Ashuri*. By that time, very few people — Daniel was one of them — still remembered the ancient script. Later when the people repented enough so that they were permitted to build the Second Temple, Ezra ordained that all sacred texts be written in this sacred square-lettered script from then on.

The Ban on the Cuthites

The Cuthites [Samaritans] continued to use the previous script for their scrolls, but they did not accept the entire Written Torah. They accepted the five books of the *Chumash* [Pentateuch] and added a book called *Yehoshua* [Joshua], which is not the same as our book of that name. The reason for this departure was their claim that they were the descendants of Ephraim, hence of the tribe of Yehoshua. The status of the Cuthites, however, involved a question far more grave than their unwillingness to accept the entire Written Torah and the enactments of the Sages. If that were all, it would have been the responsibility of the Jewish people to teach and convince them

Remains of Roman Jupiter Temple, built over Samaritan Temple, atop Mt. Gerizim near Shechem.

of the truth. But were the Cuthites truly Jewish? According to many of the Sages, the Cuthites' conversion to Judaism in the time of the First Temple was not sincere and therefore not valid. If so, they were not even Jewish. According to the opinion of other Sages, their conversion was valid, but they did not properly observe the laws of marriage and divorce, with the result that many of them were illegitimate to the extent that Jews were forbidden to marry them. For these reasons, Ezra and his court took drastic action to rule out the possibility of intermarrying with the Cuthites. In later years the Sages found it necessary to forbid the people to drink Cuthite wine or eat their bread. So seriously did the Sages of the Mishnah regard this prohibition that they strengthened it by ruling: "Whoever eats the bread of Cuthites is like one who eats the flesh of a swine" *(Shevi'is 8:10)*.

Samaritan priest displaying ancient Torah scroll (allegedly 2000 years old); Shechem.

When the Cuthites realized that they could not mingle with the Jews they built their own altar upon Mount Gerizim, near Shechem (Nablus), and from then on harassed our people at every opportunity. A small remnant of this sect and their altar exist until this day.

The following exchange is recorded in the Midrash:

> R' Yishmael the son of R' Yose went to pray in Jerusalem. As he passed that mountain [Gerizim] a Samaritan asked him, "Where are you going?"

He replied, "I am going to pray in Jerusalem." Said the Samaritan, "Is it not better for you to pray on this mountain that is blessed and not in a House that is cursed?" Said R' Yishmael to him, "You people resemble a dog attracted to a carcass. You know that there are idols buried here, as it is written: 'And Yaakov buried them [the idols of his servants] … near Shechem' (Genesis 35:4) — that is why you are attracted to Mount Gerizim" (Yalkut Shimoni, Bereishis 135).

Ordinances of the Great Assembly

The following two passages — from *Mishneh Torah*, the halachic code authored by *Rambam* (Maimonides) — throw light on two typical areas in which the *Anshei Knesses HaGedolah* legislated.

Laws of Prayer

When Israel was exiled in the days of the wicked Nebuchadnezzar, they mingled with the Persians, Greeks, and other nationalities, and children were born to them in foreign lands. The language of these children became mongrelized, each one speaking a mixture of several languages. When he spoke he could not express himself adequately in a single language, but spoke in a jargon ... When Ezra and his court saw this, they arose and composed Eighteen Blessings according to a uniform order — the first three are in praise of G-d; the last three, thanksgiving; and the intermediate ones are requests for all things, being like general categories representing the primary needs of each individual and of the entire community — that these prayers be familiar to all, that they would learn them. Then the prayers of these ill-spoken people would be as perfect as the prayers of the most articulate. For this same reason they set forth all the blessings and prayers in uniform texts in the mouths of all Israel, so that the content of every blessing would be familiar to the inarticulate (Rambam, Hilchos Tefillah 1:4).

Laws of the Sabbath

The Sages prohibited the moving of some objects (muktzeh) on the Sabbath in the same way they are moved on weekdays. Why did they set forth this prohibition? They said: If the Prophets went so far as to warn and command that your walking on the Sabbath should not be like your walking on weekdays, nor should your Sabbath conversation be like your weekday conversation ... surely one's movement of objects on the Sabbath should not be like his movement on weekdays, in order that he not regard it like a weekday, and thereby come to lift and shift objects from corner to corner or from room to room; or to put away stones and so forth. For since one sits idle and is at home, he will seek something with which to keep busy — with the result that he will not rest. If so, the intent of the Sabbath — "that he may rest" (Deuteronomy 5:15) — will be disrupted (Rambam, Hilchos Shabbos 24:12).

Shimon, Survivor and High Priest

The flourishing period of the Men of the Great Assembly was followed by a period of spiritual descent. Greece began to dominate the world and its culture spread to many lands. Like their neighbors, many Jews came under the spell of Greek culture, and drifted from the ways of the Torah.

Fortunately, G-d placed a great man at the critical juncture of the two periods. He was Shimon HaTzaddik [the Righteous]. As one of the members of the Great Assembly

he had been privileged to experience the Divine Presence among his teachers and colleagues, and he in turn reflected its splendor to succeeding generations.

During that difficult time following the sudden death of Alexander the Great, Shimon HaTzaddik was the uncontested leader of Israel. As one of the remaining Sages of the Great Assembly, Shimon was the spiritual leader of the people. He was also Kohen Gadol; and because Alexander had decreed that the Kohen Gadol should

The tomb of Shimon HaTzaddik in Jerusalem is used frequently as a place of prayer, particularly on the anniversary of his passing; and on Lag BaOmer it serves as an alternative site for the traditional first haircut of three-year-old boys for those Jerusalem families who find the journey to Meron too difficult.

be governor of the land, Shimon was the political leader, with the power to enforce his authority. He used this power to strengthen the study and observance of the Torah throughout the land.

The Talmud (Yoma 39a) tells that during his lifetime five visible miracles occurred in the Beis HaMikdash:

(1) Each Yom Kippur when he, as Kohen Gadol, put his hands into the box to draw the lots for the he-goat that would be offered on the altar, the lot inscribed "For Hashem" always came up in his right hand. This was a sign of G-d's favor upon Israel.

(2) The scarlet ribbon that was tied to the horns of the second he-goat always turned white at the moment it was pushed over the brink of a desert cliff. This was a sign that G-d had forgiven His people's sins of the past year, in accordance with the verse: "Even if your sins will be as scarlet, they will turn as white as snow" (Isaiah 1:18).

(3) The lamp of the Menorah known as the "Western Lamp" [נֵר מַעֲרָבִי] burned for twenty-four hours, even though it was filled with enough oil for only twelve hours.

(4) The fire on the altar continued to burn strongly, even though the supply of wood placed there every morning was not replenished for the rest of the day.

(5) From each of the various grain and bread offerings — the Omer, the Two Loaves, and the Lechem HaPanim — each Kohen was able to receive a small portion and satisfy his hunger with it.

Shimon Ben Sira, a poet who lived close to the time of Shimon HaTzaddik, composed a lengthy song describing Shimon in glowing terms. Among other things, Ben Sira says of Shimon: "He was the greatest of his brothers, the splendor of his people ... How glorious he was when he left the Temple, as he departed from the Most Holy, like a star shining from among the clouds, like a full moon in the festival season ..." (Ben Sira ch. 50).

5

The Rise of Greece

Look carefully, my friend; and understand;
avert your tread from snares and thorns.
Be not misled by wisdom of the Greeks,
which bears not any fruit — but only flowers.

(Rabbi Yehudah Halevi)

Settlement and Growth

At the time of King Shlomo [Solomon], when our people were settled safely in their Land and the First Temple stood in Jerusalem, most of the European continent was still uninhabited. But before long people from the East moved into Europe and settled there. They were descendants of Noah's grandson Javan [Yavan].

The island of Crete and the land of Greece were the first areas of Europe in which the migrating tribes established organized communities. The geographical conditions of Greece had an influence upon the nature of the new settlers and their way of life. Tall mountains traversed the width and length of the land, and people settled in the intervening valleys. The mountainous heights prevented the settlements from maintaining close contact with one another, leading the various settlements to regard themselves as separate nations. The emergence of independent city-states was thus the logical outcome of the geographical barriers, each city-state having its own way of life and system of government. Thus, there were as many countries in Greece as there were cities.

The coastline of Greece is sharply and frequently indented and the sea surrounds the country on three sides, cutting deep into the peninsula. Never being very far from the sea, the people soon learned to navigate it and use it as a means of commerce and conquest. They learned to build seaworthy ships, took possession of the many islands which abound in the Aegean Sea and gradually expanded the range of their ships, which sailed south to Crete, east to Asia Minor, and west as far as Italy, a considerable distance in those days.

In their expeditions the Greeks came in contact with the Phoenicians, who lived in Tyre and Sidon. From them, they acquired the letters of the alphabet and the knowledge of reading and writing. They learned also from other peoples. The Babylonians, for example, taught them astronomy and the Egyptians taught them engineering. Before long the Greeks turned from students to creative teachers in the field of science, and indeed, they are credited with being the founding fathers of modern science.

However, in the area of religion and ethics they remained on the primitive level of the other peoples with whom they came in contact. The masses continued to worship idols and believed that their many gods ate, drank, loved, and fought like people. In their personal lives there was little of today's generally accepted standards of decent behavior, and their social life had little justice and charity. Even in Athens, one of the first democracies in history, there were ten slaves for every free citizen.

The Greeks were valiant warriors and engaged in many battles with their neighbors. Archaeological discoveries on the island of Crete and along the Dardanelles eloquently testify to the destruction caused in the wars waged there by the Greeks.

The classical Greek poet Homer describes the war that the Greeks waged against the city of Troy, situated on the coast of the Dardanelles. His two historical epics, *The Iliad* and *The Odyssey,* were the treasured national heritage of the Greeks for many generations. These works contributed much to the development of their national spirit, and strengthened the bonds between the various segments of the people.

As related by Homer, for a long time the Greeks could not overcome the resistance of the city of Troy. Finally they resorted to a celebrated ruse. They withdrew from their siege, boarded their boats, and gave the impression of preparing to return home. But at the gate of the city wall they left a giant horse of wood in which were hidden dozens of Greek warriors. When the Trojans saw that the Greek army had withdrawn, they opened the gate and discovered the horse. This they interpreted as a good omen, and brought the horse into the city. During the night, while the Trojans drunkenly celebrated their victory, the hidden Greek soldiers clambered out of the belly of the horse and opened the city gates to their comrades in arms, who in the meantime had returned from their mock withdrawal. The Greek forces overpowered Troy and destroyed it.

Athens and Sparta

The two best known city-states of Greece were Athens and Sparta. Athens is situated in central Greece, near the Gulf of Corinth, while Sparta is located in the southern part of the Peloponnesian Peninsula.

There were sharp differences between these two cities, both with regard to their system of government and the mentality of their citizens. Sparta was ruled by a rigid military regime. Almost all of its male citizens were soldiers who spent most of their lives in military camps. At an early age, boys were taken from their mothers and given military training; they were taught the use of arms and were hardened to the utmost of their physical endurance. Each infant was examined at birth for physical fitness. If he showed promising signs of future military usefulness — well and good. But if not, he was thrown away to die in an open field, unless he was adopted by one of the subjugated tribes around them.

Life in Athens was altogether different — more pleasant and varied. There were, of course, soldiers, but there were also craftsmen, merchants and sailors. The most talented engaged in art and science or philosophy. Prominent among the subjects studied in schools were song, music, and gymnastics.

In the beginning Athens, like Sparta, was ruled by kings. But unlike Sparta, where the form of government remained unchanged for a long time, Athens experienced a development in the form of its government. The monarchy was followed by the rule of the aristocrats, called oligarchy. Then dictators ("tyrants" in Greek) seized control of the government. The people did not tolerate this system for long and brought about popular participation in the government, resulting in a form of government called democracy (demos in Greek is "people" and kratein is "to rule"). The people chose their rulers and all citizens took part in general meetings that were held in the public square, called the agora. In those assemblies, the more important issues, such as whether or not to wage war, were decided by a free vote and majority rule.

Athens developed art to a high degree of perfection. Its architects and builders erected beautiful buildings and adorned them with magnificent statues, many of which are still preserved in some of their ruins. Poets composed songs and dramas; scientists discovered natural facts that were not known before, as for example, that the earth was spherical. They could calculate the expected time of a solar eclipse. The philosophers speculated on the source of knowledge; they wanted to know the "why" rather than the "how." They wanted to know why a stone falls down from a height, why one building was considered beautiful while another was ugly, and why one law was just and the other was not. They taught people to look for the truth and try to improve the way they and their government behaved.

Wars with Persia

In their search for conquest and possessions, many of the seafaring Greeks crossed the Aegean Sea and settled in the coastal cities of Asia Minor But when King Cyrus of Persia dispatched his armies on his empire-building wars, he conquered these Greek colonial outposts. However, the Persian domination did not last long. With the help of their compatriots from Athens, the colonists revolted and freed themselves from the Persian yoke.

Soon thereafter, the Persians subdued the coastal cities again. This time, they decided to proceed against Athens as well and to punish her for having assisted the Greek settlers. The Persian invaders sailed across the sea with a large fleet and landed on the Greek coast, near Athens. When the Athenians saw the enemy's powerful army they were alarmed. Nevertheless, they did not wait to be overwhelmed by a Persian assault backed by a shower of arrows. With courage and brilliant strategy, the Athenians launched a surprise attack before the Persians were fully organized, and succeeded in defeating them.

The humiliation only spurred the Persians to try again. A few years later, with

King Xerxes [according to some historians, King Xerxes was Ahasuerus, the husband of Queen Esther] at its head, such a huge army set out to defeat the Greeks that there were not enough boats to carry the soldiers. Instead they marched along the coast of the Aegean Sea while the fleet sailed parallel to them and within their view. They invaded Greece from the north, planning to march south toward Athens. Although Sparta was not in the path of the Persian advance, it felt threatened. Sparta sallied forth to confront the invaders. The Spartans planned to trap the huge army in the narrow mountain pass called Thermopylae, but they failed dismally. The Spartans were killed to the last man. Now the road to Athens was open. The Athenians fled from their city and the Persians set it afire. But again the Athenians turned near defeat into victory. Their sailor-soldiers took to their boats. When the larger and more unwieldy Persian boats arrived at the bay of Athens they

THE PERSIAN WARS

- - - - -▷ Persians, First Campaign
═════▷ Persians, Second Campaign
━━━━▶ Greeks

were suddenly attacked by the smaller, yet speedier Greek boats. The clumsy Persian navy was outmaneuvered and sunk.

At the loss of his proud fleet King Xerxes despaired of victory over the Athenians. He left a small force in Greece and led most of his army back to Persia along the overland route by which they had come. Some time later the Athenians added a land victory to their naval triumphs. The outcome of this battle put an end to the famous confrontation between the small Greek nation and the mighty Persian empire.

After their great victory over the Persians the Athenians rebuilt their city, making it bigger and more beautiful than before. At the head of the government was the great leader Pericles, under whom Athens reached its Golden Age. Writers composed the famous classical dramas, architects built splendid structures, and learned men enlarged the scope of science and philosophy. The political prestige of Athens likewise rose to considerable heights as a direct result of her successful wars with mighty Persia. Many cities were anxious to come under the protection of Athens and be safe from the threat of Persian domination. Greece was no longer a small nation, but grew to be a mighty power that ruled the seas.

However, the status of Athens, and of Greece as a whole, began to fade as a result of the internal struggles between the various city-states for domination over the country. In fact Athens supremacy came to an end as the result of one such fierce encounter — the Peloponnesian War — in which the Spartans defeated the defenders of Athens and razed it by fire. Sparta, in turn, was soon defeated and displaced by Thebes as the dominant city-state. Such civil wars continued to break out until Greece, weakened by such strife, was conquered by Philip of Macedonia.

6

Alexander the Great

[During one of his expeditions, Alexander (the Great) of Macedonia] sat down beside a brook to eat a meal. When he dipped salted fish into the waters of the brook to wash off their brine the fish acquired an exceptional aroma. Said he, "This brook must originate in the Garden of Eden" ... He followed the brook until he arrived at the gates of the Garden of Eden. There he called in a loud voice, "Open the gates for me!" They said to him, "This is the gate of Hashem, the righteous shall enter through it" (Psalms 118:20). [He replied,] "I am also a king, I am an important person. Give me something [from the Garden of Eden]." They gave him a skull. He put all his silver and gold on one side of a scale and the skull on the other side, yet the skull outweighed the silver and gold. Alexander asked the Sages: "Why can I not find enough to offset its weight?" They replied: "This is the skull of mortal man, who is never satisfied. Its weight is so great because it lusts after all existing silver and gold." Said he: "How can I prove that you speak the truth?" They answered him: "Take some soil and cover the place of the skull's eye, so it cannot see. Then it will be sated" (Tamid 32b).

Macedonian Supremacy

Unlike Greece, which was wracked by civil war in its declining years, its northern neighbor Macedonia was unified. When Philip ascended the throne of Macedonia, he organized a well-trained army, which he equipped with the most up-to-date armaments and guided by original approaches to military stategy. Philip was able to expand his influence southward, conquering the Greek city-states as he advanced. Though the Greeks regarded him as a foreign invader — a "barbarian" in their language — Philip for his part saw himself as belonging to their culture. In fact he held it in such esteem that he educated his famous son Alexander according to its values, even bringing the philosopher Aristotle from Athens as a teacher.

Alexander, an unusually gifted young man, was destined for a dramatic role in history. The tales of valor which he encountered in the poems of Homer made a profound impression on him. His father introduced him at a young age to the arts of warfare and of statecraft, and when he was only sixteen years old, Philip entrusted him temporarily with the administration of the country.

When Alexander was twenty years old, King Philip was assassinated. Despite his youth, Alexander took the throne and deftly suppressed all attempts on the part of rebellious tribes in the north and the cities of the south to shake off the yoke of Macedonia. When the city of Thebes resisted him, for example, he destroyed it completely, sparing only the home of the poet, Pindar.

Having firmly established his rule in Macedonia and Greece, Alexander set out to conquer the lands of the east. He persuaded most of the Greek city-states to join him in his imperial expeditions, telling them that they now had the chance to take revenge on the Persians for the destruction they had wrought upon the temples of their idols.

G-d had shown Nebuchadnezzar in a dream the empires that would rule the world. The first part of the dream had been fulfilled — Babylonia and then Persia having played their leading roles on the international stage. The time of the Third Kingdom had come, namely the Hellenistic empire. The leading actor in this drama was Alexander of Macedonia-Greece. In his victories over the lands of

the Middle East he vanquished the Persians, and inherited their empire.

At the head of an army of 40,000 soldiers he passed through the Hellespont, the strait now known as the Dardanelles, and attacked the superior army of King Darius [the Persian; known to historians as Darius III Codomanus] at Issus. Though smaller in number, Alexander's army was better trained and armed — and it was led by a military genius. In contrast, the Persian army was composed of various and often antagonistic national elements. The lack of cooperation between them reflected the tensions and shortcomings of the imperial government. In this historical battle, the higher morale and better skill of Alexander's troops carried the day and the Persians were utterly defeated.

King Darius managed to escape and later sent word to the victor, offering to conclude a peace treaty. But Alexander's answer was unconditional surrender. This, Darius would not accept; he retreated to regroup and prepare for future battles against the Macedonian conqueror. From Issus, Alexander proceeded on his victorious march along the coastline, capturing all cities that refused to surrender. The city of Tyre alone offered serious resistance. It took seven months of siege before she, too, capitulated.

Shimon the Tzaddik and Alexander the Macedonian

During his lengthy siege of Tyre, Alexander requested the assistance of the neighboring peoples. The Jews refused because of their oath to their Persian overlords. The Samaritans, however, had no such scruples. They sent military detachments to Alexander's camp, and as their reward, asked for permission to

destroy the Temple in Jerusalem.

When the Jews heard that Alexander had granted their enemies' request, they were seized with terror. At that time Shimon HaTzaddik was still a young man, but he became the instrument of a great miracle that saved Jerusalem from almost certain destruction. Shimon was chosen to meet Alexander and convince him to change his mind. The Talmud describes that fateful encounter:

> Shimon HaTzaddik donned priestly garments and together with the notables of Jerusalem set out on his way, holding burning torches. All night, the Jews walked from one direction while the Greek army walked from the other direction until daybreak. At dawn, Alexander asked his generals: "Who are these?"
>
> They answered: "They are the Jews who rebelled against you."
>
> When Alexander reached Antipatris [near Rosh HaAyin] the sun rose and they met each other. As soon as Alexander saw Shimon HaTzaddik, he alighted from his chariot and bowed down before him.
>
> His generals said to him: "Should a great king like you bow before this Jew?"
>
> He replied: "The image of this man goes before me triumphantly in my battles." [That is to say: Shimon HaTzaddik would appear to him in a dream on the eve of battle and assure him of victory.] Alexander then asked the Jews: "Why have you come?"
>
> They said: "Is it possible that idolaters can mislead you into destroying a House where prayers are offered for your sake and that your kingdom should not be destroyed?"
>
> He said to them: "Who are they?"

This miniature illumination in a 13th-century Latin Bible shows Alexander the Great paying homage to the Kohen Gadol.

> They answered him: "These Samaritans who stand before you!"
>
> He said to them: "Behold, they are now delivered into your power" (Yoma 69a).

In grateful commemoration of that miracle, our people declared its anniversary, 25 Teves, a day of joy, when it was forbidden to fast or eulogize the dead. And in honor of Alexander, all the boys born in that year were named after him. Since then, Alexander has been a Jewish name.

Later, too, Alexander showed favor to the Jews. He appointed the Kohen Gadol [High Priest] to replace the Persian ruler as governor of the land, and extended its borders, adding to it three zones that had belonged to the Samaritans.

The Spread of Hellenistic Culture Following the Conquest of the Middle East

From the Land of Israel, Alexander continued on his march to Egypt. There he was received with open arms, for the Egyptians saw him as their liberator from the hated Persian rule. And indeed Alexander did not act like a conqueror toward Egypt. At the outset of his Middle East campaign he had intended to impose Greek culture upon the conquered peoples, but in Egypt he was ready to be influenced by the spirit and culture of the East as well. For example, he offered sacrifices to the gods of Egypt and allowed himself to be declared Son of Amen, the chief Egyptian idol. His ambition caused him to elevate himself above the level of a great general and king. Following the example of the old Pharaohs of Egypt, he declared himself to be a god.

There is no doubt that his personal ambition went hand in hand with mature and rational thinking. Alexander was determined to rule over the whole known world of his days. In order to establish this worldwide empire and rule it successfully, he knew he had to reduce as much as possible all potential areas of internal conflict and tension. He also knew that

there was no greater source of conflict than the differences of religion and culture among the many tribes and peoples of his projected empire. To avoid this he tried to merge the many different beliefs and practices of his subjects into a single culture. In the main, this was to be a Graeco-Oriental civilization, where the Hellenistic spirit — the culture of Greece — would be fused with the spirit of the Near and Far East.

To carry out his plans he founded new cities and populated them with people from different nations. An outstanding example of these hopes and intentions is the founding of the city that bears his name — Alexandria of Egypt. In it he settled Egyptians, Greeks, and Jews in the expectation that the various segments would mingle and evolve a common culture and way of life. To encourage and accelerate this process he set up facilities for the dissemination of Greek learning and wisdom side by side with temples

ALEXANDER'S CAMPAIGNS

dedicated to the pantheon of Greek gods and the polytheism of Eastern religion. The results of this attempt left their mark for many genrations among the peoples of the East, as well as those of Europe.

The spread and influence of the Hellenistic spirit reached their high point after the death of Alexander. In its wake came libraries, scientific research, and technological advance. Unfortunately, its positive aspects were overshadowed by negative by-products. The same spirit degenerated into an intensification of idol worship and the corruption of morals.

Alexander's Last Campaign

In the spring of 318 BCE (3443), Alexander set forth from Egypt to pursue the elusive King Darius. The Persian king made his stand at Gaugamela, not far from Nineveh. Again Alexander scored a great victory, but again the Persian king succeeded in escaping. Alexander and his army turned southward and reached Babylon. The city opened her gates willingly in surrender, and received him with great honor. From there he marched to Persia itself. Upon his arrival he was informed that his constant adversary, King Darius, had been assassinated by Persian princes. Losing no time, Alexander declared himself King of Persia. Neither did he give his army much rest, but continued into the interior of that vast land in order to impose his rule over all its inhabitants. Now, however, he met with enormous difficulties. The Persians did not consider Alexander a liberator but a foreign conqueror, and they offered stiff resistance to his progress. The mountainous terrain in the north of the country caused his soldiers many difficulties. This and the ever-growing distances from home created unrest in his camp and the soldiers demanded that he end the war.

Alexander's will prevailed, however, and his army advanced eastward, but when they reached the border of India they refused to go any further. This time Alexander had no choice and reluctantly turned back to Persepolis, the capital of Persia. Meanwhile, he had married a princess during one of his conquests and induced his officers likewise to marry local women. He moved to Babylonia, his mind teeming with designs and plans on how to develop his mighty empire. Many problems had developed. Many of his local governors were corrupt and Alexander himself had become vain and cruel. In the process, he lost much of his prosperity. He thought of plans to consolidate his conquests and make new ones, but it was not to be. Before he reached the age of thirty-three he fell sick with a consumptive fever and died.

Alexander's only son was born after his death, and a fierce struggle for the succession was inevitable. Three senior generals contended for the imperial inheritance. Though the power struggle lasted for many years, none of the rivals was able to prevail. They finally agreed to divide the huge kingdom among themselves. Thus Alexander's great vision of Graeco-Oriental unity was ended.

The nucleus of the Alexandrian Empire, Macedonia and Greece, fell to Antigonus. Babylonia and Syria became the possession of Seleucus, and Ptolemy inherited Egypt and the Land of Israel. One of the decisive

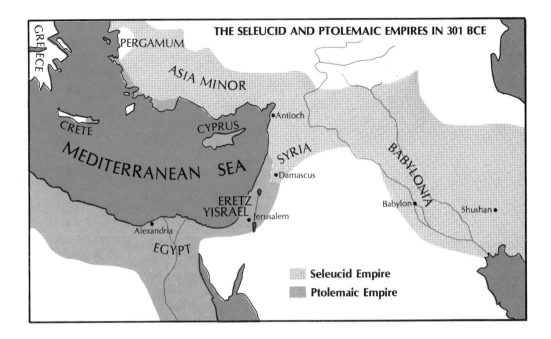

THE SELEUCID AND PTOLEMAIC EMPIRES IN 301 BCE

GREECE
PERGAMUM
ASIA MINOR
CRETE
CYPRUS
MEDITERRANEAN SEA
•Antioch
SYRIA
BABYLONIA
•Damascus
ERETZ YISRAEL
•Jerusalem
Babylon•
Shushan•
•Alexandria
EGYPT

Seleucid Empire
Ptolemaic Empire

battles which preceded this division was waged in 312 BCE (3449) near Gaza, in the Land of Israel, in which Seleucus and Ptolemy defeated Antigonus.

The struggle among Alexander's heirs continued for several years. The final battle took place near the city of Ipsus in Asia Minor in the year 301 BCE (3460). This time Ptolemy and Seleucus triumphed and from then on the Ptolemies ruled over the Land of Israel. Their rule lasted for some hundred years, until the Seleucids from the north defeated Egypt and took *Eretz Yisrael* from them. The Holy Land then became a province of Syria — until the Hasmonean revolt shook off the cruel yoke of the Syrian Seleucids.

7

The Land of Israel under the Ptolemies

We learned, R' Yehudah says: He who has not seen the dioploston (synagogue of a certain design) of Alexandria, Egypt, has not witnessed the honor of Israel ... It had seventy-one chairs of gold for the seventy-one Elders ... There was a wooden platform in the middle on which the supervisor of the synagogue stood. He had flags in his hand and when the time came to respond Amen, he waved the flags and the people said Amen. They did not sit in mixed fashion, but each trade sat by itself — goldsmiths separately, silversmiths separately, blacksmiths separately, the coppersmiths separately, weavers of wool separately. If a poor visitor came there, he recognized the men of his trade and associated with them; from there would come his livelihood and the livelihood of his family (Sukkah 51b).

Two Ptolemies, Two Attitudes

Ptolemy I, who had been one of Alexander's chief generals, was one of the three who fought each other to succeed him as ruler of the whole empire. In the compromise that ended the struggle, Ptolemy was given Egypt, but he wanted more. Particularly he wanted the Land of Israel. He set out with his army to conquer it. When they approached Jerusalem and saw how well it was fortified, he decided to capture it by means of deception rather than by open attack. He sent word that he wished to offer sacrifices in the Holy Temple and that he would enter the city on the Sabbath. The Jews agreed. Once inside, however, he turned on the unsuspecting, Sabbath-observing Jews and occupied the city.

He forcibly removed many Jews from their homeland and brought them to Egypt. Appreciating their skills and valor, he used them as servants to the court and soldiers for his army. Only years later, when Ptolemy II ascended the throne, were they freed. Most of them remained in Egypt and joined the famous Jewish community of Alexandria. Ptolemy I reigned until 285 BCE (3476), when he abdicated the throne to his son, and died two years later.

When Ptolemy II succeeded his father as king at the age of twenty-four, he inherited

A fifth-century manuscript of the Septuagint, showing a passage from Exodus.

placed them in seventy-two rooms, without telling them why he had gathered them. He went to each of them and said: "Translate the Torah of Moses your teacher for me." G-d gave each of them the same thoughts, so they all translated "G-d created in the beginning" [instead of the literal Hebrew "In the beginning G-d created", in order to prevent a mistake on the part of the gentile reader who might think that Bereishis, "in the beginning", was the name of a being who created everything, including G-d!]. They likewise wrote: "I shall make a man in My image and likeness" [instead of the Hebrew "We shall make a man," so that the gentiles should not think that there are two authorities who created man] (Megillah 9a).

The Jews of Egypt rejoiced that the translation had been done, because they were sure that their countrymen would honor the nation to whom G-d had given such a wise and great Torah, and for whom he had performed so many miracles. Every year they celebrated the day on which it was published. It was called "Septuagint," or Translation of the Seventy. However the Sages of Israel took a different view of the new situation. They knew that eventually the Jews of Egypt would study Torah only from the Septuagint, instead of reading it in the original Holy Tongue, Hebrew. Eventually they would forget the Torah and become assimilated with the Egyptians. The Sages said that on 8 Teves, when the translation was completed, "three days of darkness" descended on the world. Unfortunately, their apprehension proved to be justified.

a consolidated and tranquil kingdom that included *Eretz Yisrael*. He reigned for thirty-nine years, from 285-246 BCE (3476-3515). Warfare no longer occupied the center of the stage and people began to interest themselves in cultural matters, particularly in literature. Libraries were established in which the writings of many nations found a home. Ptolemy II loved books and built a large library. He was anxious to include in it a copy of the Torah, but it was written in Hebrew, a language he did not understand.

He had an idea. He invited sages and scholars from among the Jews and ordered them to translate the Bible into Greek. Details about this important event in the annals of our people are recorded in the Talmud:

> It happened that King Ptolemy gathered seventy-two Elders and

Influence of Hellenistic Culture on the Land of Israel

During the reign of the Ptolemaic dynasty, Hellenistic culture spread considerably. Greek-style cities were founded in Egypt, Syria, Transjordan, and even in *Eretz Yisrael*. These cities featured all the institutions and the way of life that characterized Greek culture. There were libraries that contained the writings of the Greek philosophers and writers, pagan temples, houses of entertainment, sports arenas, and so on.

These cities presented a critical stumbling block to our people. Many Jews came to them for reasons of trade and the more frivolous among them were impressed by the external beauty of Hellenism. They visited the sports arenas, where naked Greek youths engaged in gymnastics and competitive sports. They came to the Greek temples and amusement places, and participated in their wild festivities. The inevitable result was not long in coming: many Jews eventually shook off the yoke of the Torah and its commandments.

The G-d-fearing Jews did not go near these places and despised all signs of the depraved Hellenistic way of life. But they were powerless to prevent its spread among their fellow Jews.

At first the assimilationists adopted only the more external aspects of the foreign culture, such as speaking the Greek language and participating in public festivities. But one thing led to the next. Eventually they became alienated from the Jewish way of life, ate non-kosher food and participated in idolatry.

At the beginning of the Ptolemaic era, the life of the people was guided by the Torah, as expounded by the Prophets and the Men of the Great Assembly. In all communities there were synagogues where people prayed in accordance with the established ritual, read the Torah at regular intervals, and studied its explanations as transmitted in the Oral Law. Because of this strong natural attachment to the Torah, the Hellenistic Jews returning to Jerusalem and other cities from visits to the Greek towns did not dare defy the religion of their fathers publicly, but did so only in private.

These assimilationist Jews, like all those who break away from previously kept beliefs and practices, sought to rationalize their departure from them. To quiet their conscience and fear of heaven they deluded themselves by inventing some justification for their deeds.

Two disciples of Antigonus of Socho acted in this spirit. He had taught:

> Do not be like servants who serve their master for the sake of being rewarded, but be like servants who serve their master not for the sake of being rewarded (*Avos* 1:3).

Two of Antigonus' disciples, Tzadok and Baysos, were apparently influenced by the Hellenistic spirit. Their own inclinations misled them and they distorted the meaning of their teacher's words. While the obvious explanation of this Mishnaic statement is quite clear to every schoolchild, they falsified its meaning to be that there is neither reward nor punishment in the World to Come; indeed they denied its existence. The logical conclusion of this philosophy was that one's main goal should be the pursuit of pleasure in this world. They denied both the truth of the Oral Tradition and the authority of the Sages to interpret the Torah and to issue decrees. Consequently, they refused to accept any law not stated clearly in the Torah.

This so-called "theology" was only a front for the real aim of this movement — total denial of the Torah. By denying the authority of the Sages, they robbed the Torah of any precise meaning because everyone was free to explain it as he wished. Josephus Flavius' description of these people *(Wars* 2:8:14) implies that basically they were irreligious. No doubt, at this period of history they swelled the ranks of the Hellenists from whom they did not differ to a great extent.

In later generations, following the Hasmonean wars [see chs. 12-13], the number of these disbelievers increased; they were known as *Tzadokim* (Sadducees) and *Baysosim* (Boethusians).

The Hellenists Gain Power

During the reign of Ptolemy III, 246-221 BCE (3515-3540), a great change came about. The authority of the Jewish leadership became undermined and the Hellenists took advantage of the situation. Since the time of Alexander of Macedonia, the High Priest had been authorized to collect taxes from the people. Under the Ptolemies, he was required to submit to them part of this revenue in token of the overlordship of the Egyptian kings.

When Ptolemy III came to the throne of Egypt, the High Priest of the time, Chonyo II [Onias], son of Shimon *HaTzaddik,* refused to send the money to the king. Why he did so is not clear. Since the penalty for non-payment would be an Egyptian invasion and severe reprisals — as, indeed, Ptolemy threatened to impose when informed of Chonyo's refusal — it would seem to have been foolish beyond belief for Chonyo to have taken such a risk by avoiding the payment of taxes. Some historians theorize that Chonyo favored a takeover of *Eretz Yisrael* by the Seleucid kings of Syria and hoped to provoke it by antagonizing Egypt. In any case, while we do not know the reason for Chonyo's resistance, Ptolemy regarded it as tantamount to rebellion and threatened to invade Judea and punish its inhabitants.

A leading Hellenist by the name of Yosef ben Toviah, who was also Chonyo's nephew, persuaded the High Priest to allow him to go to Egypt and solve the dangerous problem.

Yosef succeeded greatly. Not only did he remove the threat of military action by giving Ptolemy extravagant gifts, he also convinced the king to appoint him tax collector of all *Eretz Yisrael* and Phoenicia (present-day Lebanon). The king even provided Yosef with 3,000 soldiers to help him in his collections.

In those days, the position of tax collector was highly profitable for unscrupulous people. The collector was allowed to keep all the money beyond what he paid the king. Cruel tax collectors would enrich themselves by demanding exorbitant taxes and pocketing most of the money. Yosef ben Toviah was such a person.

The city of Ashkelon was the first to feel the power of the new tax collector. When the residents of the city refused to pay the high taxes, Yosef had twenty of the leading Jews killed and he confiscated their property. Similar punishments were imposed in other places. The news spread quickly, and henceforth no one in the land dared to resist the demands of the new tax collector.

Many Hellenistic Jews joined forces with Yosef ben Toviah and, like him, enriched themselves from the new taxes. They now felt free and secure to openly imitate the ways of the gentiles and to disdain the laws of their fathers. The first to do so were the sons of Yosef. Other youths, including some of the *Kohanim,* soon followed their example. Later on, after the Seleucids conquered *Eretz Yisrael,* the Hellenists' power rose to the point where they forced even G-d-fearing Jews to follow their path. The threat to the integrity of the Jewish people and its religion became very real indeed.

New Spiritual Leadership

Upon the death of Shimon *HaTzaddik* his brother Elazar had become *Kohen Gadol,* while the spiritual, or rabbinic, leadership had been inherited by Shimon's disciple, Antigonus of Socho. The people then had two leaders, Elazar the High Priest who was also its political leader and had the authority to collect taxes, and Antigonus, the greatest of the Torah scholars of his time, who occupied the position of President of the Supreme Court, the Sanhedrin.

Reconstruction of one of the most impressive Hellenistic structures in Eretz Yisrael — a round tower near the summit of a hill in Shomron (Samaria), dating back to about 300 BCE.

With the death of Antigonus the authority that he represented was transmitted to his two outstanding disciples, Yose ben Yoezer of Tzreidah and Yose ben Yochanan of Jerusalem. With them began the period of the *Zugos* [Pairs], whereby the leadership of the people was shared by two outstanding sages: the *Nasi* [president of the Sanhedrin], a newly created office; and the *Av Beis Din* [dean of the Sanhedrin] an office that was now given new significance. Of the two positions, that of *Nasi* was the more powerful since it held political power, while that of *Av Beis Din* dealt with purely halachic matters.

The apparent reason for dividing the leadership between two people was the shameful transfer of the authority for collecting revenue from the High Priest, Chonyo, to Yosef ben Toviah. The Sages now felt that they could no longer entrust the undivided leadership of the people to the High Priest if he could be outwitted by a man of deceit and cruelty, as Chonyo had been by Yosef.

At the time when the rule of the *Zugos* was instituted, the spiritual level of the people was poor, and Torah study was irregular. The first difference of opinion in matters of Halachah is to be found at the period of the first of the *Zugos*. The particular question dealt with the laying of the hands [*semichah*] on a sacrifice that is brought on a festival day *(Yom Tov)*. Yose ben Yoezer forbade it, while his colleague, Yose ben Yochanan, required that it be done (see Mishnah *Chagigah* 2:2). Only much later, after the last of the *Zugos*, Hillel and Shammai, was it decided finally that *semichah* should be done.

Division in the Leadership of the People Under Egyptian Rule

King	Tax Collector	High Priest	Pres. of Sanhedrin	Dean of Sanhedrin
Ptolemy I	Shimon *HaTzaddik*	Shimon *HaTzaddik*	Shimon *HaTzaddik*	Shimon *HaTzaddik*
Ptolemy II	Elazar	Elazar	Antigonus	Antigonus
Ptolemy III	Yosef ben Toviah	Chonyo II	Yose ben Yoezer	Yose ben Yochanan

Egypt Loses Eretz Yisrael to Syria

During the reign of King Ptolemy IV, 221-205 BCE (3540-3556), the smoldering rivalry between the Seleucid and Ptolemaic kingdoms broke into the open again.

Following one of his victories, Ptolemy IV, out of arrogance, decided to visit Jerusalem and enter the Temple. The *Kohanim* tried fiercely to resist this attempt, but he forced his way inside. Miraculously, however, Ptolemy felt faint as he entered, and fell unconscious to the ground.

Returning home, he decided to make the Egyptian Jews pay for his frustration. He commanded all the Jewish notables of Alexandria to assemble in the arena of the circus. There he incited elephants to charge at the helpless Jews. Again, a miracle happened. Instead of attacking the Jews, the elephants turned against their handlers and the crowd of visitors who had come to enjoy the cruel spectacle and trampled many of them to death.

The Ptolemaic dynasty weakened considerably when Ptolemy IV was succeeded by a son, Ptolemy V, who was too young to rule effectively. Exploiting this situation, Antiochus III of Syria marched on *Eretz Yisrael* with his army, and in the year 199 or 198 BCE (3562 or 3561) conquered it from the hands of the Ptolemies.

Antiochus III, who reigned from 223-187 BCE (3538-3574), conquered the Land of Israel from the Egyptians. His contemporaries called him Antiochus the Great. He enlarged the borders of his realm and even waged war with the Romans, who were already a powerful adversary even at this early stage in their history. But in the year 190 BCE (3571) he was defeated by the Romans and was forced to pay them a heavy tribute.

At first Antiochus treated the Jews well. In order to help the city of Jerusalem repair the damage caused by the Ptolemaic-Seleucid wars, he freed the city from paying taxes for three years. He liberally contributed wine, oil, wheat, and spices for the sacrificial service in the *Beis HaMikdash* and forbade the bringing of unclean animals into Jerusalem. However, Antiochus proved to be too ambitious. His attempt to add Greece to his kingdom provoked Rome to declare war against him, a war that he lost. In the peace settlement, Antiochus was forced to agree to large payments to Rome. As a result, he was forced to increase the burden of taxes to be paid by all the peoples under his rule, including the Jews. His son Seleucus IV, who succeeded him on the throne — 187-175 BCE (3574-3586), — further increased the payment of taxes. Seeking to gain influence with the new king, the Jewish Hellenists sent word to Seleucus that the Temple treasury contained fabulous treasures, far beyond what it needed. When King Seleucus was infor-med about this windfall, he dispatched Heliodorus, one of his trusted officials, to confiscate the Temple treasury.

Upon arriving in Jerusalem, Heliodorus immediately disclosed to Chonyo III (grandson of Chonyo II), the *Kohen Gadol,* the purpose of his visit. Chonyo explained to him that the richness of the treasury had been grossly exaggerated, and that most of the funds belonged to widows and orphans, and were held in the Temple treasury for safekeeping. Chonyo argued that it would be sacrilegious to despoil the Holy Temple. However, Heliodorus refused to be dissuaded and made known his intention to enter the Temple and take what he wished.

When the *Kohanim* heard of this they prostrated themselves before the Altar and beseeched Heaven to spare them this desecration of the Temple. The people of Jerusalem assembled in throngs to offer supplication and the women donned sackcloth. The ashen color of the *Kohen Gadol* and the pained expression on his face clearly showed the anguish he was enduring.

When Heliodorus attempted to enter the Temple, a miracle happened. A divine vision in the form of a horse with an armed rider rushed at him and struck him with its forefeet. Two young men appeared and flogged him mercilessly. He fell down unconscious, became deathly ill, and had to be carried away. To the Jews it was clear that G-d had heeded their prayers for the honor of His Temple, but Chonyo knew full well that Seleucus would think otherwise. Chonyo hastened to offer sacrifices for Heliodorus' recovery so that Seleucus would not suspect the Jews of foul play. Upon recovering, Heliodorus hastened back to the king and attested to him about the Divine power that guarded the Temple in Jerusalem.

The Hellenists refused to be moved by this miracle and asserted before the king that Chonyo had influenced Heliodorus to fabricate the entire incident. Furthermore, they accused Chonyo of being loyal to Egypt, the sworn enemy of Seleucus. At that point Chonyo felt it was his responsibility to bring the affair to a head and call the king's attention to the Hellenists' lies. Chonyo now traveled to Syria to refute the charges of the Hellenists that he was siding with the Egyptian rulers. While he was waiting in Antioch to hear the king's decision, the news reached Chonyo that Seleucus IV had been murdered; the year was 175 BCE (3586). He was followed on the throne by his brother, Antiochus IV Epiphanes, who reigned from 175-163 BCE (3586-3598), and who brought the Hellenists to power in Judea and Jerusalem. Under him began the revolt that ended in the miracle of Chanukah.

8

Antiochus Epiphanes and His Decrees

All Jews are commanded regarding the sanctification of the Great Name of G-d, as it is written: "I shall be sanctified among the Children of Israel (Leviticus 22:32)," and are commanded not to profane it, as it is written: "You shall not profane My Holy Name" (ibid.). How does this commandment apply? If a non-Jew arises and forces a Jew to transgress any law of the Torah on pain of death, he should transgress and not be killed, because concerning the laws it is written: "Which man should do and live by them" [i.e., the mitzvos should cause man to live, not die] (Leviticus 18:5). ... When does this apply? With all laws, except idolatry, sexual immorality and murder. But with these three sins, if he were told, "Transgress one of them, or else you will be killed" — he should choose death and not transgress. When does this apply? When the non-Jew has in mind only his personal pleasure, such as when he forces a Jew to build his house or to cook his meal on the Sabbath ... But if his intention is only to force the Jew to transgress the mitzvos, if this occurs privately, not in the presence of ten Jews, let him transgress and not be killed. But if he forces him to transgress in the presence of at least ten Jews, let him be killed and not transgress (Rambam, Hilchos Yesodei HaTorah 5:1-2).

Hellenists Win the High Priesthood

Antiochus IV came to power in 175 BCE (3586), twenty-five years after the Seleucids conquered the Land of Israel from the Ptolemies. His courtiers, wishing to flatter him, called him Epiphanes [the illustrious]. But behind his back they called him Epimanes [the madman] — a nickname that describes him more aptly.

Antiochus believed himself to be divine. He ordered all the peoples under his rule to erect statues of him in their temples, and prostrate themselves before his image. He spent money lavishly on grandiose public entertainments, during which he behaved like a fool, even dancing naked with his royal entertainers. All this was designed to attract to himself the attention of the masses. In order to strengthen his rule he imposed Hellenism over the various peoples, including the Jews. But despite the fact that he was helped by Jewish traitors and collaborators, he did not succeed.

At the beginning of the Seleucid rule, the integrity of the Holy Temple and of the priesthood was faithfully maintained by loyal High Priests. With great effort, they had managed to keep the family of Yosef the tax collector and the other Hellenists from exerting their influence upon internal Jewish matters. When Antiochus Epiphanes came to the throne in Syria, however, things soon took a different turn. The Hellenists now had a sympathetic royal

Jason's Tomb in Jerusalem was restored from the ruins found on the site. It was first built in the first century before the Common Era, during the reign of Alexander Yannai.

ear to listen to them and help them carry out their evil plans.

The Hellenists now managed to take over even the spiritual function of the *Kehunah Gedolah*. Yeshua, a brother of Chonyo, who had Hellenized his name to Jason, offered Antiochus a generous bribe to depose Chonyo and appoint Jason *Kohen Gadol*. He promised the king another payment of tribute if he would authorize the erection of a gymnasium for the youth of Jerusalem and if he would consider the people of Jerusalem honorary citizens of Antioch, the Syrian capital. As soon as Antiochus appointed him *Kohen Gadol*, Jason set his program in motion. He established a gymnasium close to the Temple, and promoted the pagan customs of the Greek rulers to such an extent that even the *Kohanim* began to neglect the sacrificial service in favor of Jason's new centers of diversion.

Although the gymnasium was used primarily for athletics, it was a vehicle of idol worship and immorality. The exercises were performed naked and before games were held, sacrifices were offered to Heracles (Hercules). Surprisingly, however, even Jason's excesses were too mild to satisfy the more extreme Jewish Hellenists.

Three years passed and the time came for Jason to pay his tribute to Antiochus. His emissary to the king, Menelaus, made use of this opportunity to offer Antiochus a large bribe to appoint him — Menelaus — *Kohen Gadol*. Having secured the king's appointment, Menelaus, who was not even a *Kohen*, proceeded ruthlessly to oppress his people and to persecute the Jewish religion. Menelaus and his brother Lysimachus took the golden vessels of the Holy Temple and sold them to raise the money they needed to pay the royal tribute. When Chonyo, the lawful *Kohen Gadol* (who had been deposed previously by Jason), protested this act, they had him murdered. Jason apparently offered no resistance to his deposer, and bided his time, waiting for a chance to return to power.

Alarmed at the turn of events, the people of Jerusalem began to express their dissatisfaction. Lysimachus, fearing an organized revolt, fell upon the people with an armed band of 3,000 soldiers. The people fought the soldiers with sticks and stones, and Lysimachus was killed in the struggle. The Sanhedrin sent three of its members to Antioch to accuse Menelaus before the king as the instigator of these troubles. Menelaus was in great danger of being found guilty, but he managed to bribe a close advisor to the king, who saw to it that not only Menelaus was acquitted but that the three sages were condemned to death. Menelaus retained his post and persisted in his cruel ways.

The Expulsion of Menelaus and Antiochus' Decree

At this time, 169 BCE (3592), Antiochus attacked and conquered Egypt, but he failed to reckon with Rome, which had become the strongest power in the region. Rome opposed an extension of Syrian power and was strong enough to frighten Antiochus. A Roman ambassador gave him an ultimatum either to withdraw from Egypt or face attack from Rome. Antiochus retreated in disgrace. Meanwhile rumors had circulated in Jerusalem that the king had been killed in the Egyptian campaign, and Jason, taking advantage of this, attacked the city with a thousand men. He was able to penetrate the walls and Menelaus' forces had to retreat and take refuge in the Acra a strong fortification near the Temple site.

Jason entered the city and perpetrated a massacre upon its inhabitants, although they were his own countrymen. Antiochus, not yet back from Egypt, was informed of these happenings and interpreted Jason's attack as a revolt against the throne. Enraged, he stormed up from Egypt and easily took the city, which, not expecting a military action, opened its gates to him. He ordered his soldiers indiscriminately to kill men, women, and children. Forty thousand were killed and an equal number taken into captivity. Jason fled Jerusalem and died a fugitive.

Antiochus brazenly entered the Temple and stole as much gold and silver as he wanted. He entered the Holy and removed the holy vessels, the gold Altar, the *Menorah,* the Table for the *Panim* bread, the *Paroches* [curtain], and the gold ornamentation with which the front of the Temple was decorated. Menelaus was reinstated as *Kohen Gadol* and oppressed his people even more cruelly than did Antiochus.

Two years later, Antiochus sent Apollonius, the commander of the Mysians (Mysia was located in northwestern Asia Minor), to Jerusalem, with an army of 22,000 soldiers. He gained admittance to the city without a struggle, for the people did not suspect his intention. Once inside, he attacked the people and massacred great numbers of them.

The soldiers destroyed the houses and the walls guarding the city. Women and children were taken captive. Apollonius' men fortified the Acra and garrisoned it with Syrian soldiers and treacherous Jews. Until its fall to the Hasmoneans many years later, it remained a physical threat to the Jews and a danger to the neighboring Temple. In their fury against the Temple as the symbol of Judaism, the Syrians made thirteen breaches in the wall around the Temple court.

The king issued a declaration to his entire realm, but directed primarily at *Eretz Yisrael,* that it was his intention to unify the diverse national and religious groups in his empire and mold them into one homogeneous nation. Accordingly, all peoples must relinquish their own customs and religions and conform to the dominant Greek culture and creed. Disobedience would be punished by death.

A directive was sent expressly to Judea to cease the sacrificial service in the Temple. In its place, altars and temples should be set up everywhere, at which hogs and other unclean animals were to be sacrificed. As if that were not enough, Antiochus commanded that the Holy Temple should be desecrated and converted into a pagan temple! The observance of the Sabbath, festivals and Rosh Chodesh, the dietary laws, the covenant of circumcision, the laws of family purity, and the use of G-d's name were singled out for prohibition. All copies of the Torah and other Scriptural books were to be confiscated and burned. Anyone found to possess any of these books would be executed. In general, all vestiges of Torah and its observance were to be obliterated; even to profess that one was a Jew was punishable by death.

No sooner was the order given than Antiochus' Jewish lackeys, headed by Menelaus and aided by the king's forces, set about to enforce its execution with extreme brutality. On the fifteenth of Kislev 168 BCE (3594), an idol was erected upon the altar, and beginning with the twenty-fifth of that month hogs were offered upon the altar to a pagan deity.

Brave Resistance

Most of the people complied with the king's barbaric order, but many chose death rather than "desecrate the Name." Women who had their children circumcised were put to death, with their infants tied to their necks; their families as well as those who had performed the circumcision were killed.

Elazar, one of the leading sages, refused to partake of the pork which everyone was expected to eat as part of the offering ritual. Realizing he would not relent, the Syrian official took him aside and told him he would be allowed kosher meat — as long as he pretended he was eating of the offering. Elazar proudly spurned this offer and replied that "it was not becoming to one of his years to pretend — to lead many of the young people to suppose that Elazar, at the age of ninety, had gone over to the religion of the heathen ... To the young people I will leave an example of strength, to die willingly with courage for the perfect and holy Torah."

Chanah [Hannah] and her seven sons were captured and brought before the king himself to force them to partake of pig's meat. When they refused to do so even after being tortured, the furious Antiochus had them put to a slow, barbarously painful death. But these seven noble brothers defied the cruel king to the last and declared their faith in the true G-d and their determination not to transgress His Torah. Chanah herself stood by and encouraged her sons "to sanctify the Name." Then, the distraught mother climbed up on a roof and jumped to her death. A Heavenly voice proclaimed the verse [*Psalms* 113:9]: "The mother of the children is joyous" *(Gittin* 57b).

Such people served as an inspiration to their fellow Jews and played no small role in inspiring the future rebellion.

Mattisyahu and His Sons Revolt

In those trouble-beset days, Mattisyahu the Hasmonean, son of Yochanan the *Kohen Gadol,* left Jerusalem (where the persecution was strongest), and settled in Modi'in — a Judean village near Jerusalem. According to the Talmud *(Pesachim* 93b) it was 30,000 cubits (approx. 8.5-11.3 miles) from Jerusalem. However, the terror followed him even to this little town.

One day the king's forces appeared and demanded that the townspeople offer a sacrifice in the pagan fashion. They attempted to convince the aged Mattisyahu that it would be to his advantage if he would set an example for the people. Were he to comply, he and his sons would be considered the king's "friends," an official title carrying with it many

Though once attached to the soreg surrounding the Beis HaMikdash, this plaque is inscribed in Greek: it is addressed to visiting gentiles, forbidding their entry past the soreg.

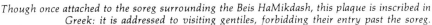

privileges, and would receive a handsome monetary reward. Mattisyahu proudly and publicly declared his determination to remain steadfast to the religion of his forefathers. As he was declaiming his defiance, a renegade Jew neared the altar to offer the sacrifice. When Mattisyahu saw this, he was filled with rage at this traitorous desertion of the Jewish nation and its religion by one of its sons. He grabbed a sword and killed not only the Jewish renegade, but the Syrian emissaries of the king.

Mattisyahu saw the desecration being perpetrated upon Judea and Jerusalem and exclaimed, "Woe is me! Why was I born to witness the ruination of my people and the ruination of the Holy City, and to have lived in it while it was surrendered to its enemies and the Temple to the foreigners? Her Temple is as a man disgraced, her precious utensils have been taken into captivity, her children have been murdered in her streets, her young men slaughtered by the enemy sword. What nation has not shared, what kingdom has not taken her spoils? All of her glory has been stolen — instead of a free women she has become a slave. Our Sanctuary, our glory and beauty, has been despoiled; the heathen has desecrated it. What is our life worth?"

Mattisyahu and his sons rent their clothing and donned sackcloth and mourned.

Mattisyahu published a proclamation: "Whoever is zealous for the Torah and is steadfast in the Covenant let him follow me!" Thereupon, he and his sons left all their possessions in Modi'in and fled to the mountains in the Judean desert. Many other loyal Jews followed their example and joined them to live in the mountain caves where they would be able to practice the Torah's precepts. The king's forces could not disregard this challenge to their authority and began to seek out these bands of loyal Jews in the mountains. The Jews were exhorted by Mattisyahu to resist the Syrian-Greeks with force, and six thousand combat-worthy, loyal Jews gathered under his banner. They began to strike back at the Syrians in nighttime raids and would demolish the idolatrous altars put up by the pagans. The die had been cast; the revolt had begun.

Mattisyahu did not live to see the result of the events he had set in motion. He died in the following year, 165 BCE (3596), but before his death he gathered his five sons — Shimon, Yehudah the Maccabee, Elazar, Yochanan and Yonasan — around him and urged them to be brave and continue the struggle against the Syrians. He bade them to follow the advice of Shimon "for he is a sagacious man," but to look to Yehudah as their leader in battle.

9

The Hasmonean Wars and the Miracles of Chanukah

Why was the passage concerning the Menorah placed near that describing the tribal leaders' offerings at the dedication of the Tabernacle? [See Numbers 7:10 — 8:4.] Because when Aharon saw the gifts of the leaders he became discouraged, since he did not participate in the dedication — neither he nor his tribe. But the Holy One, Blessed is He, said to him: "By your life, your part is greater than theirs ... There will be another Chanukah (dedication), with a kindling of lights, when through your sons I will perform miracles for Israel and bring them salvation — this will be the Chanukah of the Hasmoneans ..."

Another Midrash states that G-d told Moshe to tell Aharon, "The sacrifices are offered only as long as the Holy Temple exists. But the lights will forever burn on the Menorah" ...

Now it is clear that without the Holy Temple neither the sacrifices nor the lights of the Menorah exist. Here, however, is an allusion to the future lights of the Hasmonean Chanukah, which continue [at the annual lighting of Chanukah lamps] even after the destruction of the Holy Temple, throughout our exile (from Ramban, Num. 8:1, based on the Midrash).

Yehudah the Maccabee Leads the People

Yehudah now was the recognized leader of all G-d-fearing Jews. He was known as "the Maccabee", a word made up of the initial letters of the four words of his Hebrew battle-cry: "מִי כָמֹכָה בָּאֵלִים יְ־ה־וֹ־ה" — Who is like You among the heavenly powers, Hashem" (*Exodus* 15:11). This verse reminded him that he was the instrument through whom G-d wrought the great miracles on the battlefront which

we commemorate during the eight days of Chanukah.

Philip, the official appointed by Antiochus to administer Judea and to execute the enforced destruction of the Jewish religion, did not take the revolt seriously. Even when Yehudah's men began to venture out of the desert and audaciously attack towns under the government's control, he felt they could be contained by troops stationed in *Eretz Yisrael.*

He called upon Apollonius, who had been appointed military commander of Samaria, to help him. Apollonius tried in vain to break through to Jerusalem. The first open and large-scale battle between the Syrian army and Yehudah Maccabee's guerrilla units took place in the hilly terrain to the north of Jerusalem on the way to Shechem (Nablus). Yehudah's fighters were few and poorly trained in warfare, but G-d was with them and they defeated the attacking enemy. The second battle took place in the Judean foothills, near Beis Choron, east of Lod. In this clash, Yehudah's men won an even greater victory than in the previous encounter. Many were the slain enemies, and enormous booty fell into the hands of the Jewish victors.

Then Seron, the commander of the army in Syria, heard about Yehudah's revolt. He decided he would crush Yehudah and thereby gain prestige: "I will make myself a reputation by making war on Yehudah and his comrades — those who disobey the king's command!" He gathered a large and well-equipped army and marched to Judea. As he approached the pass of Beis Choron, a strategically located town that dominated the approach from the coast to Jerusalem, Yehudah and his men saw Seron's vast army.

In keeping with the ancient Jewish practice before battle, Yehudah's men were fasting. Frightened, they said to Yehudah: "How can we, so few in number, combat this vast multitude? We are fatigued — not having eaten today!"

But Yehudah, remembering his father's last words, was full of confidence that G-d would help them. He reassured his men as he would so many times in the coming years of fierce battle:

"It is easy for the many to be handed over to the few, for there is no difference in G-d's eyes between saving through a large force or through a tiny force. Triumph in battle does not depend on the size of an army — for strength comes from Heaven. Our enemy opposes us full of violence and lawlessness, to destroy us, our wives and our children, and to plunder us. But we are fighting for our lives and our Torah. G-d will crush them before us and you must not fear them!"

Having thus exhorted his few men, Yehudah fell upon Seron and his army, killing eight hundred of their soldiers and thoroughly routing them. After this, Yehudah's fame spread, reaching even to Antiochus himself.

Prayer in Mitzpah and Victories in Emmaus and Beis Tzur

Upon hearing about the humiliating defeat of his troops, Antiochus was enraged and commanded that his entire army be gathered. He opened his treasury and paid his soldiers a full year's wages in advance and ordered them to prepare for combat. Antiochus now realized that his military campaigns — plus his lavish spending for grandiose buildings and games — had put a severe drain on the treasury. The unrest caused by his violent tactics and unpredictable behavior had disrupted the economy of the realm and revenues had fallen off. The king was advised to go to Persia to collect tribute owed him. To head a caretaker government in his absence, he appointed Lysias, a relative, and also entrusted him with the care of the young heir to the throne, Antiochus (later Antiochus V Eupator). He equipped half of the army with war elephants, the ancient equivalent of tanks, and assigned it to Lysias' command with orders for him to march into Judea and crush the Jewish nation. Antiochus took the other half of his army and marched eastward toward Persia to raise funds.

Lysias promptly appointed Ptolemy (son of Dorimenes), Nikanor, and Gorgias, three of Syria's ablest generals, to lead the Judean campaign, and put them at the head of an army of 40,000 footsoldiers and 7,000 cavalry. They marched into Judea as far as Emmaus, a town west of Jerusalem in the Judean hills, near today's Latrun. There they pitched camp and were augmented by reinforcements from the standing armies of southern Syria and the coastal regions (Philistia). So confident were the Syrians of victory that Nikanor summoned gentile slave dealers from the coastal cities and promised to sell them Jewish slaves at unprecedentedly low prices. With the money raised from the slaves, he planned to pay the tribute the Syrians owed Rome. (Since the Roman victory over Antiochus III twenty-five years earlier, Syria had been required to pay a yearly tribute to Rome.)

Yehudah's men were not discouraged at the news of the enemy's new attack. On the contrary, they encouraged each other and prepared for the decisive battle. But first they assembled, just as their forefathers had always done in similar circumstances, to fast and pour out their hearts in prayer to G-d. Since they could not gather in occupied Jerusalem and come near the profaned Temple, they assembled in the hallowed place closest to Jerusalem — Mitzpah, which means "the lookout." On that hilltop, Shmuel [Samuel]

Mosque built atop Nebi Samwil, the traditional burial place of the Prophet Shmuel in the Jerusalem Hills.

the prophet had judged Israel and there, according to tradition, is his burial place. Indeed to this day the Arabs call it Nebi Samwil — an echo of the Hebrew *Shmuel HaNavi* [the prophet Samuel]. From there, with the Holy City and the despoiled Temple before their eyes, they cried to G-d from the very depths of their hearts to help them again in their battle with the formidable enemy.

Then they brought the priestly vestments, the tithes, the *bikkurim* [first fruit offering], and a group of Nazirites (who could not bring their required offerings to the Temple), and placed them in front of the assemblage. They all cried out to G-d: "What shall we do with these and whereto shall we bring them? Your Temple has been downtrodden and defiled ... How can we withstand our enemies if You will not help us?"

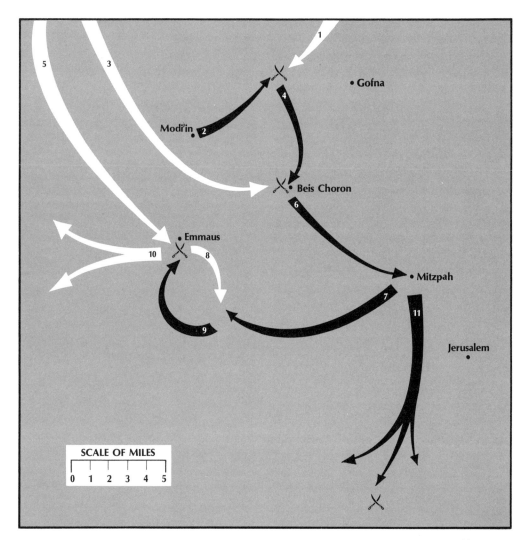

The Campaigns of Yehudah Until the Rededication of the Temple

1. Syrian troops from Samaria under Apollonius.
2. Yehudah and his fighters defeat Syrians near Gofna.
3. Seron comes from Syria to suppress revolt.
4. Yehudah surprises and routs Syrians at Beis Choron.
5. Syrian forces under Gorgias and others.
6. Yehudah goes to Mitzpah to pray before giving battle.
7. Yehudah establishes camp near the enemy forces.
8. Gorgias with 5,000 men attempts surprise attack on Yehudah's camp.
9. Yehudah slips away and attacks the enemy base.
10. The enemy is routed and flees.
11. Yehudah goes to meet the enemy in battle at Beis Tzur.

Now Yehudah divided his small army into four battalions of 1,000 men each, to be commanded respectively by himself and his brothers, Yochanan, Yonasan, and Shimon. Then, as set forth by *Deuteronomy* 20:1-9, Yehudah announced that those who had recently married, built houses, or planted vineyards, should leave the army; and he exhorted the remaining men to have trust in G-d.

"Prepare yourselves and be brave men. Be ready in the morning to fight the heathens who are gathered against us to destroy us and our Sanctuary. It is better for us to die in battle than to witness the ruin of our nation and our Temple."

Meanwhile, Gorgias had detached a 5,000-man force from his main army. With renegade Jews from the citadel in Jerusalem as his guides, he intended to lead a surprise attack against the Jewish camp. Yehudah, however, had been forewarned and, under cover of night, positioned his men for a pre-emptive attack on the enemy's main base. With daybreak, Yehudah saw that the Syrian army consisted of a large force of well-armed, seasoned soldiers. Moreover, many sentries were on guard so that any movement of his men would certainly be detected. It was probably the most critical moment for the Jews since the revolt began. Yehudah exhorted his men to pray to G-d and to be steadfast:

"Do not fear their numbers or their attack. Remember how our ancestors were saved at the Sea of Reeds when Pharaoh and his army pursued them. Let us now cry out to G-d — perhaps He will accept our prayer, remember His covenant with our ancestors, and crush the enemy camp that

faces us now. Then all the heathens will know that there is One Who rescues and preserves Israel!"

Then Yehudah ordered them to attack. His attack broke the Syrians' ranks and started them in disorderly retreat. The Jews decimated the entire rear, set fire to the Syrian camp, and pursued the fleeing enemy a long way, killing 3,000 soldiers during the chase. Yehudah cautioned his men that a large part of the enemy army was still in the mountains; the battle had just begun. But when Gorgias and his troops saw the fire rising from their camp they panicked and fled the battlefield.

After a year of licking his wounds, Lysias sent a yet stronger force of 60,000 infantry and 5,000 cavalry. Yehudah met them at Beis Tzur with a much smaller force of only 10,000 loyal Jews. Upon seeing the superior army of the enemy, Yehudah again prayed to G-d to give him a victory.

"Blessed are You, O Savior of Israel, Who halted the charge of the Philistine champion, Goliath, through your servant David and Who delivered a Philistine camp into the hands of Yonasan [Jonathan] ben Shaul and his armor bearer. Do the same to this camp — let them be ashamed of their army and their cavalry; make them cowardly; melt their boldness; make them tremble at their imminent destruction; strike them down with the sword of those who love You, and let all who know Your Name sing praises to You."

Yehudah's army attacked this strong force and was able to kill 5,000 soldiers. At this, Lysias, seeing the determination of the Jews to die rather than surrender, despaired of victory over the rebels at this time and returned to his capital, Antioch.

The Miracle of Chanukah

When Yehudah and his valiant Maccabees entered the city gates, they were overwhelmed by the sight that met their eyes: the Temple was in desolation, the Altar desecrated, the gates gutted by fire. Grass grew wild in the Temple courtyard and its chambers were in ruins. They tore their garments, put ashes on their heads, and cried out bitterly.

Yehudah sent a contingent of his men to the fortress known as the Acra, where the fleeing Hellenists from the entire city had taken refuge. The Jews were not able to dislodge the traitors from the Acra for another twenty-three years, but Yehudah's men kept them from interfering with the cleansing of the Temple that was about to begin. Yehudah sought out *Kohanim* who had remained loyal to the Torah, and gave instructions that the profaned stones of the Altar be burned and that another Altar be built from new stones. To replace the golden *Menorah* which had been stolen, they made one of iron and coated it with zinc or tin. According to some, the *Menorah* was made of wood. Later, when they could afford it, they made a *Menorah* of silver and finally, after a while, they were able to make one of gold, as the Torah prescribes.

On the twenty-fifth day of Kislev, in the year 165 BCE (3597) — three years to the day after the terrible moment on which the invaders had sacrificed to a pagan abomination in the Sanctuary — the Hasmoneans rededicated the Holy Temple and renewed the sacrificial service.

But their joy was tempered with pain. Among the ruins they had found a vessel of undefiled oil that bore the seal of the last loyal High Priest, but it contained only one day's supply of the holy oil that was needed for the *Menorah*. It would take seven days to prepare new olive oil that was valid for kindling the *Menorah*. This was the setting for the most celebrated of all the many miracles that the Hasmoneans experienced: the one-day supply of oil from that vessel continued to burn in the *Menorah* for seven more days.

This miracle of the oil clearly showed that all the preceding wonders on the field of battle were intended as a prelude and instrument to make possible the resumption of the Temple service. It also served as an eternal lesson — that the purpose of all miracles experienced by the individual Jew or the Jewish people is to enable them to observe the commandments of the Torah.

In grateful remembrance of all the miracles of the wars and the *Menorah,* the Sages of Israel set aside Chanukah as a time of joy, a time for songs of praise [*Hallel*] and prayers of thanksgiving. In memory of the unique miracle of oil, they made Chanukah eight days, during which all Jews kindle their own Chanukah lights.

Yehudah and his people searched out copies of the Torah and the Prophets, and collected them in Jerusalem to ensure the perpetuation of these holy scrolls. The Greeks, in their frenzy of persecution, had sensed that in these scrolls lay the strength of the Jewish religion and had mounted an intense campaign of scroll burning. Yehudah sent a message to all Jewish communities that scrolls were now available to all who wished to make copies of them.

It is apparent from the history up to this

Design of a seven-branched Menorah incised on two plaster fragments dating from the first century BCE and uncovered in 1969 in the Jewish Quarter of the Old City of Jerusalem.

Oil press from the time of the Hasmoneans, rebuilt near the Israel Museum from the original stones found near Modi'in.

point, and even more so from the events described below, that the triumph celebrated by Chanukah was a partial one at best. Although the Temple area had been liberated and the service reinstituted, parts of Jerusalem and nearly all of the countryside were still under Syrian-Greek and Hellenist control. Even the *Kohen Gadol* was a renegade Jew. Total independence came only many years later — but for that, no festival was proclaimed.

That a festival was proclaimed in the absence of a military or diplomatic victory in any normal sense of the word gives us an important insight into the nature of the celebration. Mattisyahu and his sons — Yehudah and his brothers — risked their lives for spiritual freedom, the purity of the Temple, and the integrity of its service, not for freedom from foreign bondage. From the first day of renewed Jewish settlement in *Eretz Yisrael* after King Darius of Persia had permitted the rebuilding of the Temple, the Holy Land had been a vassal state of Persia, Greece, Syria, or Egypt, but there was never a revolt. The sages and the people understood that dependence was a condition of the Second Commonwealth's diminished status. Only when religious freedom was wrested from them did they rebel. When it was regained, they celebrated.

10

The Rule of Yehudah Maccabee

The gentiles who still held the fortress [the Acra] caused the Jews near the Temple area a great deal of harm. Yehudah decided to lay siege to them and annihilate them completely. All his people assembled and prepared their weapons. Some of the gentiles and their Hellenist collaborators escaped, approached King Antiochus [V], and said to him: "How long will you continue to stay your hand from punishing them [the Hasmoneans] and avenging the blood of our brothers? We willingly served your father and obeyed his orders. Behold, our brothers besieged us for doing so and are hostile to us. Anyone who falls into their hands is being killed and our property is freely taken away." The king thereupon gathered all the generals of the army and with the help of his allied kings mobilized a mercenary host of 100,000 infantry men and 20,000 cavalry, and 32 elephants trained in warfare. They advanced through Edom and encamped opposite Beis Tzur (I Maccabees 6).

Yehudah Comes to the Aid of his Brothers throughout the Land

The Jews rested for more than a year from the ravages of the wars brought about by the Greek rulers of Syria. Yehudah used the time to repair and fortify the Temple and the walls of Jerusalem, as well as the walls of Beis Tzur, in the southern part of the Judean mountains. As told in the previous chapter, it was from Beis Tzur that Lysias had tried to advance on Jerusalem. The danger of another Syrian attempt to use this strategic location for an assault on Jerusalem had not passed.

While Yehudah was busy with his work, messengers from the Galilee and Gilead came and told him of widespread persecution and murder of Jews throughout the land, including Galilee, Transjordan, in the south, and along the coast. The gentiles there could not tolerate the great victories of the Hasmoneans and in their envy and hatred attacked the defenseless Jews in their midst.

Without hesitation, Yehudah came to the aid of his brethren. He divided his forces into three units. He dispatched a force of 3,000 to the Galilee under the command of his brother Shimon. The second group, of 8,000 men, went to Gilead under the command of himself and his brother Yonasan. The rest of his forces Yehudah left in Jerusalem.

The gentiles in Galilee and Gilead had been subdued, but because of their small number the Hasmoneans could not stay and govern there, so they transferred many of the local Jews to Jerusalem and other Judean towns. This solution served two purposes: first, it protected the Jews from further harassment, and second, it strengthened the Jewish community of Jerusalem and Judea.

Yehudah also waged a fierce battle against the ancient enemies of his people — the Edomites, who lived in the south. From them he wrested Hebron, the city of the Patriarchs, destroying its walls and fortifications. The inhabitants of Jaffa also felt his strong arm. From them he took revenge for his fellow Jews, whom they had forced onto boats and drowned in the sea.

Tomb of the Patriarchs in Hebron, built by Herod (as the chiseling of its stones indicates) over the Cave of Machpelah. More recent additions, such as the two Moslem minarets, are readily identifiable.

"When evildoers perish, there is joy" *(Proverbs* 11:10).

While all this was occurring, Antiochus was far away in his eastern provinces, confident that his armies had easily put down what he perceived as a minor uprising by a few Jewish zealots. He was informed that a temple in the city Elymais, in Persia, contained fabulous riches that had been stored there by Alexander the Great. He promptly went to this city and tried to rob the temple through trickery. The townspeople, however, apprised of his intentions, resisted him and forced him to flee. Antiochus sought to march to Babylon, but his spirit had been broken and he was greatly depressed by the reversal in his fortunes. Then, a messenger brought him the news that his forces in Judea had been shamefully routed and that the entire country was in turmoil.

Realizing that his entire empire was crumbling, the king fell into a deep depression and his nerves were further shattered. As his mental capacities declined, so he also deteriorated physically and contracted a mysterious disease. According to one account *(II Maccabees 9:5-12)* the disease was precipitated by a fall from a speeding chariot. He gradually lost the use of his limbs and acquired such a foul smell that nobody wanted to come near him. Feeling that his end was near, he called his close advisors and expressed his regrets that he had oppressed the Jews needlessly and had despoiled the Holy Temple. "I remember the wrongs I committed in Jerusalem ... it is because of this that misfortune has overtaken me. Now I am dying in a strange land."

He bade Philip, his closest confidant, to supervise the education of his son the crown prince Antiochus V Eupator, and to raise him to be king. Antiochus died friendless and deserted in Ecbatana (Hamadan), Persia, in the year 163 BCE (3598). When the news of the king's death reached Lysias, he crowned the prince and named him King Antiochus V Eupator.

Under the stress of his illness, Antiochus apparently forgot that he had earlier appointed Lysias to be the regent of Syria during his absence. It did not take long before Lysias and Philip began to quarrel over their respective roles in guiding the boy king.

The Enemy at Jerusalem, and Divine Intervention

Some time after the land had calmed down from continuous struggle and warfare against external and internal enemies, the Hellenists again began to assert themselves. In the very heart of Jerusalem, not far from the Temple, was the Acra, a fortress that the Hellenists turned into their stronghold. They turned a blind eye to all the miracles through which G-d had saved His people, and could not admit their own defeat. From their fortress they sent word to Lysias in Syria, begging him to rally to their aid.

Lysias responded to their plea. He promptly organized a vast army of 100,000 foot soldiers, 20,000 cavalry, and many elephants. The battle elephants were the ancient counterpart of the modern tank —

each of them carrying on its back four soldiers in a small turret, a vantage point from which they were in control of the surrounding area. Each elephant was surrounded by dozens of cavalrymen and hundreds of foot soldiers. Accompanied by the young Antiochus, Lysias advanced toward Jerusalem along the same southern route as before. Again, they encamped in front of the fortified walls of Beis Tzur.

In the face of such an army, Yehudah's chances to win were poor indeed. Elazar, his brother, tried to turn the tide by rushing to the leading elephant, mistakenly thinking that it carried the king, and driving his sword deep into the animal's belly. The mortally wounded elephant collapsed, burying the Maccabean hero underneath.

The Syrians captured Beis Tzur, and after another victory at Beis Zechariah the army reached the gates of Jerusalem and laid siege to Mount Zion. The situation of the defenders of Jerusalem became very difficult. Because of the fact that it was the Sabbatical Year — *Shemittah* — and the fields were not worked, food was in short supply. With the overwhelming Syrian army before their eyes, their courage began to give way to fear and despair. It appeared that Jerusalem would fall again into the hands of the enemy. But at this critical moment G-d intervened.

Lysias received word from Syria that a rebellion was in the making and that his rival, Philip, was trying to wrest control over the country from him. He therefore decided to call off the siege of Jerusalem and march his army back to Damascus in order to protect his rule. This he did successfully, executing Philip in the process. Before he lifted the siege he turned to his men and said:

"We are getting weaker with every day. Food is scarce and the place against which we are encamped is strongly fortified. And we are concerned with royal matters. Let us therefore extend our right hand to these men and make peace with them and all their people. Let us allow them to observe their religion, as they have always done, because it is only in defense of their religion, which we have suppressed, that they arose and acted as they did" (I Maccabees 6).

Accordingly, Lysias made a peace pact with Yehudah and abolished officially all the decrees of Antiochus, which had not been enforced in practice since the victories of the Hasmoneans. Yehudah and his men then permitted Lysias to enter the city. When he saw the mighty fortifications of the walls he broke his promise and ordered his soldiers to tear them down. Only then did he leave Jerusalem and return to his homeland.

Despite Lysias' final act of treachery, Jerusalem was now safe and at peace. The lifting of the siege was celebrated as a miraculous salvation, as related in *Megillas Taanis*:

On the twenty-eighth (of Shvat) King Antiochus (V) was removed from Jerusalem; for he tyrannized Israel and came to destroy Jerusalem and to exterminate the Jews. Jews were able to come and go (in and out of Jerusalem) only at night. But he heard bad tidings, left and fell in his place. That day on which they eliminated him from there (i.e., Jerusalem) they (the Sages) designated a festival.

The Day of Nikanor

When Antiochus III was defeated by the Romans at Magnesia some 27 years before the lifting of the siege against Jerusalem, the terms of the armistice forced him to leave members of his household in Rome as hostages to guarantee that Syria would not again attack Rome. The hostages could be rotated as long as someone was always held by Rome, and this arrangement continued for many years. One such rotation of hostages took place just before the assassination of Seleucus, the eldest son and successor of the defeated Antiochus III. In 175 BCE (3586) Seleucus' younger brother Antiochus IV, who was to become the arch oppressor of Israel in the Chanukah era, was released by Rome and replaced by Demetrius, son of the soon-to-be slain Seleucus. As crown prince, Demetrius was the lawful heir to the crown, but Antiochus IV took advantage of his absence to hurry to Syria and usurp the throne.

In the year 161 BCE (3600), three years after the Chanukah miracle, Demetrius I managed to escape from Rome. No sooner had he landed on Syrian soil than he proclaimed himself king. In a short while he managed to win over the influential people in the country and establish himself as ruler; Lysias and Antiochus V were executed.

With Demetrius' accession to the throne, the peace agreement reached just months earlier between Yehudah and Antiochus was now null and void. Shortly thereafter, the present leader of the Hellenizers, Alcimus, a *Kohen* who aspired to the post of *Kohen Gadol*, came to the new king and convinced him to attack Yehudah the Maccabee. The king appointed Bacchides, one of his most trusted officials, to lead the fight and gave the *Kehunah Gedolah* to Alcimus. Bacchides and Alcimus now marched with a great force to Judea. Upon arriving they sent messages of peace to Yehudah and his people, giving them assurances under oath that they would not be harmed. The Jews, not suspecting that a fellow *Kohen* would betray them, sent a party of sixty sages and devout people to meet them. No sooner had they arrived in the Syrian camp than they were executed. Bacchides also rounded up many Jews who were suspected or accused of having fought against the Syrians in the uprising and executed them.

Believing he had reestablished the Syrian domination in the land, Bacchides left Alcimus with an armed force and returned to Antioch. Alcimus, now with the help of his fellow renegades, proceeded to take over Judea and oppress the loyal Jews even more barbarously than the gentiles had done.

Particularly harsh treatment was meted out to the Torah sages. Typical is the story related in *Bereishis Rabbah* (65:22) about Yose ben Yoezer, the leading sage of the period. Yose was condemned to death and, as he was being led to the gallows, his nephew, Yakim of Tzroros, rode in front of the illustrious Yose. Yakim taunted Yose saying, "Behold the horse upon which my master mounts me and see the horse upon which your Lord mounts you!"

Yose responded, "If this fate is accorded to those who perform His will, then surely it will be so to those who anger Him!"

Yose's words had such a profound impact upon the renegade — the matter penetrated him like the poison of a snake — that he went and committed suicide out of remorse for his sinful ways. Although according to some, Yose's execution took place before the time of Alcimus, this is typical of how the murderous, tyrannical Hellenist rulers acted.

Apparently, Yehudah's force had disbanded after the successful conclusion of his peace with Antiochus. Thinking that Bacchides had come on a peaceful expedition, Yehudah would have no reason to recall his men to arms; perhaps he was not even in Jerusalem at the time. Now, however, Yehudah realized that he could not rest on his laurels, but had to take up the fight again.

When Alcimus realized he had as his opponent the implacable Yehudah, he hastened to Antioch and requested the king's help. Demetrius now sent Nikanor — an old foe of Yehudah who had taken part in the campaign of Lysias during the rule of Antiochus IV — with a great army to wage war against Yehudah, and to obliterate the Jewish resistance to Hellenism. In his first engagement with Yehudah, five hundred Syrians fell and Nikanor retreated hurriedly to Jerusalem. In Jerusalem, the Kohanim came out of the Temple to greet him and to show him the sacrifices they were offering for the king. But Nikanor rebuffed them haughtily and swore that if he succeeded now in conquering Yehudah he would return and burn the Temple.

Nikanor marched his force to Beis Choron (a few miles north of Jerusalem) where he rendezvoused with an additional Syrian army. Yehudah encamped nearby with an insignificant force of 3,000 devout Jews, but his faith in G-d never weakened.

As always before battle, Yehudah prayed: "It was You, G-d, Who sent an angel in the time of King Chizkiyahu [Hezekiah] of Judah, and he destroyed 185,000 in the blaspheming camp of Sennacherib. Now, too, Master of the Heavens — send an angel before us carrying fear and terror. May Your strong right arm strike down those who blaspheme against Your holy people."

After offering his short prayer, Yehudah beset the Syrian forces. Nikanor was one of the first to fall. His troops, seeing their leader die, panicked. They threw down their arms and began a disorderly fight. Many loyal Jews in the surrounding towns of Judea, seeing the enemy's rout, poured out of their homes and joined the fight. Nikanor's once proud army was wiped out on that day; none of his 35,000 soldiers survived. Yehudah and his men went up to Jerusalem and offered thanks to G-d Who had again delivered them. Yehudah and the Sages designated the day of victory, the thirteenth of Adar, as a festival.

On the thirteenth [of Adar] is the Day of Nikanor. They [the Sages] said: Nikanor was one of the nobles of the Greek kings; every day he would wave his hand toward Jerusalem and the Holy Temple and blaspheme, accuse, abuse, and say, "When will they fall into my hands so that I will demolish this tower?" When the noble house of the Hasmoneans gained power and defeated them [the Greeks], they penetrated his armies and killed them until they reached his chariot. They cut off his head and the fingers of his hands and feet and hung them up opposite [the gates of] Jerusalem and wrote beneath them: "The mouth that spoke haughtily and the hands that waved at Jerusalem and the Holy Temple — this is the vengeance inflicted on them!"

That day on which they [the Hasmonean warriors] did thus to him, they [the Sages] designated a festival (Megillas Taanis; the account given in Talmud Yerushalmi, Taanis 2:12 differs in a few details).

Death of Yehudah

Yehudah realized that all his victories over the Syrians were only temporary solutions and that the danger from the north was always present. He therefore decided to seek support from the dominant power of the day — Rome. He sent messengers to Rome to conclude a treaty of mutual aid in case of war.

The pact with Rome proved to be of no value to Yehudah. The Syrians soon launched another army against Jerusalem, but no Roman help was forthcoming.

For Yehudah to seek Rome's help was a mistake, even though it brought no ill results at the time. Many decades later, two of his descendants brought Roman power into *Eretz Yisrael,* with results that eventually led to the Destruction of the Temple. *Ramban,* in his commentary to *Genesis* 32:4, alludes to the grievous error of inviting Rome — which descended from Esau — to help Yaakov, i.e., Israel.

After a few months, Demetrius sent yet another army, an even larger one, under Bacchides and Alcimus. They confronted Yehudah's camp near Elasah, west of Jerusalem. Most of Yehudah's men, upon seeing the mighty army of the enemy, lost heart and deserted him; he was left with only 800 men. Yehudah refused to flee, however, and gave battle. In the ensuing contest many fell on both sides, but when Yehudah himself was killed the remnants of his force fled the fray. Yonasan and Shimon carried their brother to Modi'in for burial. All Israel mourned for him a long time. They lamented his death, saying, "Woe, for the hero of battle has fallen, the strength of Israel and its protector."

After Yehudah's death in 160 BCE (3601) the Hellenist party was greatly strengthened. Just then there was a great famine and most of the devout, out of necessity, chose to make peace with the Hellenizers. Bacchides appointed Alcimus and others of his party to administer the country. These renegades used the opportunity to avenge themselves upon those loyal to Yehudah; they were brought to Bacchides to be tortured and executed.

The death of Yehudah the Maccabee gave the Hellenists and their sympathizers new confidence. Once again, those who were disloyal to G-d and the Torah were unafraid, and they renewed their attempts to turn Jerusalem into a Syrian outpost.

SUMMARY

I. The Wars of the Hasmoneans before the Miracle of Chanukah

1. Against Appolonius — in the north.
2. At Beis Choron — in the northwest.
3. Against Gorgias at Emmaus — in the west.
4. Against Lysias at Beis Tzur — in the south.
5. The dedication of the Temple, the miracle of the oil, and the end of the enforcement of the decree forcing the Jews to accept Hellenism.

II. The Events from Chanukah until Yehudah's Death

1. The wars against the enemies in Galilee, Transjordan, Edom, and along the coast.
2. The death of Antiochus in Persia.
3. The heroic death of Elazar in the battle against Lysias at Beis Tzur.
4. The miracle that caused Lysias to lift his siege against Jerusalem.
5. Lysias officially nullifies Antiochus' decree.
6. Demetrius becomes king and sends an army under Bacchides and Alcimus to reoccupy Judea.
7. Yehudah defeats Nikanor's huge force.
8. Yehudah killed in battle against Bacchides and Alcimus.

11

Yonasan and Shimon

"The scepter shall not depart from Yehudah" (Genesis 49:10) … When for a long time Israel crowned kings from other tribes, king after king, and they did not return to the reign of Yehudah, they violated the testament of their ancestor [Yaakov] and they were punished for it … This was the punishment of the Hasmoneans who ruled in the time of the Second Temple. They were extraordinarily devout men; if not for them the Torah and its commandments would have been forgotten from Israel. Nevertheless, they were afflicted with a severe punishment. Four sons [of Mattisyahu] the elder, devout Hasmonean, who reigned one after the other, despite all their heroism and success, fell by the sword of the enemies (Ramban, Genesis 49:10).

After the Death of Yehudah

The surviving devout Jews assembled and entreated Yonasan to reorganize and lead the resistance against the Hellenists and Syrians. Bacchides was informed of this new development and sent a force to capture Yonasan.

Yonasan, together with his brothers Yochanan and Shimon and their loyal followers, fled to the Judean desert near the southern end of the Jordan River. While on a mission, Yochanan was captured and killed by one of the Transjordanian tribes. Bacchides was told of the location of Yonasan's hideout and marched there with a considerable force. Yonasan was surrounded and forced to fight his way out of the trap in order to flee across the Jordan. Bacchides lost 1,000 men

in this battle and Yonasan made his way to safety. The Syrians returned to Judea and refortified the fortresses of the land.

Alcimus was now in full control of the country. He began to demolish one of the walls surrounding the Temple Court, but he was suddenly stricken with paralysis and lost his speech (probably he had a stroke) and died shortly thereafter in 159 BCE (3602). With his death the persecutions against the devout Jews ceased; Bacchides returned to Syria and the land enjoyed a well-deserved peace of two years' duration.

However, the Hellenists refused to rest as long as Yonasan was alive and posed a threat. In 157 BCE (3604) they again prevailed upon King Demetrius I to send

Bacchides with a force to destroy Yonasan. The loyal Jews had gained control of one of the towers near Bethlehem and fortified themselves. Bacchides besieged them but could not gain a victory. The Maccabees began to press the Syrian army strongly and, deciding he could not win, Bacchides retreated with the intention of returning to Syria. Just then Yonasan sent messengers with offers of peace and assurances that the Syrian captives would be returned if the wars would end. Since Bacchides had lost heart for his mission to *Eretz Yisrael*, Yonasan's offer came at a perfect time. The Syrian accepted the terms and returned to his land, never again to molest *Eretz Yisrael*. Yonasan went to Michmash, north of Jerusalem, and established a base there. Around that nucleus, the Hasmoneans would soon build their kingdom.

Yonasan as High Priest

Five years later, Divine Providence caused a change that brought long-lasting benefit to the Jews. A dramatic event occurred in Syria. Alexander Balas appeared on the scene, claiming to be the son of Antiochus IV and the legitimate heir to the throne. Well-informed people knew he was an impostor, but his marked resemblance to Kings Antiochus IV and V lent credence to his claim. The hoax was supported by the neighboring kings of Pergamum, Egypt, and Cappadocia, all of whom wanted to topple Demetrius. Alexander won backing and proclaimed himself king in Acre with the connivance of his backers, the kings who opposed Demetrius.

Finding himself isolated, Demetrius reached out for Yonasan's support. Afraid that Yonasan would use his forces to back the usurper, he quickly sent him a message inviting him to be his ally. He gave Yonasan permission to raise an army and to gather arms.

Yonasan did not accept nor reject the offer, but he realized that the political situation in Syria would prevent Demetrius from interfering with Jewish independence. Yonasan left his stronghold in Michmash immediately, went up to Jerusalem and began to refortify the city. The Syrians, who garrisoned the fortresses built almost ten years before by Bacchides, were now faced with a Yonasan who was acting as Demetrius' ally, so they left their

Akko (Acre), with its seawall dating from the Crusader period.

posts and the country.

When Alexander heard of these developments, he would not be outdone in bidding for Yonasan's friendship. He sent Yonasan a gold crown and a purple mantle (a gesture equivalent to formal recognition in our days) and appointed him *Kohen Gadol*.

Finally, Judea had ceased to be the oppressed victim of its more powerful neighbors and enjoyed the opportunity to consolidate its Jewishness while the rival Syrian monarchs competed for its favor. Having experienced Demetrius' cruelty and sure that he could not be trusted, Yonasan donned the vestments of the *Kohen Gadol* and performed the service in the Temple. At the festivities in honor of Alexander's marriage to Cleopatra (a common name found often in the Ptolemaic family), the daughter of King Ptolemy VI of Egypt, in 150 BCE (3611), Alexander ordered Yonasan dressed in the royal purple and rebuffed the Hellenists who had come to complain about Yonasan's growing power. Although Judea was still a vassal state of Syria, Yonasan's shrewd diplomacy had achieved a degree of independence and power greater than any Judea had known for many years.

Yonasan's Downfall

During the next few years the Seleucid Empire was considerably weakened and thrown into turmoil through the incessant struggle for the throne occasioned by the claims and counterclaims of a half dozen usurpers. Alexander had defeated Demetrius in battle and killed him, but Alexander proved to be a despotic and unpopular king. His own father-in-law, Ptolemy of Egypt, turned against him. Against this background, Demetrius II, a son of the dead king, came upon the scene and, in 146 BCE (3615), led a successful rebellion against Alexander. Ptolemy took his daughter away from Alexander and married her to Demetrius II. Having lost both his kingdom and his wife, Alexander fled to the king of Arabia, who killed him, in 145 BCE (3616).

Yonasan used this opportunity to wrest further concessions from the new king. Three provinces of Samaria were annexed to Judea, and a relaxation of tribute and taxes was granted. But Syria was still not tranquil. Tryphon, a former official of Alexander, capitalized on Demetrius II's unpopularity. Tryphon brought the dead Alexander's baby son Antiochus out of hiding, toppled the king, and set himself up as regent for the baby king Antiochus VI. A message was sent to Yonasan in the name of the new king recognizing all the privileges granted Yonasan by Demetrius. Yonasan used the general unrest to further expand his realm to the southern coast (Gaza, Ashdod) and Galilee.

Tryphon, having usurped the throne for all practical purposes, now set his sights on greater things. He dreamed of restoring the Seleucid kingdom to its former glory and boundaries. A primary object in his plans was to crush the growing power of Judea. He marched into Judea with a sizable force and was met in Beis She'an by Yonasan at the head of an army of 40,000 men. Realizing that he would be defeated in battle, Tryphon resolved to gain by treachery what he could not win in war. He convinced Yonasan that his intentions were peaceful, and that Yonasan should come to Acre with a token force, where he and Tryphon would confer. Tryphon promptly arrested Yonasan and demanded an exorbitant ransom for him.

Shimon, Prince of Judea

Shimon was the last remaining son of Mattisyahu. When he heard the news of his brother's capture and the massacre of his men, he set out to fight Tryphon. The Syrian general sent word to Shimon that he was prepared to release his brother Yonasan in exchange for a ransom. Shimon agreed and sent the money, but Tryphon murdered Yonasan and sent his body to Shimon. Yonasan was buried in the family's gravesite in Modi'in.

The war continued, and Tryphon led his troops in an advance against Jerusalem. Once again, Jerusalem was saved through a miracle. Heavy snows fell upon the Judean hills and stalled Tryphon's march. Unable to continue due to the unusually harsh winter and the impossible roads, Tryphon was forced to retreat.

In retaliation for Tryphon's treachery, Shimon now supported Tryphon's rival, Demetrius II. In return, Demetrius recognized Shimon as ruler over Judea and freed the land from all taxes. Now, for the first time in the history of the Second Temple, Judea was fully independent. Later on Shimon was proclaimed *Nasi* [Prince]. He had coins minted which indicated both Judea's independence and his new title. Some of these coins were recently discovered during archaeological excavations in various parts of Israel.

Jaffa, which had already been occupied under Yonasan, was now settled by Jews and officially annexed to Judea. To make sure of uninterrupted passage between Jerusalem and Jaffa, Shimon captured the stronghold of Gezer which commanded the main road. He also took possession of Acra, the fortress in Jerusalem in which the Hellenists had established their headquarters when Yehudah Maccabee had liberated Jerusalem from the Syrians.

During the rule of Shimon the people were privileged to enjoy an era of peace. Now the leadership could more fully concentrate on intensifying the study of the Torah and the observance of its commandments among the people. Material well-being also increased, and the people dwelt securely, without fear and anxiety, in their homeland. This is the way the author of the Second Book of *Hasmoneans* describes the blessings of this period:

> And they tilled their soil in peace; the land yielded its crop, and the trees gave their produce. Old people sat in the courtyards and spoke of pleasant things, and the young were dressed richly, even in garments of war. Shimon laid up food in the cities, and weapons in case of war, and his fame spread far and wide. He brought calm and confidence, and Israel was glad and rejoiced. And they dwelt — "everyone under his vine and fig tree" with no one to make them afraid. The voice of war was not heard throughout the land and the arrogance of the despots was subdued. And he raised the honor of His Sanctuary and increased the number of the holy vessels in the Temple.

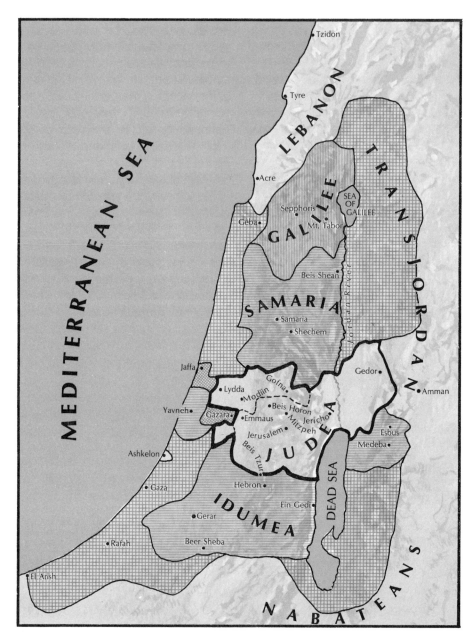

The expansion of the Hasmonean Kingdom

Area controlled by Yonasan

Area conquered by Shimon

Area conquered by Yochanan Hyrkanus

Area conquered by Aristobulus

Area conquered by Alexander Yannai

12

Yochanan Hyrkanus and His Contemporaries

The sages of the court put him [the Kohen Gadol] in the custody of the sages of the priesthood who took him up to the Avtinas family's upper chamber, administered an oath to him, took their leave and went their way.

They said to him, "My lord Kohen Gadol, we are emissaries of the court and you are our emissary and the emissary of the court. We ask you to swear by Him Who domiciled His Name in this House, that you will not change anything of all that we have told you."

He would turn aside and weep [for they had suspected him wrongly of being a Sadducee], and they would turn aside and weep [for they had suspected an innocent man] (Mishnah, Yoma 1:5).

Shimon's Family

Antiochus VII of Syria begrudged the successes of the Hasmoneans, and wanted to recapture the cities they had occupied. Upon learning of the king's intention, Shimon the son of Mattisyahu sent him the following declaration: "The land that we conquered anew is the inheritance of our fathers and no alien has any part or inheritance in it. Our enemies had plundered our inheritance, holding it through injustice and deceit, and now that G-d has made our way successful, we have retaken the inheritance of our fathers, and settled it" (*I Maccabees* 15:33-34).

But Antiochus refused to accept Shimon's words. Instead, he dispatched his army to recapture Jaffa and its surroundings. The two armies met near Yavneh, facing each other from both sides of the Sorek River. At the head of the Jewish army stood Yehudah and Yochanan, the sons of Shimon. They led their soldiers across the rushing waters of the river, attacking the Syrians head on. Their resistance crumbled and they began to flee, with the Jewish army pursuing them all the way to Ashdod.

The victory increased the prestige of Shimon, Prince of Judea, both among his own people and among all the surrounding nations. Foreign officials came to visit his ornate palace. Although the people crowned him as their *Nasi* [prince] he did not have the title of king. Presumably he neither sought nor was offered this title, because, according to the final testament of Yaakov, only the tribe of Yehudah could hold the kingship of Israel. Among his visitors was Ptolemy, son of Abuvi, whom he took as his son-in-law.

As his daughter's dowry, Shimon gave Ptolemy the city of Jericho with its environs. But Ptolemy's ambitions were much bigger. He wanted no less than to rule over all of the land of Judea, and he did not shrink from treachery in order to gain his objective. With the help of Judea's enemies, Ptolemy plotted to eliminate his father-in-law, while simultaneously his allies would move against Jerusalem. The opportunity came in 135 BCE (3626), when Shimon, accompanied by two of his sons, Yehudah and Mattisyahu, came to Jericho to visit his daughter and son-in-law. In the middle of the festive meal, Ptolemy and his men fell upon Shimon and his entourage and assassinated them.

After this foul deed Ptolemy hired assassins to murder Shimon's son, Yochanan Hyrkanus. However, Yochanan discovered the plot in time and killed the would-be assassins. Then he rushed to Jerusalem to defend it and to take the place of his father as ruler of the country.

As soon as the government was securely in his hands he left the city to go to Jericho, there to avenge the murder of his father and free his mother who was held captive by Ptolemy. Yochanan reached the fortress where Ptolemy and his garrison were entrenched, and laid siege to it. Ptolemy's defense was his cruelty. To force Yochanan to break off the siege, he took the mother of his own wife and of Yochanan to the top of the wall and there, in her son's sight, beat her repeatedly and threatened to kill her, if Yochanan would not withdraw his forces. This he did day after day. The heroic widow and mother cried out to her son not to give in, even at the cost of her life, and to avenge his father's death.

Finally, having heard that Jerusalem was in new danger, Yochanan lifted the siege and returned to the city to defend it against a new onslaught from Syria. This did not save his mother's life, however, for the vicious Ptolemy killed her nevertheless, and then fled the country.

Yochanan — Conqueror and Kohen Gadol

The new Syrian siege against Jerusalem, mounted by Antiochus VII, was a very serious one. It lasted for a long time and caused heavy suffering to its inhabitants. Hunger increased and the strength of resistance weakened. Yochanan came to a surprise decision — he offered to negotiate a surrender.

Antiochus demanded a treaty of friendship which would include the following conditions: The Jews must

(a) lay down their arms;

(b) pay tribute to Syria for all Jewish-held territories outside of Judea proper (e.g.,

such cities as Jaffa);

(c) admit a Syrian garrison into Jerusalem.

Yochanan agreed to the first two demands, but refused to open Jerusalem to foreign soldiers. Instead, he offered a sum of silver and hostages to assure Antiochus that the Jews would not attack Syrian forces. Antiochus accepted these terms.

In fulfillment of this treaty, Yochanan provided troops to aid Antiochus in a war against Parthia. Interestingly enough, at one point in his victorious campaign,

Antiochus halted hostilities for two days to allow his Jewish soldiers to observe *Shabbos* and Shavuos, which fell on a Sunday that year.

Before long, Yochanan's surrender was vindicated. He was able to exploit the constant internal strife in Syria to regain Judea's independence and even to enlarge the borders of the land.

Yochanan was anxious to extend Jewish control to all of *Eretz Yisrael,* as it was before the country was split up into two kingdoms in the time of Rechavam [Rehoboam], son of King Shlomo [Solomon]. The capital of the ancient northern kingdom had been Shomron [Samaria]. Yochanan wanted to conquer this city from the Samaritans, Judea's implacable enemies. To that end he sent his army commanded by his two sons. One day, while performing the service in the Holy Temple, Yochanan suddenly heard a voice saying: "Your two sons who went forth to battle with the gentiles have won the war."

His next objective was the Negev, the southern part of Judea. Here, too, he was successful and wrested the land from the Edomites, who had taken possession of it during the Babylonian exile.

One problem worried Yochanan a great deal. Many non-Jews lived within the expanded borders of Judea, and now the Edomites had been added to their number. He feared that in a future time of war the aggressive Edomites would join forces with the enemy and rebel against the rule of the Jews. Again, his solution was a surprising one: he forced the Edomites to convert to Judaism, even though conversion under duress is against the Halachah.

From these converted Edomites there later emerged Herod [Hordos], a man who caused untold harm to our people and country.

Like his father before him, Yochanan bore dual responsibility as *Nasi* of Judea, and *Kohen Gadol.* In addition to his military achievements and the extension of the national borders, he improved the spiritual and material standards of his people. Their way of life was molded by the Torah, and the Supreme Court — the Sanhedrin — functioned in the Chamber of Hewn Stone in the Temple precinct, and decided on questions of law in all areas of individual and collective import.

Although Yochanan, like Shimon before him, held the title of *Nasi,* the Sages continued to appoint a *Nasi* as the leading member of the Sanhedrin, so that civil authority would belong to those who interpreted the Torah.

The *Nasi* of the Sanhedrin at the time was Yehoshua ben Perachiah, while Nitai of Arbel held the title of *Av Beis Din,* the head of the Sanhedrin.

Yochanan Hyrkanus is known to have ordained certain statutes of a religious nature. He instituted regulations to ease the service of the priests in the Temple service, and he forbade the sound of the hammer and the noise of work to be heard in Jerusalem during *Chol HaMoed,* the intermediate days of the festivals. The Sages did not agree with all his ordinances, a fact which was exploited by the Sadducees, the partial heirs of the Hellenists, who tried to induce Yochanan to side with them in their confrontation with the *Perushim* [Pharisees], or Rabbinic party.

Sadducees, Heirs of the Hellenists

During the reign of Yochanan Hyrkanus a growing party of law defiers came to the fore. Mainly the descendants of the Hellenists, they were disciples of Tzadok and were therefore known as *Tzadokim* [Sadducees].

How did the Sadducees differ from the Hellenists? Both denied the divine origin of the Oral Law and both cast off the "yoke of the Commandments." Primarily they differed in their political concepts. The Hellenists were assimilationists who saw no reasons for existence of a Jewish nation. They advocated complete integration into the surrounding peoples and an end to Judean independence. Not so the Sadducees. They were only too well aware of the spiritual and political achievements of the Hasmonean period. They knew that their contemporaries, who were the eye-witnesses of miracles and divine intervention, would not easily forsake their G-d and their Jewish pride. Hence, they gave the impression that they, too, were nationalists who were dedicated to the independence of their country.

The Sages saw them for what they truly were and tried to keep them from exercising any influence in Jewish life. The Sadducees retaliated by openly opposing the Sages. They argued that there was no need for Sages in order for one to know the laws. According to them the written Torah was to be taken literally; it was an open book that everyone could read and understand. This was a declaration of war on the fundamentals of Jewish belief in that it denied the divine origin of the Oral Law and the unbroken transmission of Torah interpretation stretching from teacher to student since Moses received it at Sinai. Furthermore, the Sadducees denied that the Sages had the authority to pronounce ordinances and decrees.

The fact is that despite their declared allegiance to the letter of the Written Torah, the Sadducees were lax in its observance, even when there could be no dispute regarding the meaning of a given commandment. Often, when it was clear that a given commandment could be performed properly only according to the tradition of the Oral Law, the Sadducees did it in such a way that their performance of it was actually a non-compliance or even a violation according to the true Halachah.

Some of the better known examples of Sadducean deviation are:

— They did away with the ritual of pouring water on the Altar on Succos [נִסּוּךְ הַמַּיִם], because it is not explicitly mentioned in the Torah.

— Contrary to the interpretation taught by the Oral Law, the Sadducee High Priest set fire to the Yom Kippur incense before — instead of after — entering the Holy of Holies.

— Instead of counting Shavuos as the fiftieth day from the second day of Passover, the Sadducees began their count from the first Sunday after the beginning of Passover.

— The Sadducean courts administered justice in a particularly cruel manner. The Oral Law teaches that "an eye for an eye" means that an assailant must give monetary compensation for any wound he may have inflicted. The Sadducees, however, interpreted the verse literally. If someone had blinded another man, they would blind him in retribution. If he had broken his victim's leg, the Sadducees would break his leg.

In addition, following their master, Tzadok, the Sadducees denied the existence of the World to Come, ruling out any reward and punishment in the life after this. Hence, no fear of consequences would deter them from any sin. Their only concern was to enjoy physical pleasures to the full while alive in This World, for there was nothing after death. In time they grew strong enough to boldly and bodily strike back at their fellow Jews who were loyal to the Torah. Much blood was shed in the confrontation between the Sadducees and the loyal masses of the people and their leaders, the Sages.

The success and prosperity that Judea enjoyed at that time played right into the hands of the Sadducees, who emphasized the pleasures of this life. In this end they even influenced Yochanan Hyrkanus, the Prince and High Priest, to side with their party. Thus they gained the upper hand in shaping the affairs of the country.

All his life Yochanan had been loyal to the Torah. True, he had enacted some statutes of which the Sages did not approve, but on the whole, he was devoted to them. Nevertheless, toward the end of his life the Sadducees prevailed upon him and he became their supporter. It may be that Yochanan was displeased that the Sages repudiated some of his enactments, and this caused him to become a Sadducee at the end of a long and otherwise honorable career. Whatever the reason for Yochanan's change, it caused the Sages to teach: "Do not trust yourself until the day of your death" (Avos 2:4). Yochanan ruled Judea for thirty-one years, 135-104 BCE (3626-3657).

True Leaders and Deviant Sects

The true leaders of the Jewish people throughout the generations were and are its Torah scholars and Sages. The time of Yochanan was no different. He reigned in the period of the *Zugos*, when two sages shared the spiritual leadership. The two people in office during Yochanan's time were Yehoshua ben Perachiah and Nitai of Arbel. They were disciples of the previous "Pair," Yose ben Yoezer and Yose ben Yochanan, who functioned during the troublesome years of the conflict between the Hasmoneans and the Hellenists.

In the Mishnah we learn what they both taught:

Yehoshua ben Perachiah said: "Appoint yourself a rabbi; acquire a friend; and when judging a person,
give him the benefit of the doubt."

Nitai of Arbel said: "Keep your distance from a bad neighbor; do not associate with an evildoer; and do not lose faith in ultimate justice" (Avos 1:6-7).

In Nitai's words, there sounds an echo of his age. At that time, "keep your distance from a bad neighbor" meant to avoid the Sadducees. And if a Jew were disturbed at the sight of a prospering evildoer and a successful Sadducee, Nitai reassured him, "Do not lose faith in ultimate justice," know that all the evildoers will eventually get their punishment and that there is no grain of truth in their teachings and beliefs.

All the laws of the Torah at that time were clear and undisputed, and there was

The 2000-year-old Scroll of Isaiah displayed beneath the dome of the Shrine of the Book, Israel Museum.

The First Isaiah Scroll from Qumran, showing 38:8-40:2, which can be readily deciphered with the aid of a Tanach. The bottom line begins with the well-known passage of consolation, Nachamu, Nachamu ami, read as the haftarah on the Sabbath following the Ninth of Av.

no difference of opinion among the leading Sages. Whenever local authorities could not decide important questions, the Torah commands, "You must go to the place that G-d will choose," and ask, "The judge who will be in those days" (Deuteronomy 17:8-9). The "place" was Jerusalem and the "judge" the Sanhedrin. Only one difference of opinion on the highest scholarly level is reported during those days. It dealt with the laying of one's hands on the sacrifice on a festival. The Nasi of the Sanhedrin and the Av Beis Din had opposing views on the question.

But later on, during the years of bitter clashes with the Sadducees, some laws were forgotten, or not properly transmitted. Fortunately, in every generation there arose spiritual giants who "restored the crown of the Torah to its former glory," and re-established the correct Halachah — men such as Shimon ben Shetach, Shemaya, Avtalyon and Hillel.

Most of the people followed the Sages and remained loyal to the laws of the Torah. The Sages were called Pharisees [Perushim], which means "those who separate themselves." This title signified their very strict adherence to the most stringent requirements of the laws of ritual purity [טֻמְאָה וְטָהֲרָה]. The observance of these laws often caused them to refrain [separate themselves] from activities or avoid people and places that were permitted under ordinary Halachic interpretation.

The title chaver was awarded to a learned person who was known to observe the Halachah scrupulously, particularly with regard to the laws of ritual purity and tithes.

A delicate operation — opening and restoring one of the Dead Sea scrolls (1955). Also found in the Qumran Caves: letters in Aramaic written on papyrus, and clearly signed "from Shimon bar Kosiba [Kochba]"; and a letter written on four wooden tablets, in which Bar Kochba gave stern orders to his subordinates and which he signed: "From Shimon Bar Kosiba, Nasi al Yisrael [Prince of Israel]."

These clay tables and benches were reconstructed from remnants found in the scriptorium (writing room) at Qumran.

The common people were called *ammei haaretz* [earthy people]. They cleansed themselves from ritual contamination only when they were about to go up to the Temple Mount, such as before the Three Pilgrimage Festivals, or before bringing a sacrifice. Though unlearned and therefore prone to error in some areas of Halachah, these people remained followers of the Sages.

While the Sadducees openly opposed the Torah, there arose in those days still another group that departed from the clear path of Torah and the Sages. These people were not as brazen as the Sadducees, but they, too, undermined the foundations of Torah tradition.

These people were called Essenes. The name is derived from the Aramaic word *assia* which means "a healer," for indeed many of them engaged in medicine. Generally, they withdrew into isolated areas, far from other communities. They lived a communal life and adopted various restrictions not required by the Halachah. Their common meals had rites that have no basis in the Torah, they did not live a family life, and did not offer sacrifices in the Temple.

It has been conjectured that from their teachings later arose the Christian religion, which throughout the centuries caused untold harm to the Jewish people.

From 1947 onwards, a number of scrolls were found in the Cave of Qumran, in the Judean desert near the Dead Sea. They were written and hidden by a sect that called itself "The Sons of Light and the Sons of Darkness." Some researchers believe that there exists a connection between this group and the Essenes.

13

Domination of the Sadducees

[Once a cynical, lawless man named Elazar ben Poera managed to convince King Yannai that the Sages opposed him. Elazar advised Yannai to test them by expressing his intention to serve as Kohen Gadol. The Sages asked Yannai to withdraw because there was a doubt as whether he was qualified by birth for the priesthood.]

Elazar ben Poera said: "Could a common Jew be insulted this way? You are the king and Kohen Gadol and this is how you are treated?!" "What should I do?" [asked Yannai]. "If you heed my advice — trample them!" "But what will become of the Torah?" [asked Yannai]. "It [the Torah scroll] is rolled up and lying in a corner. Whoever wishes to learn, let him come and learn."

Said R' Nachman bar Yitzchak: "At that moment, heresy penetrated the king..He should have replied: 'That is satisfactory concerning the Written Law; but what about the Oral law?' "

Immediately, the evil was unleashed by Elazar ben Poera, and all the Sages of Israel were killed. The world became desolate, until Shimon ben Shetach came and restored the Torah to its former glory (Kiddushin 66a).

Yehudah Aristobulus Assumes Kingship

Aristobulus, son of Yochanan Hyrkanus, ruled only one year over the Land of Judea, 104 BCE (3657), but in this short period of time he managed to do much harm. He, too, was hostile to the Sages, as was his father toward the end of his rule, but he pursued them with even greater ruthlessness. Aristobulus was a suspicious person who feared anyone who might compete with him for power; he attacked even his closest relatives.

Before he died, Yochanan had commanded that his rule be passed on to his wife, but Aristobulus paid no attention to his father's testament. He imprisoned his mother and brothers and seized power for himself. Only his brother Antigonus he left unharmed, and appointed him head of the army.

Aristobulus was not content to call himself "prince" like his successors; he was the first Hasmonean ruler to call himself "king." Antigonus followed his father's military policy and fought the non-Jewish inhabitants of his land, particularly the Galileans, and forced the Galilean gentiles to convert to Judaism, as his father had compelled the Edomites to convert. The joy of his victory, however, was shortlived.

Upon returning home from the successful military campaign, Antigonus was received by the people with great honor. The men of the royal court were envious of him, however, and played upon the fears of the ever-suspicious King Aristobulus. They slandered Antigonus, accusing him of plotting to usurp the kingship. King Aristobulus began to fear for his very life, and ordered his guards to kill anyone who would come to the palace carrying arms. Despite the lies of his courtiers, the king loved his brother, and sent word that he should come to see him unarmed. The conspirers seized the opportunity to do away with Antigonus. They induced the messenger to tell him that the king wanted him to come in his battle dress. When Antigonus came to the palace adorned with his military gear, the soldiers of the guard followed orders — they killed him.

This tragedy deeply affected Aristobulus, who was a sick man. He died in 103 BCE (3658) without leaving any children.

King Yannai, Warrior and Oppressor

After Aristobulus' death the government was headed by his widow, Queen Shlomis [Salome] Alexandra, also known as Shlomtzion. Shlomis was a sister of Shimon ben Shetach, the leading sage of the period, and she remained loyal to him even when married to a monarch who was an archenemy of the Sages. The first thing she did when her husband died was to free his brothers from prison. The oldest among them, Alexander Yannai, married Shlomis, his childless brother's widow, in accordance with the law of the Torah; he later succeeded his brother to the throne.

Under the influence of his wife, the queen, Yannai halted the suppression of the Pharisees and the Sages for a time, so that he could be free to do what he was most capable and eager to do, namely, to pursue the war against the hostile non-Jewish enclaves in the Land of Israel. This he did throughout most of the twenty-seven years of his reign. He was motivated not by the interests of his people, however, but by lust for battle and glory. In his large army were many foreign mercenaries, and as time went on he used these foreign soldiers to suppress his own people and hunt down the Pharisees.

His major objective was the conquest of the coastal cities. Knowing that they could not hold out against the Jewish king, the cities turned for help to Ptolemy VIII Lathyrus, who was ruler of Cyprus at the time. He had been co-ruler of Egypt with his mother, Cleopatra, but she had deposed him in favor of his brother. Ptolemy responded to the plea of the coastal cities. He defeated Alexander Yannai and took possession of the entire coastal zone and the southern lowland of Judea up to the Egyptian border.

Knowing that Ptolemy hated her for having dismissed him from the Egyptian throne, Cleopatra was now afraid that after this great victory her ambitious son would dethrone her and take possession of Egypt. Against him, she dispatched an army commanded by two Egyptian-Jewish generals. Ptolemy was defeated and was forced to relinquish the fruits of his victory. The entire coastal territory was restored to Yannai. Thereafter he moved against Transjordan and captured many towns there.

The Sadducees tried by all possible means to extend their domination throughout the expanding borders of the country, and to keep the Pharisees away from any position of power. They knew that they could best succeed in winning the king over to their side by provoking him to anger at the Pharisees, with whom he maintained a generally friendly relationship. To gain their objective they used half-truth and slander.

They knew that the Pharisees were displeased with Yannai's desire to be High Priest. His eligibility for this sacred office was in question because there was evidence indicating that his mother was disqualified to be married to a *Kohen*. A cunning Sadducee leader, Elazar ben Poera, sought a way to incite an open clash between the Pharisees and the king. The occasion soon came. Yannai invited the leading sages of Israel to a festive gathering to celebrate his victories. Elazar ben Poera

persuaded the king to appear before his guests wearing the gold headband of the High Priest on his forehead. Yannai seemed to indicate publicly that he was a qualified *Kohen,* when in fact his status was questionable.

As expected, the Pharisee Sages protested. One of them, Yehudah ben Gedidiah, called out: "King Yannai, the crown of royalty is enough for you. Leave the crown of priesthood to the descendants of Aaron!"

The king was incensed. The charge against his mother was investigated and proved to be unfounded. Yehudah ben Gedidiah received lashes, the punishment given a slanderer under Rabbinic law. But Elazar continued his incitement of the king. He argued that lashes might be sufficient punishment for one who slandered a common man, but if one slandered the king, the punishment ought to be much more severe. Moreover, if the Pharisees were satisfied with such a slight punishment to Yannai's slanderer, this proved that they meant to show their disregard for the king. In the end he prevailed upon Yannai to kill many of the Sages and to exile the others from the country.

Shimon ben Shetach Restores the Torah

The persecution of the Pharisees lasted for a few years. The surviving Sages and their students fled the country and the Sadducees' ascendancy was complete. They even constituted the membership of the Sanhedrin. As their knowledge of the law was far from sufficient, they based their decisions on their personal ideas of right or wrong. Their insistence on the literal

meaning of the Torah caused them to misinterpret verses and issue rulings that were gross violations of the Torah interpreted by the Oral Law.

With the rise of the Sadducees, the spiritual level of the populace declined sharply. Without teachers there were no students, whether young or old. Even Shimon ben Shetach, brother-in-law of the king, had to go into hiding to escape Yannai's rage.

Aside from his general fury against the Pharisees, Yannai held a particular grudge against Shimon ben Shetach. This resulted from an incident in which three hundred Nazirites asked for financial assistance to purchase their required offerings. Shimon ben Shetach turned to the king and asked him to join in helping them. The king agreed and provided sacrificial animals for half the Nazirites. Shimon, however, had found a Halachic basis to release half of the Nazirites from their vow and, hence, from the need to bring sacrifices. When the king heard about it he was furious, thinking that Shimon ben Shetach had tricked him. Shimon escaped from the city and went into hiding (Yerushalmi, Nazir 5:3).

After the king's anger subsided, an opportunity arose for Queen Shlomis to bring Shimon back. Once again he became an honored guest at the royal court and used his influence to restore Torah to its rightful place. The Talmud relates how it happened:

> King Yannai and the queen sat at a banquet. Since he had killed the Sages there was no one to recite the grace. Yannai turned to his wife and said: "Who can get us a man to recite the blessing?" She answered: "Swear to me, that if I bring you such a man, you will not cause him anguish." He swore. The queen then brought in Shimon ben Shetach, her brother. He sat down between the king and the queen. Said the king to him: "Do you see what honor I show you?" He answered: "It is not you who honors me; it is the Torah that honors me" … They brought him a cup of wine to recite the grace. He said [since he

> had not eaten with them]: "Shall I recite, 'Blessed is He from Whose bounty Yannai and his companions [instead of "we"] have eaten?' " So he drank that cup and they brought another cup over which he said the blessings (Berachos 48a).

Taking advantage of the relative easing of Yannai's attitude toward Torah scholars, Shimon ben Shetach wanted to restore the prestige and authority of the Torah. His main efforts were on two fronts: to enhance the authority of the Sanhedrin and to educate the young. With extraordinary tact and skill, he gradually replaced the Sadducee members of the Supreme Court with genuine Sages — the Pharisees. In the education of children, Shimon understood very well that "If there are no kids there will be no goats." He instituted a system of public education, requiring that all young boys attend school. In this activity he worked together with his colleague Yehoshua ben Gamla, who also served as Kohen Gadol.

The Talmud (Bava Basra 21a) says that were it not for Yehoshua ben Gamla, Torah would have become forgotten among the Jewish people. In earlier times — since the Torah makes fathers responsible to teach their own children — those without fathers, or whose fathers were unlearned, went untaught. Then an academy was set up in Jerusalem for teen-agers, but even then, fatherless boys had no one to bring them there. Later, similar academies were established throughout the land, but that, too, was not a solution: the sixteen and seventeen year olds who came to study were often not willing to accept a teacher's discipline. Finally Yehoshua ben Gamla introduced a new plan — the first comprehensive system of public education in history. He arranged for teachers to be placed in every town and for all boys to be taught from the age of six.

Open Warfare against the Pharisees

Becoming alarmed over the rising influence of the Pharisees, Yannai and his Sadducee allies decided upon a bold act that would lead to an open and violent confrontation between the people and the king. Until then they had not dared to tamper with the service in the Holy Temple, for they knew that this would rouse the entire people against them. But now that they had decided on a drastic measure, it was in their interest to incite the people so that Yannai would have a pretext to retaliate severely and suppress the Pharisees and their popular following completely.

It happened during the festival of Succos. As he customarily did, Yannai was officiating in the Temple. The people were gathered in their masses in the courtyard, each holding his *lulav* and *esrog,* awaiting the moment when the High Priest would pour the water on the altar. But instead of pouring the water on the altar, Yannai poured it at his feet. He wanted to demonstrate his disregard for this *mitzvah* whose source is the Oral Law, and for the people's feelings.

The purpose of the king and his Sadducee consultants was achieved. Witnessing this public sacrilege, the people could not contain themselves. Spontaneously they pelted the king with their *esrogim.* In anticipation of a violent reaction, Yannai had stationed his mercenary troops around the Temple. They hurled themselves at the defenseless people, with the result that more than 6,000 people were killed in the Temple

area. This was Yannai's declaration of war against the Sages and their followers, a violent suppression that lasted for six years, in the course of which some 50,000 Jews lost their lives. At the beginning of Yannai's rule, his army had fought the enemies of the Jewish people; now it fought the people itself.

In their desperation to rid themselves of the tyrannical Yannai, the people turned for help to the Syrian king Demetrius III [Eucerus], son of Antiochus IX, for help. He accepted their plea, and with joint Jewish-Syrian forces they defeated the army of Alexander Yannai, who himself fled the battlefield and found refuge in a mountainous wilderness. This took place in 88 BCE (3673).

Then the people had a surprising change of heart. Out of fear of the Syrian alliance and out of pity for the homeless and isolated refugee king, they recalled him to Jerusalem, in the confident hope that Yannai, in response to the people's good will, would now rule them justly. This expectation proved to be a cruel illusion. As soon as Demetrius returned to Syria and Yannai had the reins of power firmly in his hands, he imprisoned 800 Pharisees and tortured them in a horrible manner, according to the custom of the Romans. While the victims were suffering excruciating pain, he had their wives and children killed before their very eyes. Then the prisoners were executed. Yannai himself witnessed the gruesome spectacle.

Finally, the long-awaited news of Yannai's death arrived. During a military expedition he became seriously ill. Before dying, he transferred power to Queen Shlomis, and advised her to make peace with the Pharisees. He told her:

> Do not fear the Pharisees, nor the non-Pharisees, but only the hypocrites, who masquerade as Pharisees. For their deeds are like Zimri's but they demand a reward like that of Pinchas (Sotah 22b).

Yannai finally realized where his Sadducean connections had led him, and saw that Shlomis was right in trying to help the Pharisees. He had reigned for a turbulent twenty-seven years, until either 77 or 76 BCE (3684 or 3685).

14

Rule of Shlomis Alexandra

It happened in the days of Shimon ben Shetach and Queen Shlomtzion [Shlomis] that rain fell every Friday night, until the wheat grew as big as kidneys, the barley like olive kernels, and the lentils like dinars of gold. The Sages gathered some of them and preserved them as an example for future generations, to demonstrate how much harm sin causes and to confirm what is written: "Your iniquities have turned away these things, and your sins have withheld good from you" (Jeremiah 5:25; Midrash Vayikra Rabbah 35:8).

Peace and Calm under Shlomis Alexandra, c. 76-66 BCE (3685-3695)

With Shlomis the reigning monarch, the persecutions and murders that were rampant under Yannai came to an end. Calm and tranquility returned to the land, and every man dwelt "under his vine and under his fig tree" (I Kings 5:5). G-d's blessing could be seen in all the queen's activities, and within a short time she succeeded in reversing the situation that had prevailed under her husband.

The Sadducees — who had been so influential, had controlled the Temple service and had dominated the Sanhedrin — were removed from all their positions of power and replaced by the Sages who returned from their exile abroad and their secret hiding-places. Again they con- stituted the membership of the Sanhedrin and the lower courts. Shimon ben Shetach took his rightful place as the head of the Sanhedrin, and Yehudah ben Tabai, who had returned from his exile in Alexandria, Egypt, was elected its *Nasi*.

Those few years were distinguished by an ideal partnership between the royal power of the queen and the wise counsel of her great brother, Shimon. Every area of religious, social and political activity benefited from this fruitful combination of secular and spiritual authority. Shimon imposed the rule of the Torah on the land, appointed the leading Pharisees to the Sanhedrin, reinstituted the Temple service in its properly ordained manner and corrected other deviant practices of the Sadducees.

In order to forestall any Saducean attempt for return to power, Shlomis arrested the Sadducees who had advised King Yannai to put 800 Pharisees to a cruel death. The criminals paid with their own lives for the murders they caused.

The queen built a strong army, made up largely of Jewish soldiers, and supplemented by mercenaries from other lands. Unlike her husband, her goal was not to seek personal fame through military conquests, but rather to safeguard the security of her country. Here, too, she succeeded. G-d cast the fear of the Jewish people upon all their gentile neighbors and during her reign none of them dared to attack the country. She was privileged to see the fulfillment of the cherished blessing: "And I will grant peace in the land" (Leviticus 26:6).

The Last Days of Shlomis Alexandra

Toward the end of the righteous queen's life, matters took a marked turn for the worse. This change is responsible for very serious consequences in the history of our people.

Shimon ben Shetach died, leaving no one capable of taking his place, either as the queen's close relative, or sagacious counselor. Shlomis was old and did not have the strength to suppress the manipulations of the Sadducees who tried to regain their lost power. She had two sons. The older one, Hyrkanus, was of a quiet disposition and served as Kohen Gadol. But Aristobulus, her younger son, was different. He was a hot-tempered, stormy, ambitious man. For this reason his mother had not appointed him to a position of power. The Sadducees shrewdly reasoned that they could gain power by winning and manipulating the unstable Aristobulus. When they approached him for help, he eagerly responded to their request, thinking that he could use them as stepping stones to the throne.

Aristobulus went to his mother and demanded that she turn over all the fortresses in the land to him and the Sadducee leaders. He threatened that should she refuse, he and his associates would ally themselves with Aretas, king of the Arabs and a bitter enemy of the Jews.

The old queen lacked the strength and energy to withstand her son's pressure and complied with his request. Only three fortresses, in which the royal treasure was kept, remained under her control.

Not long thereafter, Shlomis Alexandra was stricken with her final illness. Now, Aristobulus decided, was the time to act decisively. He knew that his mother would bequeath the kingdom to Hyrkanus, her first-born son. He therefore demanded of the Sadducee army commanders that they seize the remaining fortresses and hand them over to him. He used the vast fortune that was stored there to build up an army and with its help planned to seize the throne.

The Pharisee leaders protested vigorously to the sick queen about Aristobulus' action, but she lacked the power to act against her headstrong son. She authorized the Sages to do whatever they deemed advisable. The rabbis realized that the use of force could lead to only one result — civil war. To avoid this calamity, they decided to withdraw altogether from affairs of state and instead to turn all their energies to strengthening the inner life of the people, the only true guarantee of the continuity of a flourishing Jewish life.

The death of Queen Shlomis Alexandra ended the only golden era during the time of the Second Temple, and it ushered in a century of almost unrelieved disaster. The feared civil war *did* break out, pitting the two brothers, Aristobulus and Hyrkanus, against each other. The outcome of this confrontation was bloody warfare, the end of Judea's independence, the destruction of the Holy Temple, and the long and still unfinished exile of the Jewish people from its homeland.

The New Leaders of the People

In the troubled times following the death of the beloved queen the broad mass of the people concentrated around the Sages for leadership and guidance. New leaders came to the fore — Shemaya as *Nasi* of the Sanhedrin, and Avtalyon, as *Av Beis Din.* One of the favorite expressions of Shemaya was: "Love work; hate lordship; and do not become intimate with the government" *(Avos* 1:10).

In the last words of Shemaya we detect an unmistakable echo of the new attitude of the Sages — to withdraw from political and governmental matters. Avtalyon, too, cautioned the Sages to be very careful in expressing political opinions, lest they be forced to seek exile. If the teachers were forced to find refuge in the surrounding Hellenistic cities the students who followed them would be exposed to non-Jewish influences that would eventually lead to a desecration of the Name of G-d *(Avos* 1:11).

The Talmud tells a revealing story which clearly shows the people's attachment to the great teachers of the Torah in preference to the political leaders, among them even the High Priest, who fought each other for power and position:

> The Rabbis taught: It happened once that a High Priest left the Holy Temple (at the end of Yom Kippur) and all the people followed him. But when they saw Shemaya and Avtalyon, they left the High Priest and followed Shemaya and Avtalyon. Later the two Sages came to the High Priest to take their leave from him. He said to them: "May the sons of the foreign peoples go in peace" (thus reminding them spitefully that they were the sons of converts). They answered him: "May the sons of foreign peoples go in peace, for they walk in the footsteps of Aharon, but may the son of Aharon not go in peace, for he does not walk in the footsteps of Aharon" (Yoma 71b).

15

Civil War, 68-63 BCE (3693-3698)

When the soldiers of Hyrkanus laid siege to the Temple Mount they brought Choni the Circle-Maker to curse the men of Aristobulus who had fortified themselves in the Temple area. It was well-known that Choni's prayer was accepted in Heaven and so they brought him by force to the scene of battle between the two brothers. When Choni saw that he could not get away from there, he spoke as follows: "Master of the Universe! Those who lay the siege are Your people and those who are besieged are Your priests. I plead before You: do not heed the prayers that either side offers to You — to do evil to the other side!" (Josephus, Antiquities).

Hatred between Brothers and Foreign Intervention

The power struggle between Hyrkanus and Aristobulus had its beginning while their mother, Shlomis Alexandra, was still alive. After her death, the dispute erupted into open war. Aristobulus was under the influence of the Sadducees, who supported him in his fight against his brother. Hyrkanus became friendly with Antipater, the Edomite, a cunning power-hungry man whom King Yannai had appointed governor of Edom. By exploiting his alliance with the soft-hearted Hyrkanus, Antipater expected to further his own ambition, which was no less than to become ruler of the land himself. Thus the Jewish people became pawns in a power struggle between their spiritual enemies — the Sadducees — on one side, and the scheming Edomite on the other.

The last testament of Queen Shlomis declared Hyrkanus to be the legal ruler of the land, but he held power for only three months. Aristobulus put a large army into the field against his brother. The military encounter took place near the city of Jericho, and Aristobulus emerged victorious. The brothers made peace between themselves. Hyrkanus abdicated the throne and withdrew from public life. As the only brother of the new king, he enjoyed a special status, honor and riches. Private life suited him well, as he was a man of mild character who lacked the decisiveness and sense of responsibility demanded of a monarch.

The scene was now set for life to return to its previous serenity, but it was not to be. The villain was Antipater, the Edomite, who plunged the country into a cruel and prolonged civil war.

Antipater began by provoking Hyrkanus into reopening the war against his brother. On the Edomite's advice, they both left Jerusalem secretly and traveled to the Arab king Aretas. They asked for his support in their war against Aristobulus, and in return promised to restore to him the cities that Alexander Yannai had conquered in Transjordan, as well as some areas on the western side of the Jordan. Aretas readily agreed to this proposal, hoping that by cooperating with such traitors he would finally impose his rule over the entire land of the Jews. With his large army, he crossed the Jordan and marched to the very gates of Jerusalem. Seeing Hyrkanus at the head of the army, his supporters opened the gates of the city to the invading Arabs,

One of the facades hewn out of the solid rock in the first-second centuries CE at a site called Petra, in Edom (Transjordan), 60 miles north of Eilat; this one, known as al-Khazna ("the treasury"), imitates a Hellenistic theater. Petra was the capital of the Arab kingdom of the Nabateans, with whom Hyrkanus allied against his brother Aristobulus after the death of their mother Shlomis Alexandra.

forcing Aristobulus and his soldiers to retreat behind the massive fortifications of the Temple Mount. To prevent the invaders from following them, Aristobulus' forces demolished the bridge that connected the Temple Mount with the Upper City, leaving a deep valley between themselves and their attackers.

The hatred between the royal brothers reached its ugly climax during these days of siege. Hyrkanus' party brought Choni the Circle-Maker to their camp and demanded that he curse their enemies. He was famous as the righteous man whose prayers had brought rain in time of drought. Once, as he prayed, he drew a circle in the sand and said that he would not leave it until it rained. Almost immediately a deluge began. That was the origin of his nickname, "the Circle-Maker." Now, when Choni was called upon not to help Jews but to curse them, he refused.

As the numbers of livestock for the Temple sacrifices dwindled, the besiegers were ready to supply the animals, but only for an enormous price. Finally came an incident which the Talmud reports in three different places:

The Rabbis taught: When the Hasmonean family fought one another, Hyrkanus was outside and Aristobulus inside. Every day they lowered a basket with dinars and in turn lifted the animals for the daily sacrifices. There was an old man, learned in Greek wisdom, who told the besiegers: "As long as they continue the Temple service, they will not be delivered into your hands." The next day, the defenders lowered the basket with dinars, but they sent up a pig. When it reached half the height of the wall, the pig stuck its hooves into the wall, and the Land of Israel shook over an area of 400 parsos by 400 parsos (Sotah 49b, Menachos 64b; but Bava Kamma 82b states that Hyrkanus was inside and Aristobulus outside).

"And our enemies are judges" *(Deuteronomy 32:31)*

The pig that stuck its feet to the wall of the Temple was a shocking indication of evil days to come. Soon after this event imperial Rome appeared on the scene. Rome, which had been likened to a pig, also plunged its claws into the walls of Jerusalem and the Holy Temple itself.

At the time when the two hostile camps were facing each other from inside and outside the Temple walls, the famous Roman general, Pompey, was marching his legions throughout the lands of Asia Minor, subduing them one after the other. In 63 BCE (3698) the two brothers turned to Pompey's proconsul in Damascus and asked him for Rome's intervention in their dispute. Rome's representatives were notorious for their greed, and when the messengers of Aristobulus offered the larger bribe, the Roman decided in his favor and commanded King Aretas and Hyrkanus to lift the siege and leave Jerusalem.

The bitter end to the civil war came when Pompey returned to Damascus after completing his victorious military campaigns. The two brothers appeared personally before the great Roman general to lay their cases before him. Aristobulus argued that the kingdom belonged to him, as he was by far the more qualified of the two to be a ruler. Hyrkanus' claim was presented by Antipater, who argued that the late queen had willed her older son, Hyrkanus, to be her successor to the throne.

Pompey, of course, was guided neither by justice nor the claims of the two brothers, but by the interests of Rome. Because he intended to impose the imperial rule of Rome upon the land of Judea, he preferred Hyrkanus, the weaker and more submissive of the two brothers. Pompey declared that Hyrkanus was to be both king and High Priest, and he demanded that Aristobulus surrender to him all the fortresses in the land. Aristobulus meekly gave in to these harsh demands. Only later did the full meaning of his surrender dawn upon him — that he had delivered his country to a foreigner. At the last moment he tried to save at least the independence of Jerusalem, and rushed to the defense of the city. But when Pompey commanded him a second time to appear before him, he lost heart and submitted again to the dictates of the Roman. His men, however, decided to defend the city against the approaching Roman army.

The Roman Eagle on the Temple Wall

Even when the Roman legions were marching on Jerusalem, the camps of the two hostile brothers refused to unite. Hyrkanus' men, who considered Pompey their ally, opened the city gates to him, while Aristobulus and his soldiers withdrew behind the fortifications of the Temple Mount. The Temple Mount had a natural protection on three sides — on west, east, and south it was surrounded by steeply-sloped valleys. Only on its northern flank the terrain before it was flat; it was from there that the Romans launched their attack. Because their northern flank was so vulnerable, the Jews had always built their main defenses there. It was protected by a deep and wide moat and a high wall, fortified with towers and turrets.

The Romans employed their battle-tested siege techniques. They built high earthen ramps upon which they positioned catapults, machines that could hurl stones over the top of the walls. They built a crane-like device that held a huge ironclad battering ram with which they incessantly pounded the wall until they breached it. The struggle lasted for more than two months. The defenders put up a heroic resistance. From time to time they made surprise attacks against the enemy and demolished some of his war machines. All the while, the priests continued the service in the Temple, even though they were often pelted with stones and arrows from the enemy outside.

But the end was inevitable. The Romans succeeded in breaching the wall and put up ladders upon which they climbed over the wall into the Temple area. The officiating *Kohanim* were the particular target of Roman cruelty, yet the service was maintained as long as was humanly possible. As soon as one *Kohen* was murdered, a second immediately took his place. The bloodbath went on for a whole

Reconstruction of a Roman catapult (above) used for hurling stones over the defense walls of a besieged city. The stone ammunition (below) was used during a Roman siege: the large, rough boulders were rolled downhill by the defenders; the smaller, smoother stones were hurled upward by the attackers' catapults. From the Masada exhibition at the Israel Museum.

day, during which some 12,000 *Kohanim* and defenders were killed. Pompey and his soldiers even entered the Sanctuary, but they did not desecrate it and its holy vessels — the Table, the *Menorah,* and the Golden Altar, which was used for incense. The next day they left, and the Temple service was resumed.

After his victory Pompey left the Land, but not before he had instituted a new order. Hyrkanus, who had assisted him in his war, was reaffirmed as High Priest. The captured officers were executed in a cruel spectacle and Aristobulus and his two sons and two daughters were taken as captives to Rome, so that Pompey could parade them in a victory procession before the eyes of the Roman populace. One of Aristobulus' sons managed to escape on the way to Rome. He returned to his homeland and encouraged the people to continue their resistance against the invader.

Pompey thus put an end to Judean political independence and imposed a tributary tax upon the land. The coastal cities — Gaza, Jaffa, Dor, Ashdod and Yavneh — as well as those of Transjordan, were torn away from Jewish rule. All that remained of the Jewish state was Judea, part of Edom, Galilee and a narrow stretch of land in the south of Transjordan. But even in this limited territory Jewish rule was not sovereign, for it came under the jurisdiction of the Roman proconsul in Damascus.

16

Ascendancy of Rome

Rabbi Yehudah said in the name of Shmuel, "At the moment when Shlomo married the daughter of Pharaoh, the angel Gabriel descended and rammed a staff into the sea and surrounded it with stones and mud — and on it was built the great city of Rome" (Shabbos 56b).

Rome, an Aggressive Nation

By the time the bitter family feud culminated in Pompey's conquest and desecration of the Holy Temple, Rome was already a great power, casting its imperial shadow upon many lands and provinces. That Jerusalem would be ultimately destroyed, but only by a mighty king, was predicted by the prophet Yeshayahu, as interpreted by the Talmud:

[Rabban Yochanan ben Zakkai told the Roman general:] If you were not to become king, Jerusalem would not be given over into your hands, as it is written: "And Lebanon [a reference to the Holy Temple] shall fall by a mighty one" (Isaiah 10:34; Gittin 56b).

The First Temple, too, had been destroyed by the then mightiest king — Nebuchadnezzar.

As the saying goes, "Rome was not built in a day." Its ascendancy to a world power was a process that started with modest beginnings and lasted for a few hundred years. This development, too, was foreseen by the prophets of Israel:

[G-d said of Edom (Edom symbolizes Rome):] "... Behold, I made you small among the nations. ... Though you soar aloft like the eagle and though you set your nest among the stars, from there I will bring you down," says Hashem (Obadiah 1:2,4).

Briefly, this is the history of Rome, which grew by stages to become "the rod of G-d's wrath."

The founding of Rome goes back to the time of the First Temple. The city is on the Tiber River, approximately in the middle of the Italian peninsula, near its western coast. Rome was built on one of the seven hills that rise from a large and fertile valley west of the Apennines. As the city grew, it spread over all the seven hills, and conquered the people of the nearby villages.

Around the beginning of the Second Temple era, Rome's political and military skills asserted themselves, as she gradually imposed her will upon all the tribes of the peninsula. In a series of wars, most of them successful, the Romans pushed northward and southward until, in 275 BCE (3486), they succeeded in bringing the entire peninsula under their control.

The first rulers of Rome were kings; a few of them were not even Romans, but came from unfriendly tribes, such as the Etruscans. But when the kings imposed increasingly heavy burdens on the populace, the people rebelled and put an end to the monarchy. They replaced it with a new system of government based upon popular participation in the affairs of state. They called it a republic, from *res publica*, a Latin term that means matters of the public. The term monarchy comes from the Greek, and it means the rule of one.

The new regime emphasized military strength above all. The leaders of Rome succeeded in developing and maintaining an army that was superior to the armies of all other lands. It won almost all of its battles and even when it lost a battle it never surrendered. The Roman legions were famed and feared, first throughout Italy and later on, far and wide beyond its borders.

Our Sages often refer to Rome as Edom, and they teach that the Romans are descendants of Esau the ancestor of Edom. Indeed, the aggressive warriors of Rome fulfilled Yitzchak's blessing to Esau: "By your sword shall you live" *(Genesis* 27:40).

At the head of the republic were two consuls, who were responsible to lead the people in battle and to conclude treaties with other countries. Their influence upon matters of state was severely limited by the fact that their term of office lasted for only one year, after which they became proconsuls and were sent to the various foreign countries and provinces under Roman control.

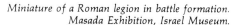

Miniature of a Roman legion in battle formation.
Masada Exhibition, Israel Museum.

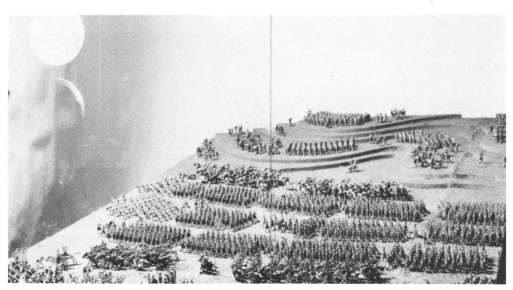

The Common Man Struggles for his Rights

Real power was vested in the members of the Roman Senate. Its members were elected to their position for an unlimited term. The senators exercised the legislative, judicial and, to some extent, executive authority of the state. They appointed the high officials of the administration and the senior generals, and decided on all political matters, such as whether or not to declare war. The consuls were required to carry out their decisions.

This system worked well for a long time. Both the consuls and the senate knew their respective spheres of authority and cooperated with each other. But in the course of time the legal limits became more obscure and men who were hungry for power tried to impose their will upon others. Severe friction and violent confrontation between the consuls and the members of the senate became common. In the end the republican system was abolished and in its stead emerged the autocratic rule of one man — the Roman emperor.

Not all the inhabitants of Rome had the same political rights and privileges. Only those who belonged to the oldest families of the city — its founding fathers, who were called patricians (*pater* in Latin means "father") — could lay full claim to them. People who had come to Rome from conquered villages and provinces were second-class citizens and suffered discrimination.

These common people, who were called plebeians, had more duties than rights — in particular, the duty of serving in the army — but in political matters they had no say. As Rome was almost always fighting wars and more and more of the common people were taken to the army, they felt the inequality and discrimination more keenly. A veteran who returned home after many years of bloody warfare would ask resentfully why he should shed his blood for Rome, when his country denied him full citizenship.

The smoldering resentment against the proud patricians finally broke into the open. Gradually, after a long and bitter struggle, the plebeians won: they were given equal rights and full Roman citizenship.

Two of their important objectives were conceded to the plebeians at the beginning of their struggle. They were: (a) The right to elect representatives of their choice to whom they could bring any complaint against the government and its

Lupa Romana, Roman she-wolf, symbol of the founding of Rome.

officials. The men chosen were called tribunes. They participated in sessions of the senate and whenever a resolution to the disadvantage of the common people was voted upon the tribune could rise and say: "Veto," which means: "I forbid" — and the resolution was defeated. (b) The basic laws of Rome were engraved on special tablets and displayed in the center of the city. Now everyone could readily find out what were his rights and duties. A person thus felt better protected against high-handed and discriminatory decisions of government officials and judges.

Rome Turns to the Mediterranean

After the Romans had conquered Italy they began to look beyond its borders. The Roman proclivity for conquest was about to make it the major power in the immediate area and then the Near East, where it would become the dominant factor in the destiny of Judea.

Across the Mediterranean Sea loomed the huge coast of Africa. There, to the southeast, not very far from the southern tip of Italy, was the great and rich kingdom of Carthage, near present-day Tunis. The seafaring traders of Rome, trying to establish commercial bonds with the inhabitants of the Mediterranean isles, found themselves in serious competition with the traders of Carthage, whose navigational and commercial skills were nurtured by hundreds of years of experience. The commercial rivalry between Rome and Carthage resulted in the three great Punic Wars ("Punic" comes from the word Phoenicia, the original homeland of the Carthaginians), which lasted for some 120 years and ended with the total destruction of Carthage.

During the period when Rome was founded, seafaring merchants from Tyre and Sidon (the Biblical צוֹר and צִידוֹן) had already established Carthage on the northern coast of Africa, not far from the island of Sicily. As Carthage grew, its rule extended to include the entire northwest coast of Africa to Gibraltar; parts of Spain, Corsica, and Sardinia, and the western part of Sicily, uncomfortably close to the expanding borders of Rome. In order to meet and defeat the looming Carthaginian challenge, Rome was forced to built a battle-worthy navy.

The focus of the clash between the two contending seafaring powers was the island of Sicily, where their commercial and political interests met head on, and brought about the First Punic War, which lasted twenty-three years, 264-241 BCE (3497-3520). The military engagements between Rome and Carthage were fought mainly on the sea. Although the Carthaginians were more experienced mariners than the Romans, neither power succeeded in consistently defeating the other. The seesaw struggle at sea went on for years, with first one and then the other country gaining the upper hand.

But the Roman genius for military strategy devised a plan that would give them an advantage at sea. They equipped their ships with long, wide wooden planks and sailed as close as possible to the boats of the enemy. Then the Romans placed the ends of these boards upon the parallel Carthaginian ships and, using them as bridges, stormed across to do battle in their accustomed manner. The first three attempts to use this new strategy ended in failure, as the Carthaginian navy sunk three Roman fleets. The Romans, however, did not despair. Their pride was challenged. At great cost and exertion they built a fourth fleet — with the help of the contributions of Roman citizens — and this time decisively defeated the Carthaginians.

Carthage was forced to pay a heavy price to the victorious Romans. They had to cede Sicily and pay a huge annual tribute to Rome. Two years later, the inhabitants of Sardinia rebelled against Carthage. Exploiting this development, Rome declared war on Carthage, despite Carthaginian protests. Before long, Carthage was forced to cede Sardinia and Corsica to Rome and pay it another indemnity.

Carthage Fights Back

Despite its defeat, Carthage was still a strong kingdom, and Rome, despite its victory, had learned to respect this strength. Each looked for new conquests, but tried to avoid another conflict between the two of them. Avoiding a new southern adventure that would pit them against Carthage, Rome turned northward, where the fertile valley of the River Po was occupied by the Gauls. Long before the Gauls had defeated Rome, but now the powerful Roman army attacked and

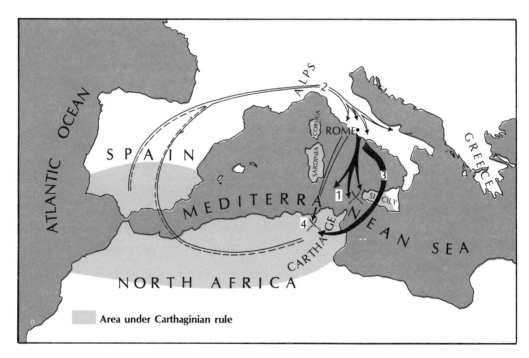

Area under Carthaginian rule

1. **First Punic War:** Romans fight naval battle near Sicily.
2. **Second Punic War:** Hannibal's forces penetrate Italy.
3. Roman forces attack Carthage.
4. Hannibal returns to Carthage, meets Roman, and is defeated.

defeated them. In northern Greece, too, Rome conquered a number of places.

Carthage, avoiding a new conflict with Rome, turned northwest to Spain. Under the leadership of Hamilcar, Carthage sent a large expeditionary force that re-conquered the southern part of Spain, which had a number of valuable silver and copper mines. The income from these gains made up for the loss of their Sicilian mines. The Romans tolerated Carthage's conquest of southern Spain, but in order to prevent any further move northward, they concluded a treaty with Hasdrubal, Hamilcar's son-in-law and successor, which did not allow for any expansion beyond the borders of Spain. The treaty remained effective until the assassination of Hasdrubal.

When Hamilcar's son Hannibal suc-ceeded his brother-in-law Hasdrubal, the relationship with the Romans again became tense and hostile. It is related that while he was yet a child, his father had made Hannibal swear that he would not rest until he avenged Rome's defeat of Carthage. Hannibal remained faithful to his oath, and looked for an opportunity to renew the war against Rome. He ignored the conditions of the treaty that his brother-in-law had concluded. When he dared to violate the treaty openly, the Romans took up the challenge and demanded the extradition of Hannibal into their hands. Carthage's refusal to comply with this request set the stage for the Second Punic War, which lasted 218-202 BCE (3543-3559).

Hannibal, commander of the Carthagi-nian army, is considered to have been one of the greatest generals of all time. When war was declared, he did not wait for the Romans to come and attack him. He decided to surprise the Romans by attacking them in their own country. Unlike the previous war, this was to be a war by land. In an incredible feat, he marched his army through Spain into southern France and over the Alps into Italy. Through treacherous, unmapped passes, he had to cross the tall Alpine mountains which were covered with snow and ice, over terrain which only very few had ever passed, at the head of an army of 40,000 soldiers and 36 battle elephants, together with all their equipment and provisions. All along the way, he was harassed by hostile tribes who tried to block his progress, but he persisted. Upon reaching the lowlands of Italy, he prepared his army for battle.

The Romans were shocked. They never imagined that Hannibal could strike from the north, for they had always relied on the Alps as their natural defense. Yet they quickly rallied to fight off the invader, only to be defeated time after time. The decisive battle was fought in 216 BCE (3545) at Cannae, a small town in southeastern Italy. In brilliant tactical moves Hannibal and his soldiers encircled the Roman army and annihilated it completely, causing the Romans some 70,000 casualties.

Hannibal's army was smaller than Rome's, he fought far from his home in the enemy's territory, and his lines of supply were overextended; nevertheless, he continued to win victory after victory throughout the length and width of Italy. For fifteen years, his army remained in Italy, winning triumph after triumph. Only the city of Rome itself he dared not attack. Instead, he tried to weaken her by provoking her various allies into severing their bonds with Rome and rebelling against her mastery.

The end came for Hannibal when the Romans, under the leadership of a very able general, Scipio, used Hannibal's own strategy against him. Scipio transported a new army across the sea and invaded Carthage itself. The Carthaginians turned in fear to Hannibal, requesting his immediate return home. He did so and again the two armies clashed in decisive battle near Carthage. This time, Scipio defeated Hannibal, and the Second Punic War ended in a decisive Roman victory.

The Roman conditions for peace were very harsh indeed. They demanded that Carthage hand over its fleet, that it surrender its rule in Spain, and that it undertake not to wage war with neighboring tribes without the permission of Rome. In practice, this last condition brought the independence of proud Carthage to an end.

The End of Carthage

For fifty years there was peace between Rome and Carthage. The Romans turned their attention to the eastern part of the Mediterranean. Among others, they fought Antiochus III, father of Antiochus Epiphanes, the despot of the Chanukah story. Gradually they brought almost all the peoples of Greece and Asia Minor under their dominion. Their main target in this part of the world were the three leading powers — Macedonia, Syria and Egypt. One of their favorite tactics was "divide and conquer" — which enabled them to achieve their objective without waging war. To that end they encouraged and stirred up the smaller peoples and tribes to rebel against their overlords. This explains the very friendly reception that the Roman Senate accorded to the delegation of little Judea, when Yehudah Maccabee sought to gain Roman support in his struggle against the Seleucid empire, Rome's great adversary. In this way Rome's diplomatic skill extended her sphere of influence to the lands of the eastern Mediterranean, after the western Mediterranean had been brought under her rule.

Carthage, Rome's old enemy, was the only independent state on the Mediterranean coast. Though weakened and subordinated, Carthage was still a thorn in Rome's ambition to dominate all the Mediterranean lands and islands. When a conflict broke out between Carthage and an ancient tribe of Berbers, who inhabited today's Algeria, Rome had a pretext to crush its old adversary once and for all. The Roman army set out for an invasion of Carthage. Knowing that it was outmatched, Carthage submitted to Rome and was ready to accept all her conditions for peace; all — except one. The Romans demanded the complete destruction of the city of Carthage and its rebuilding at a site some ten miles from the coast.

This condition they could and would not accept. They preferred to fight instead to the bitter end. They withdrew behind their walls and defended themselves against the mighty Roman army for three years. Finally, in the year 146 BCE (3615), the Romans breached the walls, entered the city and destroyed it to its very foundations. Carthage ceased to exist.

17

Rome — a World Power

Ten measures of riches descended to the world; nine of them the ancient Romans took and one measure the rest of the world took (Kiddushin 49b).

The Curse of Rome's Stolen Riches

Rome made the conquered peoples feel the full might of her imperial fist. The various tribes and peoples in Italy proper, she considered her allies. With them she concluded treaties of peace and friendship, although they were not granted Roman citizenship. But those outside Italy were oppressed and exploited. Their lands — Sicily, Spain, Carthage, Greece, Macedonia, and so on — were called provinces.

For every province the Senate appointed a governor; as a rule he would be a consul whose term of office had expired. He was called a proconsul and he served abroad for one year with absolute power over his province. As a rule, the Roman proconsuls considered their provinces to be sources of personal enrichment. They amassed large treasures and used them to strengthen their political standing in Rome. And a proconsul had to hurry, as one year was not a long time.

Cruel indeed was the lot of the conquered peoples abroad. First came the soldiers. They conquered and plundered the land and took many of its inhabitants captive, in order to sell them as slaves to Rome. Then came the Roman officials, who continued the policy of exploitation and oppression. They imposed heavy taxes upon the population and had no scruples about outright robbery. When the local people, in distress and vexation, turned to the Roman senators for help, their pleas usually fell on deaf ears, for they too shared in the gains from the provinces, and supported the proconsuls.

The huge sums of money that streamed from the provinces into Rome had a far-reaching and negative effect upon the way of life of its own citizens. When Rome was still small, its people lived a simple, unsophisticated life centered around the family unit. The children would honor their father, the head of the family. The men drew their livelihood from honest toil, whether in agriculture or in handiwork. Their houses were small and unassuming.

With the huge influx of foreign wealth, this picture changed completely. Now that they had the means to do so, many of the people turned to idleness as a way of life. And idleness spoiled their virtues. The modest houses of yesteryear gave way to sumptuous villas. The pursuit of luxury became an end in itself. The availability of tens of thousands of foreign slaves corrupted their morals even further. This corruption had its most vivid expression in the form of popular entertainment they loved so dearly; they took amusement in violence, human suffering and bloodshed. Roman stadiums were filled with thousands of people watching public spectacles of men — slaves — fighting hungry lions, or gladiators fighting each other with the naked sword until one of them succumbed, while the spectators would passionately accompany the gruesome "sport" with wild cheers of appreciation.

The Decline of Farmers

Not all Romans benefited from the influx of riches from the conquered territories. The rich and those close to the government became richer, but the masses of the common people and the farmers lost their sources of income and turned into proletarians, that is, people owning nothing.

Most of Rome's soldiers were recruited from the class of the farmers. They spent many of their best years of manhood in the army and when they returned home, they often did not find much to return to. Many of the villages were completely ruined in the wake of Hannibal's victorious march up and down the Italian peninsula during the Second Punic War. Many farms were lost to rich moneylenders; farming families could not repay the loans they had taken, because the main breadwinners were away fighting. Consequently there developed a landless proletariat, while the rich in-

The Colosseum of Rome — originally called the Flavian Arena — was built between 72-80 CE by slave laborers captured during the Destruction of Jerusalem.

creased their landholdings on a large scale.

Even those farmers who succeeded in holding out, or in reestablishing themselves after military service, were no longer the only food producers. Rome now imported huge quantities of cheap grain from Sicily and North Africa. The Italian farmers could not cope for long with such competition. They left their farms and moved into the big city. There they roamed the streets and expected the Senate to feed them and their families. The Senate had no choice. They had not had the foresight to help these destitute people while they still owned their land and were working hard trying to make a living; now they had to be provided for when there was no real hope of making them self-sustaining.

These unemployed farmers increased the numbers of idlers in the streets of Rome. They had one cry and demand: "Bread and circuses!" With nothing productive to do, they wanted only food and entertainment. The city fathers tried to fill their demand for a selfish reason: the idlers had votes and they would give them to those who could make them happy. The politicians did not have the welfare of the common people at heart; they used the masses only as a means to secure themselves positions of power and wealth, as consuls or tribunes.

Tiberius Gracchus was an exception to the rule. He too wanted to be a tribune, but only in order to improve the lot of the poor and to redress the wrong that was done to them by Rome's high society. In the year 133 BCE (3628) he was elected tribune. He legislated an agricultural law which forbade anyone from owning more than about 310 acres of land. Those who had more land had to relinquish it for the benefit of the landless farmers, so that they could return to a normal and productive life. But Tiberius Gracchus' reform ran into serious opposition from many members of the Senate, who were themselves large landowners and who worked their estates with cheap slave labor.

Tiberius Gracchus' one-year term of office came to an end, but his land reform law had still not been enacted. He had been reelected for a second term by the people, despite it being against all custom and tradition. But members of the Senate who feared for their power and position killed him that same year.

The Rise of the Generals

Although Tiberius Gracchus had not succeeded in having his reform bill become law, his efforts were not in vain. He had started a movement that affected Roman history for centuries to come. The popular dissatisfaction weakened the authority of the Roman Senate and strengthened the potential of popular self-expression. Ten years later, Gaius Gracchus, a younger brother of Tiberius, began another drive for a land reform. It too, failed, but the attempt further eroded support for the Senate. This in turn prepared the ground for the emergence of strong military leaders who, with the personal loyalty of the army, imposed their will upon the Senate.

Rome's continuous preoccupation with military matters led to the development of a standing army, composed of professional soldiers and officers whose loyalty was primarily to their commanders. The generals led their troops to victories and enabled them to take the spoils of war. Even when being demobilized after many years of service, they knew that their commander would remain loyal to them and look after their interests.

One of Rome's greatest generals was Pompey. More than other officers, he knew how to use his position to gain political ends. In his time Rome was beset with many difficulties and dangers, both internal and external ones. Indeed, her very existence was threatened.

In the city, violent power struggles in which many people died took place. Tribes in central and southern Italy became restless and revolted, because they had not been granted full citizenship. Thousands of slaves, under the leadership of Spartacus, escaped from their masters and threatened to invade the city of Rome itself. Pirates roamed the Mediterranean Sea and endangered Roman ships. They even attacked coastal cities and dared to challenge the Romans at their very doorstep, the mouth of the river Tiber. Rome also had its troubles in Asia, where

King Mithridates IV of Pontus (a kingdom in northern Asia Minor) successfully challenged the might of Rome. He set up an independent kingdom between the Caspian Sea and the Euphrates River. To subdue him the Senate dispatched an army under Crassus, but it failed to achieve its mission.

Various generals tried to quash the resistance to Rome's rule. The one who distinguished himself most was Pompey. He dealt ruthlessly with the rebellious slaves and in a few months liquidated the pirates of the sea. Then he went to Asia, where he defeated the Persians, driving them back into their vast hinterland. On his way back he crossed Syria, and noting the weakness of the Seleucids, he ended Syria's independence and turned it into a Roman province.

At that time the two Hasmonean brothers, Aristobulus and Hyrkanus, were locked in bitter civil strife and, as we have seen above, they turned to Pompey for arbitration. The Roman took quick advantage of the situation and imposed his will on Judea. True, it had not yet lost its independence, but the Roman presence in the land was felt and feared.

Julius Caesar and Pompey

Pompey returned home a national hero. In a great triumphal parade he displayed the captives he had brought back from his wars. Prominent among them were Aristobulus and his son, whom he had captured in his war against Jerusalem.

The Senate was concerned at the great popularity of Pompey and feared lest he assume power that had until then belonged exclusively to the Senate. In

order to express its superior authority and put Pompey in his place, the senators did not confirm the rules and regulations he had imposed in the countries of the East. They also refused to grant his demand that land should be distributed to his demobilized soldiers.

Pompey decided to act on his own, but he knew that alone he was not strong enough to challenge the Senate. He found two powerful allies with whom he formed a triumvirate — that is, a rule of three men. One was Julius Caesar, a great orator and a born leader; the other was Crassus, who was not only a general but one of the richest men of Rome. Although the youngest of the three, Caesar became the dominant figure of the triumvirate.

The Senate bowed to the will of the three men. Caesar was made consul and his first act was to force the Senate to pass Pompey's order in the provinces and distribute free land to his veterans. A year later Caesar became proconsul of southern Gaul, which is the valley of the River Po. There he revealed himself not only as a superior statesman but also as a brilliant general. At the head of an army he moved northward and after ten years of warfare he succeeded in vanquishing all the tribes that inhabited Gaul — today's Belgium, France, southern Netherlands and northern Italy. He conquered all of the continent west of the Rhine River and even crossed the English Channel to establish a foothold in the British Isles.

The tales of Caesar's successes in Gaul slowly overshadowed Pompey's achievements and Pompey became jealous and apprehensive of Caesar's ultimate ambition. He decided therefore to close ranks with the members of the Senate and other politicians in order to forestall Caesar's bid for power. In March of the year 49 BCE (3712) Caesar's proconsulship came to an end. He was ordered by Pompey, the

Julius Caesar

present consul, to return to Rome and present himself before the Senate as an ordinary citizen without any military escort.

Caesar knew what awaited him in Rome. He did not hesitate. At the head of part of his army, he crossed the Rubicon River and before the Senate and Pompey could organize for war, he marched into Rome and took control of it. Pompey and some senators escaped to Greece. Caesar could not allow his major rival for power to be free and he pursued him. In 48 BCE (3713), in a military encounter near the Greek city of Pharsalus, Pompey was defeated and fled to Alexandria, Egypt. There he was murdered by the Egyptians who wanted to find favor with Caesar. After four more years of struggle with his remaining opponents Caesar emerged victorious and triumphantly returned to assume undivided power.

Caesar's Rule and its Aftermath

Julius Caesar was destined to rule the Roman Empire for only seven months, but during this short period of time he accomplished a good deal. He distributed free land and rewards to his many soldiers.

He began building a number of public projects, in order to occupy the unemployed. Many impoverished farmers were resettled in the provinces. The people responded to his military genius and

Marcus Brutus

constructive statesmanship with trust and affection.

One contribution of Caesar, the Julian Calendar, had an important and lasting influence to this day. This calendar replaced a haphazard system of dating that gave the consul complete control of the calendar. He could add days to any month and could add a month to any year. Since a consul's term of office was limited to one year, some consuls abused their authority by lengthening the year to enable them to stay in power longer. By the time Julius Caesar became consul, March fell in the middle of autumn. In 46 BCE (3715) he established a new calendrical system — one almost identical to the system used today. Caesar's system remained in general use for more than sixteen centuries, until it was slightly modified in 1582, by Pope Gregory XIII. The only difference between the two calendars is in the frequency of leap years. In the Julian calendar, every fourth year without exception is a leap year with a twenty-ninth day added to February. In the Gregorian Calendar, century years (1600, 1700, 1800, 1900) are not leap years unless they are divisible by 400. Thus in both systems 1600 was a leap year. However, in the Gregorian, 1700, 1800, 1900 were not leap years.

Yet Caesar had opponents, too. Among them were Cassius and Brutus. They did not hate him personally — Brutus had enjoyed Caesar's special affection — but as a symbol of an autocratic ruler whose dictatorial regime meant the end of the republican form of Roman government. Caesar was careful not to declare himself king or sole ruler, but in practice all power was concentrated in his hands. Convinced that they had to save the republic and restore the authority of the Senate, Cassius and Brutus decided to act. On the 15th day of March, 44 BCE (3717), when Caesar came to a session of the Senate, they fell upon him and struck him dead. His last words were: "And you too, my son?"

A triumvirate was formed, but the actual rule was in the hands of two strong men who vied to inherit Caesar's power — Mark Antony, who had been Caesar's right-hand man, and Octavian, who was Caesar's adopted son. First, however, they had to deal with Caesar's assassins and their party, who also wanted to seize the reins of government. Antony and Octavian joined to fight the forces of Brutus and Cassius. Caesar's people soon prevailed, and Brutus and Cassius committed suicide.

As neither Octavian nor Antony commanded enough strength and support to seize sole power, they decided to divide the imperial inheritance in the following manner: Octavian remained in Rome to rule over Italy and Western Europe, while Antony went to Alexandria and from there ruled the lands surrounding the Mediterranean Sea.

Octavian was the younger of the two men, but he possessed greater qualities of leadership and a more rational approach to problems than his colleague. While Antony gave himself over to a life of luxury at the palace of Cleopatra, queen of Egypt,

Octavian worked energetically to strengthen his position at home. When Antony was accused, wrongly or rightly, of intending to hand over parts of Italy to the Egyptian queen and to make Alexandria the capital of the Roman empire, enough popular resentment against him was stirred up to give Octavian the chance to confront him in open battle. In a great naval engagement at Actium, Octavian's ships defeated the combined fleet of Antony and Cleopatra. Now the road to sole power over the Roman empire was open before Octavian.

After the sea battle, Octavian ruled for some forty-three years, from 30 BCE to 14 CE (3731-3774). But he was careful not to repeat the mistakes of Julius Caesar with regard to the Senate. He treated it with respect and courtesy.

Octavian was a grandson of Julius Caesar's sister, and had been adopted by Caesar in 44 BCE (3717). At that time his name was changed from Gaius Octavianus to Gaius Julius Caesar Octavianus. The Senate was so delighted with the recognition bestowed upon it by Octavian that they continually added titles of honor to his name. In 29 BCE (3732) he was made imperator [from which the word emperor is derived]; in 28 BCE, princeps; in 27 BCE, Augustus [splendid; august]; and in 12 BCE (3749) pontifex maximus [high priest]. At that time the month Sextilis was renamed August in his honor. Later rulers of Rome also added the title Caesar to their names, so that the name Caesar became synonymous with Imperator, or Emperor.

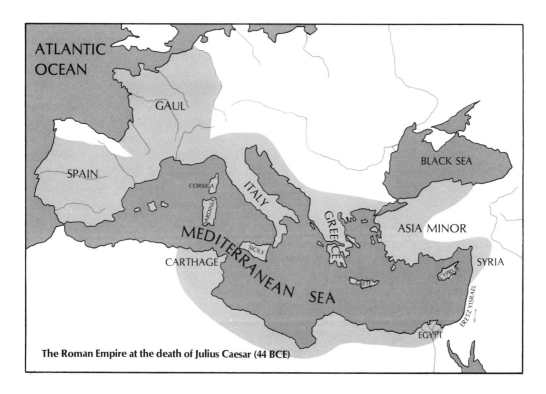

The Roman Empire at the death of Julius Caesar (44 BCE)

18

Beginning of Roman Rule
over the Land of Israel

The stranger who is in your midst will rise above you — higher and higher, and you will descend lower and lower (Deut. 28:43).

Rome Tightens Its Grip

We will now return to the history of the Jewish people and note the lasting impact Pompey's intervention had upon the Jewish state.

To place the events in historical perspective, we will note two events from our history and one from the history of Rome:

(a) In the year 63 BCE (3698) Pompey was invited to intervene in the civil war between Aristobulus and Hyrkanus. He did so and conquered Jerusalem.

(b) In the year 57 BCE (3704) Gabinius [see below] divided the country into five provinces, each governed by a Jewish council. His purpose in doing so was to destroy the authority of the Sanhedrin. He also turned over control of the coastal cities to their Greek inhabitants.

(c) Exactly in between these two dates, in the year 60 BCE (3701), three important Romans — Crassus, Pompey, and Julius Caesar — concluded an alliance, thus creating the triumvirate that assumed supreme power in Rome.

In the process of conquering Jerusalem, Pompey's soldiers perpetrated a bloody slaughter in the Temple area (chapter 15). With that done, Pompey established a new order for Judea, which went a long way in undermining its independence.

In deciding which of the two warring brothers to favor, Pompey chose to install the weak, pliant Hyrkanus in power as governor. The more dangerous Aristobulus, with his two sons, Pompey took to Rome in captivity. In effect, Hyrkanus' cunning Edomite advisor, Antipater, held the real power. The city of Jerusalem suffered much from the conquest. Its walls were torn down and a heavy tax was imposed upon its residents.

Although this Roman intervention violated the national self-respect of the people and caused economic hardships, it did not lead to open defiance. As long as the Roman proconsuls did not overstep the harsh decrees of Pompey, the Jews accepted their lot quietly. But with the appointment of Gabinius as Roman proconsul for Syria and Judea the political situation deteriorated considerably. He rebuilt the Greek cities throughout the land and settled many non-Jews in them. The Jews feared that the time would come when the foreigners would outnumber them and would claim ownership of the whole country.

On the way to Rome, Aristobulus' son Alexander had eluded his captors and returned to Judea. Jewish bitterness against Rome had grown to the point of resistance, and 10,000 Jews rallied behind Alexander to fight for the overthrow of the foreign yoke. As bases they used the old Jewish fortresses that had survived Pompey's earlier onslaught, but they were no match for the Roman legions. Alexander surrendered, and in order to save his life he took his mother's advice and turned his fortresses over to the Romans. During the next twenty years, 57-37 BCE (3704-3724), several attempts were made to regain Judean independence, but all of them were quelled.

After Alexander's defeat, he was again sent to captivity in Rome, but he refused to accept his defeat.

He escaped from Rome a second time and again rallied his compatriots for an uprising against Rome. They fought the Romans in a great battle near Mount Tabor, but were defeated with the loss of some 10,000 Jewish fighters. Alexander was captured and this time, at the order of Pompey, he was executed. The year was either 49 or 48 BCE (3712 or 3713).

Alexander's first rebellion proved to the proconsul Gabinius that, despite Pompey's conquest, the Jewish spirit of unity and independence had not been weakened. He searched for the source of Jewry's spiritual strength, realizing that only if he

could break the people's spirit could he be assured of mastery over their bodies.

Gabinius came to realize that Israel's greatest spiritual center was the Sanhedrin which, as the Oral Law commands, sat in the Chamber of Hewn Stone on the Temple Mount. If he could destroy the power of the Sanhedrin he was sure that the people would soon become as tame and submissive as the other nations under Roman dictatorship. Antipater — the treacherous, ambitious Edomite — seized this opportunity to enhance his own standing. He advised Gabinius to strip all authority from the sages of the Sanhedrin and transfer their power to Hyrkanus. In effect, this meant that Antipater, who controlled Hyrkanus, would hold what authority the Romans left in Jewish hands. In 57 BCE (3704) Gabinius published his decree dividing the land into five provinces and abolishing the Sanhedrin.

The seventy-one sages no longer sat in the Chamber of Hewn Stone adjacent to the Holy Temple. Their functions were handed over to local councils made up of Sadducees and their followers, which Gabinius and his collaborators, Hyrkanus and Antipater, set up in five cities — Jerusalem, Jericho, Gezer, Safed, and Chamas in Transjordan.

The Talmud gives us a brief but vivid account of the impact the abolition of the Sanhedrin made upon the people: "When the Sanhedrin was abolished, songs were no longer heard at banquet halls" (Mishnah Sotah 9:11).

As long as the Great Sanhedrin convened, its authority was unquestioned. But without it there was fear that the nation's morality and piety might deteriorate. In order to avoid this, the people stopped singing at celebrations;

too much rejoicing could easily lead to lightheadedness. Another explanation for the cessation of songs is that it was a reaction of pain and mourning to the abolition of Israel's Supreme Court. One of the lamentations of Tishah B'Av (Ninth Day of Av) says that we still mourn: "For the council that is desolate, and for the abolition of the Sanhedrin."

In 56 BCE (3705), after Caesar had become famous as an outstanding general for his victories over the Gauls and Germanic tribes, the triumvirate met and decided that Crassus would become governor of Syria in 54 BCE (3707). On his way to Syria, Crassus stopped in Jerusalem and robbed a large part of the Temple treasures. A year later he received his punishment — he was killed in battle against the Parthians.

An Edomite Gains Power

One year after Alexander's unsuccessful attempt to expel the Romans from the land, his father Aristobulus escaped from captivity in Rome and returned home. He, too, organized a Jewish army and tried to dislocate the Romans, but also to no avail. He was recaptured and brought back to his exile in Rome.

After another seven years of captivity, it seemed for a brief moment that his great opportunity had arrived — to return to his land and even to his former power. In the year 49 BCE (3712) the smoldering jealousy between Caesar and Pompey broke into open war. Caesar quickly seized Rome and all of Italy, but to take possession of the lands in the East was a different matter. There, Pompey's allies held power, supported by a Roman garrison in Alexandria and King Ptolemy XII, a boy king, who was controlled by a Roman court official. Caesar therefore decided to release Aristobulus from his Roman captivity and put at his disposal two Roman legions, with whom he would reconquer Judea from Pompey's command. Had he succeeded he probably would have become lord of Judea again, but before Aristobulus reached the shores of the Land

of Israel he was poisoned to death by hirelings of Pompey.

The decisive battle between Caesar and Pompey took place at Pharsalus in central Greece in 48 BCE (3713). Caesar won a great victory and continued on to Egypt in his conquest of the lands of the Middle East. Antipater and Hyrkanus, who had been allies of Pompey, had reason to fear for their future, but the sly and resourceful Antipater knew a way out of the dilemma. He learned that Caesar was besieged in Alexandria by Pompey's Roman and Egyptian allies. Convinced that his advantage lay in helping Caesar, Antipater came to the Roman's aid with 3,000 Jewish soldiers. He also prevailed upon the Egyptian Jews not to oppose Caesar's troops.

Soon thereafter, Antipater and Hyrkanus appeared before Caesar to claim their reward for helping him in his battles. At the same time Antigonus, the second son of the slain Aristobulus, came, claiming his right to be installed ruler of Judea because of his father's earlier support of Julius Caesar.

Caesar, who was a shrewd statesman, decided in favor of Antipater and

Hyrkanus. This was not because he was concerned over the issue of gratitude for services rendered. It was rather that experience had taught him the lesson of perpetual Jewish resistance to direct Roman rule in their homeland. He therefore reckoned that with the help of a man like Antipater, who was of non-Jewish origin, Rome could better control matters in Judea.

He bestowed upon Antipater almost unlimited authority. To conceal the painful fact that an Edomite was now the factual ruler in Judea, he officially conferred upon Hyrkanus the title of *Nasi* with the right to pass on the office to his descendants. He also confirmed his status as High Priest. Thus, although Hyrkanus was the figurehead leader of Israel, the actual power was in the hands of Antipater.

Altogether, Julius Caesar displayed a liberal attitude towards the Jews in Judea and in the other countries of his empire. He annulled the harsh Pompeian order that had been installed after the abolition of the Sanhedrin. He allowed a central Jewish government in Jerusalem, permitted the rebuilding of its walls, and restored to the Jewish state the port city of Jaffa and other cities.

Herod — Governor of Galilee

Antipater treated the Land of Israel as if it were his private property. His older son he appointed governor of the Jerusalem area, and his younger son, Herod, he made governor of Galilee in the north.

Galilee was known for its patriotism; its people would not reconcile themselves to direct or indirect Roman rule of their country. They continued to resist the collection of taxes for the benefit of Rome and organized themselves into an underground movement against Rome and its local representatives. Chizkiyahu [Hezekiah] the Galilean was their leader.

Herod immediately revealed his brutal nature. He arrested many of the young patriots together with their leader Chizkiyahu, and without any semblance of a trial executed them.

With this mass murder Herod forfeited his life. According to Jewish law he should have been tried before a court of twenty-three Sages, but Roman law left the Jewish courts without the power to compel the accused to appear before them. The community leaders and the relatives of the slain turned to Hyrkanus, the *Nasi* and High Priest, and did not desist until he agreed to convene a special court in Jerusalem composed of distinguished leaders and sages. Such a court would have the prestige and authority to judge a governor and friend of Rome.

Hyrkanus presided over the special court. Among the recognized sages who participated in its proceedings was Shammai, the disciple of Shemaya and Avtalyon, who was already known as a leading scholar.

Herod accepted the summons, but he was not ready for a free and honest trial. Knowing that his guilt was beyond doubt, Herod decided to frighten his judges into releasing him. He appeared before the court wearing royal garments of purple and escorted by a retinue of soldiers. This open affront to the dignity of the court had its desired effect. Many of the judges were afraid to speak up and looked down in embarrassment. Only Shammai remained strong. He stood up from his seat and turned to his colleagues and to Hyrkanus with these stirring words: "Members of the Court and you, O King: Surely, neither I, nor you have ever seen an accused man appear before a court of law in such a manner. All the accused who have come before the court have done so with trepidation and fear, and dressed in black. But Herod, who is accused of mass murder and was summoned here as a major criminal, has come before us dressed in purple, his hair festively groomed,and escorted by soldiers — to threaten us with death, if we were to convict him. But I do not so much blame Herod, who wants to maintain his life rather than the law; I blame you members of the court — you and the king, who have permitted him to behave this way. Know then, that G-d is mighty and there will come a day, when this man whom you wish to acquit in order to find favor with Hyrkanus, will turn against you and the king and punish you severely" (Josephus Flavius, *Antiquities*).

Shammai's words had their desired effect and the members of the court were ready to sentence Herod to death, but Hyrkanus came to his aid. He ordered the verdict to be postponed until the next day. He did so not only because the accused was the son of his friend and confidant, but because he feared the vengeance of the Roman proconsul in Damascus.

During the night, on the advice of Hyrkanus, Herod fled to Damascus. The special court could not recall him to appear before it to be sentenced, because the Roman proconsul in Damascus had immediately appointed Herod the military commander of Lebanon.

Now Herod had nothing to fear. As the commanding general of Lebanon, he marched on Jerusalem at the head of a Roman troop, intending to avenge himself on the Jewish leaders who had dared to judge him. But this plan appeared too brazen even to his father, Antipater. He advised Herod to desist from it and return with his soldiers to Damascus. Not many years later Herod did take his revenge and murdered his judges, just as Shammai had predicted.

19

Herod's Rise to Power

"Herod became king like a fox. He ruled like a tiger and died like a dog."

From Tax Collector to Ruler

In the year 44 BCE (3717) Julius Caesar was assassinated by Brutus and Cassius. In order to prepare himself for the expected war with the heirs of Caesar — the Second Triumvirate composed of Antony, Octavian and Lepidus (who had been a consul under Caesar) — Cassius came to Syria. The cost of paying and outfitting an army would require enormous expenditures, much more than he could afford. He levied exorbitant taxes and looted wherever he could. Cassius sold the inhabitants of four Judean towns into slavery to raise money. Always looking for ways to enhance their own power and wealth, Antipater and his sons came to Cassius' aid, although he was responsible for the murder of Caesar, their great benefactor.

Antipater and his sons were given the office of tax collectors by Cassius. They pursued their task with great efficiency and cruelty and collected great sums of money from the hapless Jews. Those who could not or would not pay were sold as slaves.

The resentment of the people against the rule of the Edomite family grew more

and more fierce. What added fuel to the fire was the rumor that Cassius had promised that upon winning his war against Antony, he would appoint Herod as king over the Jews. Even Hyrkanus became afraid for his future, and one of his friends poisoned Antipater.

Many hoped that the death of Antipater would bring a change for the better. But they soon realized how wrong they were. Immediately, and with customary cruelty, Herod suppressed all attempts to throw off the rule of his family. Moreover, Cassius appointed him and his brother Phasael as rulers of the Land of Israel.

A new chance to get rid of Herod's evil rule presented itself when the triumvirate defeated the forces of Cassius and Brutus at Philippi in 42 BCE (3719). The three divided the empire among themselves, with Antony becoming governor of the Middle East. The Jews sent three delegations to Antony, pleading for Herod's removal, on the grounds of cruel oppression of the people. Like those before him, Antony turned a deaf ear to the people's request. He even put the first delegates into prison. When the Jews continued to send other delegations to him, he killed all of the old and most of the new delegates.

Antony's motives were coldblooded, but easy to understand: Herod was a willing collaborator with his Roman masters; and Herod offered a bigger bribe. But Hyrkanus' attitude to Herod is beyond comprehension. He actually advised Antony to appoint Herod as ruler of the entire country, even though this would remove power from Hyrkanus himself.

Later he even agreed to give Miriam [Mariamne], his granddaughter, in marriage to Herod.

The reason Herod was anxious to marry Miriam is obvious. He knew how much the people despised him and that, as a non-Jew, he could not be accepted as a legitimate ruler of Israel. By marrying into the House of the Hasmoneans, he hoped to legitimize his claim to power and to raise his prestige in the eyes of the people who considered only the Hasmoneans as worthy of ruling over Israel.

Herod's Fall and Return

The events affecting Rome and its subjugated countries followed each other at a dizzying pace. Only two years after the defeat of Cassius and Brutus, a new development held out a promise to remove Herod, the evil genius, from the government of the country. It came about in the year 3721 (40 BCE) when Parthia, a kingdom near the Caspian Sea, defeated the Roman army. The Parthians offered to help Antigonus the Hasmonean (son of Aristobulus) take advantage of the Roman dilemma to regain the freedom of Judea. He rushed an army to Jerusalem to retake it from the hands of Rome and Herod. At the news of the Roman defeat in Parthia, there was a general uprising of the Jews and many rallied to swell the ranks of Antigonus' army.

Herod and his men fled behind the walls of his fortified palace in Jerusalem. Their position worsened with the approach of the festival of Shavuos, which brought masses of Jews from all over the country to the Temple in Jerusalem. The pilgrims swelled Antigonus' army.

After a short while, Herod realized his position was hopeless and surrendered to the Parthians, but he managed to escape without being taken captive. Hyrkanus was captured by the Parthians, but not before Antigonus had cut off both his ears, thereby disqualifying him from ever again being High Priest. Phasael, Herod's brother, committed suicide. For a while it appeared that the rule of the Edomite family was over.

There was general rejoicing when Antigonus the Hasmonean became king and High Priest in 40 BCE, but it was not to last. Antigonus ruled for only three years, much of which was spent in fighting Herod.

Herod fled to Egypt and from there to Rome. There the Roman Senate, at the recommendation of Antony, proclaimed him king over the land of the Jews, but Herod had to defeat Antigonus before he could retake the government.

Herod came to Syria, where the Roman proconsul in Damascus provided him with a large army. Marching through the Galilee he faced stiff resistance from the local population, who hated him bitterly from his early days as governor there. They harassed his powerful army from concealed caves in the mountains, and only after great efforts was he able to overcome their fierce opposition and continue on his march to Jerusalem.

After bloody fighting in the Jordan River valley, Herod and his Roman army arrived at the gates of Jerusalem. Antigonus and his men decided to resist to the end. By the time the attackers could breach one wall, the defenders had put up a second one. Only after five months of siege and intense and cruel battles did the city fall. The Roman soldiers perpetrated a bloodbath among the defenders of the city and the civilians alike. When Herod saw the gruesome sight, he called to his soldiers: "Do you want to make me a king over a city of corpses?"

Herod achieved his objective. He had become king of the Jews, but he never was a Jewish king. Antigonus was taken alive and sent in chains to Syria. There, at the behest of Herod, Antony put Antigonus to an ignoble death: he had him beheaded.

Southwestern tower of the citadel popularly known as David's Tower (Migdal David), with minaret of later date; originally part of Herod's palace this corner was called the Phasael Tower after Herod's brother.

To strike fear into the hearts of the people, Herod put forty-five friends of Antigonus to death. Now he also felt free to avenge himself upon the judges who years ago had tried to sentence him to death. He had them and the city fathers killed. Only Shammai, due to his great prestige, was spared from Herod's wrath.

The Beginning of the Destruction

Herod assumed supreme and total power over the land of the Jews about 105 years before the Destruction of the Second Temple. His rule lasted thirty-two years, from 36-4 BCE (3725-3757),* a long period of time during which the Jews endured much from this tyrant. They did not even dare to cry out and protest, for fear of swift and ruthless retaliation. Only after his death, Jewish delegates came before the Roman Senate and described the anguish Herod had inflicted on them. Suffice it to quote only part of the emotional plea of the Jewish delegation, in order to understand how evil this period was in the painful history of our people: "Even if a raging beast had reigned over us, the calamity would not have been as enormous as the disasters that were inflicted upon us during the period of Herod's rule. In ancient days too, Israel saw many dark days and terrible disasters; and we were exiled from our homeland. But what happened to the Judeans in the days of Herod has no likeness and no counterpart. Nor does the history of other peoples know of anything like it" (Josephus Flavius, *Antiquities*).

The accounts of the Jewish emissaries make plain that Herod was a man of unusual cruelty and lack of scruples. As we shall see, even his closest friends and relatives were not safe from his brutality and selfishness.

Herod wore the kingly crown by the grace of Rome, because through him Rome could better control the affairs of the Land of Israel. But he went beyond the intentions of his overlord. Rome was only concerned that the Jews should not exercise political independence as a nation. Herod however undermined their cultural and spiritual independence as well. He introduced into the land customs and practices from other peoples of the Roman empire, that were alien and forbidden to the Jewish people. His long rule planted the seeds that ultimately led to the destruction of the Holy Temple and the long and bitter exile.

The Murder of the Hasmonean Family

Though Herod fully realized that he became king only by the swords of the Roman legions, he craved for recognition and acceptance by the Jews. For this

---

* The year 37 BCE is most commonly given as the year of Herod's ascension to the throne, but the Talmud (*Avodah Zarah* 9a) states that Herod's reign began 103 years before the Destruction. Thus Herod's conquest of Jerusalem must have occurred in 35 BCE (3726). [See appendices regarding counting of dates BCE, and the date of the Destruction; the year of the Destruction itself is not counted in these calculations.] Since, however, Josephus dates this event as 23 Sivan (Antiquities 14:16:4) it stands to reason that Herod's reign was counted from the following Tishrei: Thus, it is assumed that the 23 Sivan mentioned was in the year 36 BCE (3725). Although Josephus' chronology is ambiguous and confusing, he does indicate that Herod's conquest of Jerusalem came 27 years after Pompey's [in 63 BCE (3698)], which agrees with the above calculation.

reason he had married Miriam, the granddaughter of the old Hyrkanus. Being related to the Hasmonean family, he imagined that the people would honor him as they did the other Hasmoneans. When reality proved otherwise, his disappointment turned into anger and hatred.

When Herod became king four members of the Hasmonean family were still alive: the aged Hyrkanus; his daughter, Alexandra; and her two children, Queen Miriam and Aristobulus (by Alexander, son of Aristobulus II). Hyrkanus was unfit to be High Priest because of the physical defect inflicted upon him by Antigonus, who had cut off his ears. There remained only one candidate for the high office — the seventeen-year-old Aristobulus. At first Herod prevented Aristobulus from becoming High Priest and appointed a Babylonian Jew instead. But Aristobulus' mother, Alexandra, who was also Herod's mother-in-law, did not desist until Herod transferred the high priesthood to her son.

On the festival of Sukkos, Aristobulus made his first appearance as High Priest in the Holy Temple. The lad's handsome and aristocratic bearing deeply impressed all who saw him and the masses of people who had assembled there greeted him with tears of joy and festive blessings. At this sight Herod was filled with deep resentment and jealousy. He could not but contrast this with the contempt and hatred of the people when he made a public appearance in the streets of Jerusalem, escorted by his bodyguard of Gallic and other northern mercenaries.

He decided to act in his customary manner — swiftly and brutally. At the conclusion of the festival, Herod invited his friends and family to his palace in Jericho.

He persuaded his brother-in-law Aristobulus to join his Gallic soldiers in the swimming pool, to refresh himself from the heat of the day. At a prearranged signal, the bathing soldiers held Aristobulus' head under water, as if in play, until he drowned.

A heartfelt mourning descended upon the people. To remove suspicion from himself, Herod also pretended to mourn, but he could not deceive the grieving mother, Alexandra. She turned to Antony, who was then in Egypt, and accused Herod of the murder of her son.

Antony summoned Herod to appear before him and explain his conduct. Fearing that Antony might convict him and have him executed, Herod left instructions with his faithful finance minister Joseph to kill Queen Miriam in case any misfortune befell him. Not that he hated his wife; on the contrary, he loved her passionately. But his jealousy was so great that he could not tolerate the thought that upon his death she might marry another man.

In fact Herod had nothing to fear from the unscrupulous Antony. He readily accepted Herod's bribe and acquitted him of all charges.

A more serious threat arose some five years later. Octavian, who took the name Augustus, defeated his imperial partner Antony in the battle of Actium, in 31 BCE. Herod knew that Augustus had punished all those who had allied themselves to Antony. Knowing that his logical replacement would be the eighty-year old Hyrkanus, Herod had him killed on a trumped-up charge. Then — instead of waiting for the blow to fall upon his head — Herod took the initiative of meeting the threat head on, and blunting it. He traveled to the Isle of Rhodes, where

Aerial view of Herodium fortress, seven kilometers southwest of Bethlehem, dating from 20 BCE. The fortified round towers can be clearly seen.

Augustus was at the time, and with great cunning and flattery managed to find favor with him. He returned to Jerusalem a proud and happy man.

His joy was short-lived. He could win the trust of an Augustus, but in his own palace he was miserable. Queen Miriam could neither forget nor forgive what he had done to her family, and she showed him her feelings. Herod, who could not tolerate criticism, grew angry, and lent an ear to the insinuations and slanders of his Edomite family, who were jealous of the proud and beautiful Hasmonean princess. They told Herod that Miriam wanted to poison him. Despite his fierce love for her, Herod finally submitted to the slander of his courtiers and put his wife on trial for her life. Anxious to ingratiate themselves with the powerful and ruthless king, the judges sentenced her to death.

As soon as Miriam was put to death, Herod regretted the deed. He turned mad with grief and had her judges put to death, but he could not bring his queen back to life. He was on the verge of insanity.

Though he concentrated all power in his own hands, he suffered from a persecution complex, forever suspecting plots and conspiracies against his life. He tried to drown his mental derangement in the pursuit of cruel edicts and physical pleasures, but nothing helped. He fell into a severe emotional illness, from which he did not recover for many months.

His mother-in-law Alexandra tried to take advantage of Herod's illness by inducing his generals to revolt against the man who had killed her father, son and daughter. But her intentions became known to Herod and from his sickbed he gave the order to kill her, too.

According to the Talmud (Bava Basra 3b) there was still one surviving Hasmonean, a young girl whom Herod now wanted to take as his queen. Knowing what sort of man he was and what he did to the rest of her family, she jumped from a rooftop to her death. From then on, the Sages ruled that anyone who claimed to be a Hasmonean should be considered a descendant of non-Jewish slaves, since the Edomite Herod, who tried to pass himself off as a Hasmonean, had been a servant of the Hasmonean family.

Herod recovered from his illness and with a more settled mind attended to the business of administering his large and rich kingdom. This period saw a relaxation in his domestic policies, but he was no more accepted by the Jews than before. They continued to look at him as a foreign intruder and, legally speaking, a servant of the Hasmoneans. Only his fellow Edomites and the non-Jewish population of the Hellenistic coastal cities and of Transjordan considered him their king.

Openly, no one dared oppose him. He was constantly surrounded by bodyguards who were recruited from among his foreign mercenary soldiers. To root out any secret intrigue he circulated spies and informers among the people, whose task was to report any hostile move or criticism against him.

Many were caught by these informers and brought openly or under cover to one of his fortresses and were killed in a gruesome manner, the like of which was not heard even in ancient times. Those who were left alive envied the dead, because of their constant fear for their families, their property, and their very lives (Josephus Flavius, The Jewish Wars).

The people gritted their teeth and bore the ordeal silently, but there were people who could not contain their wrath and tried to assassinate the tyrant. One such attempt is reported to have occurred about the year 24 BCE (3737). Ten men conspired to kill Herod. A spy informed on them and they were all caught and put to a cruel, painful death. But the spy paid for his act. He was seized by the people, who tore him to pieces and threw his body to the dogs.

Herod wanted more than silent and unquestioning obedience from the people. He demanded that everyone swear an oath of personal loyalty to him. Those who refused were threatened with death. Six thousand Torah scholars of Jerusalem — disciples of Hillel and Shammai — refused to do so. So great were the authority and prestige of these two sages, however, that Herod recoiled from carrying out his threat against their students.

20

"When a Servant Reigns"

For appearance's sake Herod was called King of Judea, but in reality the policy of his rule was conducted with cruelty to uproot and destroy the people.

All the cities of our neighbors, all the cities of the foreigners, he beautified with large and splendid buildings to the extreme detriment of Judea. When short of money, he squeezed the substance out of the sons of Judea, even if they collapsed under the burden and were reduced to nothing (Josephus Flavius, the Jewish Wars).

Herod the Builder

After Augustus confirmed him as king, Herod began a frenzy of construction. He built magnificent cities, temples, gymnasiums, and palaces. To build on a Herodian scale, in the Land of Israel and beyond its borders, cost huge sums of money. The money came from one unfailing source — the people. Herod imposed all kinds of taxes on all classes of the people and collected them with utter ruthlessness. Josephus put it this way: "The people of Judea, who at the beginning of his rule were in a good economic situation, were humbled to the ground and turned into miserable paupers. He had the leaders of the people killed, in order to confiscate their property" (The Jewish Wars).

In Jerusalem, the seat of his government, he built himself a splendid palace and surrounded it with a wall, to serve as a fortress in case of need. The palace was in the western part of the city and in its northern wall he built three strong and lofty towers: One was called the Tower of Miriam, in honor of his wife; the second he called the Tower of Phasael, in honor of his brother; and the third was called the Tower of Hippicus, in honor of a friend. One of these towers is still standing; it comprises part of the complex known as the Tower of David. North of the Temple Mount was a fortress first built by Yochanan Hyrkanus. Herod strengthened it and renamed it Tower of Antonia in honor of his Roman benefactor, Antony.

Outside of Jerusalem he built many palaces and fortresses, in order to have secure places of refuge in case of a general uprising against him. They were strategically located, as the ruins of four famous ones still testify eloquently to this day: Masada, near the Dead Sea; Herodium, near Bethlehem; Sebastia, in Samaria; and Antipatris, near Rosh HaAyin.

In Jerusalem he also built two theaters or circuses for the performance of the cruel Roman gladiatorial contests and the like. There, foreign visitors came for entertainment, but the Jews detested these abominable reminders of similar entertainments in the time of Antiochus Epiphanes.

On the coast, Herod build a large city, with a port second to none among the many Mediterranean harbors. It took twelve years to complete. To its dedication festivities he invited none less than Augustus Caesar [Octavian], in whose honor the city was named Caesarea. It was a magnificent city that boasted many splendid buildings, theaters and pagan temples. Most of its inhabitants were non-Jews.

Herod wanted to make Caesarea the capital city of the land and thus symbolize that the new Jewish state stood for the values of Herod and Caesarea, not David and Jerusalem. Had he succeeded in making the Jewish people accept Caesarea as their capital, Herod would have gone a long way toward convincing Jews that Esau/Edom — as represented by the Roman government and the Edomite king, both of whom were based in Caesarea — were superior to Israel. The Talmud expresses the contrast between Jerusalem and Caesarea with a telling statement:

> Caesarea and Jerusalem — if someone will tell you, "Both are destroyed," do not believe it. If someone will tell you, "Both are settled," do not believe it. But [if someone will tell you], "Caesarea is destroyed and Jerusalem is settled," or "Jerusalem is destroyed and Caesarea is settled" — you may believe it (Megillah 6a).

Part of David's Tower (left), originally known as the Phasael Tower, and the Hippicus Tower (right), the foundation of which dates back to the Herodian period; photographed in 1968 from the interior court of the citadel.

With Jewish money Herod also built palaces and theaters in other countries. Thus, by means of robbery and bloodshed, Herod entered the annals of ancient Rome as one of the great kings of the empire.

Herod Rebuilds the Temple

Nearly all of Herod's grandiose building projects were intended to impress foreigners in and around *Eretz Yisrael*. He did very little for the benefit of the Jews. Only once did he feel a genuine desire to find favor with the Jewish population — when he rebuilt the Holy Temple.

The Temple had been built about 330 years earlier by the returnees from the Babylonian exile, but it had not been as imposing a building as Shlomo's Temple even when it was new. During its long life, it had been looted and damaged many times by foreigners and Hellenists, with the result that it had fallen into disrepair. Why would Herod, a non-Jew who hated what the Temple stood for, have wanted to rebuild it in magnificent splendor? The Talmud *(Bava Basra* 3b-4a) tells how this happened:

Herod had learned that the Torah requires that a Jewish king may be only a person "from among your brethren" *(Deut.* 17:15), which implies that a non-Jewish slave — like Herod — could not become king of Israel. Not surprisingly, Herod became furious at this interpretation that disqualified him from the monarchy. "Who taught this?" he demanded. When he heard that it was the Sages, he ordered that they be killed. Hardly a sage was left by the time his rage had stilled. For his own benefit, he permitted his advisor, Bava ben Buta, to survive, but even Bava was not spared Herod's cruelty. Herod had him blinded and forced him to wear a painfully prickly leather crown at all times.

Once Herod tried to test Bava ben Buta. The king came to the blind sage without revealing who he was and spoke as if he were a fellow Jew who hated Herod. He said that Herod was an "evil serpent" and urged Bava ben Buta to curse him. Bava refused to utter a curse no matter how much his visitor provoked him.

Finally, Herod revealed his true identity and exclaimed to Bava: "It is I! Had I

Mosaic floor in the entrance to the bathhouse of Herod's palace at Masada.

A miniature reconstruction of Jerusalem in late Second Temple times, including this view of the inner courtyard of the Second Temple as rebuilt by Herod, has been built in the grounds of the Holyland Hotel in Jerusalem according to plans prepared by the late Prof. Michael Avi-Yonah. (Other scenes from this model appear on pages 139 and 160, where they are referred to as "the Holyland model.")

known that the Sages are so careful, I would not have killed them. Now — how can I make amends?"

Bava answered that by murdering the Sages, Herod had made the world blind, because the Torah Sages show people the proper way. Now, Herod should do something for the Holy Temple, which is also called the "eyes for the world," for the prophet Yechezkel referred to the Temple as "the desire of your eyes" (*Ezekiel* 24:21).

Josephus reports that many Jews who heard of Herod's plan were shocked; they feared that he would destroy the old building and not build a new one. Herod was sincere, however. He prepared all the necessary building materials in advance and only then was work begun. Some 10,000 laborers were employed in the restoration of the Temple. The work progressed rapidly, and within three years, the building stood ready in all its glory, more beautiful now than when it was first built by the exiles returning from Babylon.

Indeed our Sages stated: "He who did not see Herod's building has never in his life seen a truly grand building" (Bava Basra 4a).

But when the building of the Temple was completed, Herod offended the people in a brazen manner. Over the gate of the Temple he mounted a golden eagle, the symbol of Rome's might. This was intended to demonstrate Herod's admiration of Rome and to remind the Jews that even their House of G-d was subject to the grace and control of the Romans.

When Herod fell ill for the last time, two fearless sages and their disciples sought to defend the honor of Heaven. Defying Herod's henchmen who were stationed there, they publicly tore down the eagle and smashed it to pieces. The two elders and forty of their disciples were arrested and dragged to Herod's bedside. When he demanded that they explain their action they replied with dignity:

> We are commanded to safeguard the honor of the House of G-d. Since we have studied the Torah, it is no wonder that its laws, given to us by G-d, are more important to us than your laws. With joy we shall accept any of your punishments, for we know that we shall be killed not for any evil we have committed, but because of our love for righteousness and our zeal for the word of G-d (Josephus Flavius, The Jewish Wars).

The tyrant was incapable of understanding the heroic stand of these Sages of Israel, and gave the order to have them and some of their disciples burned alive.

Herod's Last Days

Toward the end of his long reign, Herod again became enmeshed in wild suspicions of his own family. The time came for him to consider whom he should recommend to the Roman emperor as his successor. Originally he had wanted to bequeath the kingdom to the two sons of his wife Miriam. To that end he had sent them in their youth to Rome, there to acquire the training suited to young princes. When they returned home, they were so enthusiastically received by the people that Herod became jealous and tensions arose between father and sons. A malicious individual spread a false rumor that they intended to poison their father and thus come quickly to power. Characteristically, Herod believed the story and ordered that his own, once-beloved sons be executed (approx. 8 or 7 BCE).

The plotter behind this tragedy was Herod's son Antipater, born to his Edomite wife. The reason for this was obvious — he wanted to inherit the throne himself after Herod's death. After his success in doing away with his competitors, Antipater's ambition ran away with him, and he plotted to kill Herod. His plot was uncovered, however, and he was sentenced to death.

Perhaps Hillel, who lived in Herod's time, had such events in mind when he said: "Because you drowned others, they drowned you, and in the end those who drowned you will themselves be drowned" (Avos 2:6).

Herod had three more sons from other wives: Archelaus, Antipas and Philipus (Herod Philip). In his last testament Herod divided the land between these three

Herod's Palace in the Holyland model (see caption, p. 137), showing (left to right) the Hippicus Tower, and the Mariamne and Phasael Towers.

The Division of Eretz Yisrael among Herod's Heirs

SYRIA

GALILEE

BASHAN

Tiberias

MEDITERRANEAN SEA

TRANSJORDAN

Caesarea

SAMARIA

Jaffa

Yavneh

JUDEA

Jerusalem

Amman

Ashkelon

Gaza

IDUMEA

Archelaus' Territory
Phillip's Territory
Antipas' Territory
Salome's Territory
Annexed to Syria

sons: Archelaus was to be king over Judea and Samaria [Shomron], Antipas over the Galilee, and Philipus over the Argov and Bashan in the northeastern part of the country, east of the River Jordan.

After the execution of the two sages and their disciples for having torn down the golden eagle from the Temple gate, Herod's illness grew worse and he suffered excruciating pain, but even then he did not repent his wickedness. On the contrary, he summoned a number of leading Jews to his bedside in Jericho. First he admonished them for their failure to appreciate what he had done for the Jewish people. He then had them imprisoned, and issued his last command — that they all be executed the moment his death became known throughout the land.

Herod knew well that his death would be an occasion of rejoicing for the Jews, and his satanic plan was to turn that day of joy into a day of mourning for the killed leaders. The vile king's last act of cruelty never took place, however. His powerful and influential sister Salome and her husband Alexas had the prisoners freed before Herod's death became known.

The Wicked Rule of Archelaus
4 BCE-6 CE (3757-3766)

Herod was dead and the Jews hoped that better times were now ahead. They asked Archelaus, who was to assume the rule over Judea and Samaria, to free their brethren who had been imprisoned by his father during his reign, and to ease the heavy burden of taxation. Archelaus first gave the impression that he would comply with their requests. Reassured and thinking that they need no longer fear the dead tyrant's soldiers and spies, the people publicly mourned the martyred sages who had removed the idolatrous eagle from the Temple gate. They even dared to ask Archelaus to replace the present High Priest, who did not observe the Torah and who had received his high office only through Herod's personal support.

The people soon learned to their distress that their hopes were unfounded; the son was no better than the father. It happened on the eve of Passover. Masses of Jews went up to the Temple to sacrifice the Passover offering, when suddenly, in the midst of the festive proceedings, the new king's mercenary soldiers broke into the Temple court. The people tried to resist their entry, but to no avail. The foreign soldiers killed some 3,000 Jews and drove the others away. Archelaus was sure that this was the best way to impose fear of his royal authority upon the Jews — by the same method his father had used.

After Pesach, Archelaus went to Rome to be confirmed as king of Judea and Samaria. Archelaus was opposed by other members of Herod's household, chiefly Antipas and Salome. One of their arguments against him was his unlawful slaughter of the people in the Temple. Archelaus, trying to find favor with the emperor, slandered the Jews, claiming that they always wanted to rebel against Roman authority. He tried to convince Augustus that only through such terror could he guarantee that there would be no Jewish rebellion against Rome. With this argument he tried to gain two objectives: to have the emperor confirm

1 2 3 4 5

From the Maritime symbols on the first three of these coins minted by Archelaus one may guess at some of his activities: (1) galley (trilepton); (2) prow (perutah); (3) anchor (perutah). Another trilepton, (4) shows a cornucopia, the horn overflowing with the fruits of the field, which since ancient times has been a common symbol of prosperity; and the perutah (5) engraved with a wreath, standard symbol of the victor, shows the Greek title which Archelaus bore — etnarches (in English, "ethnarch"), meaning governor of a province or people.

Herod's testament and to justify the mass murder as a sign of his loyalty to Rome.

On Shavuos, again, Archelaus called upon Roman soldiers bloodily to assert his authority upon Jerusalem. After this new demonstration of Archelaus' unscrupulous power lust, a Jewish delegation was dispatched to Augustus. The Jews presented their case in stirring words. They described their sufferings under the Herodian regime and requested restoration of the Sanhedrin as the final authority in purely internal matters, while political control should be in the hands of the Roman consul in Damascus. This would be better than living under the rule of a local governor, like Herod and Archelaus, who suppressed them more than the emperor required them to.

The future of the Jewish people and of Judaism was hanging in balance on the divinely-held scales of history. Had Augustus accepted the plea of the Jews, life in their homeland would have returned to what it had been in the days of the Men of the Great Assembly, when the Sages of the Torah directed the life of the people, while foreigners controlled external and political matters. But Heaven decided otherwise. The days of the Men of the Great Assembly would never again return and the Holy Temple was destined to be destroyed.

The emperor confirmed Herod's testament and divided the land among his three sons. However, he did not appoint Archelaus as king, but gave him a lesser title, "Ethnarch" or governor. The people's delegation returned home to *Eretz Yisrael,* empty-handed and broken-hearted.

Archelaus ruled Judea and Samaria for nine years. Throughout this time the people continued to complain to the Roman emperor about the cruel treatment they received at the hands of the king. However, when even the Samaritans joined the Jews in their complaints against Archelaus, Augustus Caesar was convinced. He removed Archelaus from his position and banished him to Gaul (modern-day France).

Judea and Samaria were placed under the jurisdiction of the Roman proconsul in Damascus. To attend to the daily administrative matters in the land, a special commissioner, the procurator, was appointed with headquarters in Caesarea. Thus began the chapter in Jewish history known as the era of the Roman procurators. [See chapter 22.]

Torah Sages — Leaders of the People

If we but turn our eyes from this nightmarish spectacle (Herod's era), if we but want to forget for a moment the Edomite monstrosity and the foreigners who oppressed through him, and turn our face to the other side — behold, there is light and life, there is the spirit of Israel in all its magnificent strength, national vitality, Jewish life, spiritual power, and radiant strength (Doros HaRishonim).

The New Leaders

Previous chapters described the stormy events that overwhelmed our people after the death of Queen Shlomis Alexandra and throughout the Herodian regime. During the many decades when the Jewish monarchy failed to provide proper leadership, the people looked for guidance to the Sages, especially the *Zugos* — the *Nasi* and the head of the Sanhedrin. In the beginning of that period, during the civil war of the two Hasmonean brothers, the people were led by Shemaya and Avtalyon; the two leaders during the period of Herod and Archelaus were Hillel and Shammai.

Acting upon the advice of Shemaya and Avtalyon, the Torah scholars of the time did not involve themselves in political matters. This enabled them to continue the study and teaching of the Torah even under the most trying circumstances, and thus assured that the Jewish people would pass on the heritage of Sinai from generation to generation.

Yet the study of Torah in troubled and turbulent times cannot be compared with its study in calm and peaceful times. There were many interruptions in the years of study that a person needs in order to reach maturity and mastery in Torah knowledge. Even when studies continued, the constant fear of the government made concentration difficult. Thus there were many students who knew only the explicit Halachah as revealed to Moshe *Rabbeinu* and recorded in the Mishnah. However, intricate details of the law and of the Rabbinic enactments that are mastered only through long and steady personal association with great teachers were not learned thoroughly enough and some were forgotten.

When Gabinius abolished the great Sanhedrin there was no institution to decide on matters which were crucial to the people as a whole, such as the calendar. In those days there was no fixed calendar, and the new months were proclaimed — as the Torah prescribes — by the Sages, on the basis of testimony by witnesses who saw the new moon. Consequently, the observance of the festivals depended on a periodic decision regarding the beginning of each new month and the fixing of leap years.

True, after a number of years the Sanhedrin returned to the Chamber of Hewn Stone in the Temple, but it lacked authority and could not act independently with fear of intervention by Roman officials who, directly or indirectly, ruled the land. The Sages therefore thought it advisable to hand over some of the basic functions of the Sanhedrin, including determination of the calendar, to one of the most respected families in Jerusalem,

the family of Beseira. This was only an emergency situation, and it was hoped that the Sanhedrin would soon return to its full functioning.

As long as the Edomites ruled the land, the Sages realized that there was little reason to believe that in the foreseeable future the Sanhedrin would be restored to its former power. They therefore sought a more effective way to administer the religious and moral life of the people. The opportunity came with the arrival of Hillel on the scene of Jewish history. A few centuries later the Talmud put it this way:

In the beginning, when the Torah was forgotten by Israel, Ezra came from Babylonia and reestablished it. Later the Torah became forgotten again. Then came Hillel the Babylonian and reestablished it (Sukkah 20a).

Hillel becomes the Nasi

Hillel and Shammai received from Shemaya and Avtalyon the authority to interpret and transmit the Torah. Shammai, who was a native son of the Holy Land, was their outstanding disciple, and when his teachers died he was the undisputed head of all the Torah scholars in the country. We have seen his quality of leadership in the famous trial of the young Herod, where he showed that his love for truth was greater than the fear for his life. He continued to teach Torah during the most difficult times. He was venerated by the people to such an extent that even Herod did not dare to harm him as he did the other leading scholars and dignitaries of the people.

Hillel was born in Babylonia, and his family traced its descent from King David.

From his early youth, he studied in the *yeshivos* which had existed in Babylonia since the days of Ezra and Nechemiah. There he concentrated on gaining a thorough understanding of the entire body of the Halachah. When he found that he had a number of halachic questions to which he could find no answer in Babylonia, Hillel migrated to the Land of Israel, where the central authority in matters of Jewish law was transmitted in an unbroken chain — from Moshe *Rabbeinu* to Yehoshua and so on, down to his own generation.

His devotion to the study of the Torah became a model for all times. The Talmud describes it vividly:

They said of Hillel that every day he

used to work and earn half a dinar. Half of it he gave to the doorkeeper of the House of Study [as his entrance fee to study], and with the other half he supported himself and his family. One day he could not earn anything and the doorkeeper did not let him enter. He climbed to the roof and sat at the skylight so that he could hear the words of the living G-d coming from the mouths of Shemaya and Avtalyon. People tell that that day was a Friday. It was in the winter month of Teves, and snow fell on him from heaven. At dawn [in the morning], Shemaya said to Avtalyon, "My brother, every day the hall is light and today it is dark. Perhaps it is a cloudy day?" They looked up and saw the outline of a man over the skylight. They went up and saw a layer of snow three cubits thick. They brought him down, washed him, rubbed his body with oil and sat him near the fire. They said, "For his sake it is proper to desecrate the Sabbath" (Yoma 35b).

Upon the death of Shemaya and Avtalyon, Hillel returned to Babylonia. When he came back to the Holy Land many years later, the land was in the grip of Herod's despotic rule. Hillel lived modestly within the "four cubits of the Halachah," and despite the fact that he was the greatest Torah sage, he was not well-known among the masses because of his humble avoidance of public office.

He became recognized as the leading sage of the time when only he could give the answer to a question of Halachah to which the sons of Beseira had no answer. The day before Pesach fell on a Sabbath, and the people came to inquire whether the Pesach sacrifice that is offered on the day before the festival may be brought even on the Sabbath, when slaughter and cooking are forbidden. The sons of Beseira did not know. They were informed that Hillel the Babylonian, who had studied under Shemaya and Avtalyon, would surely know. The sons of Beseira asked that he be summoned immediately.

The question was put to him, and he gave convincing proof that the offering must be brought even on the Sabbath. Seeing that Hillel's knowledge of the Torah was superior to their own, the sons of Beseira stepped aside and appointed him as the *Nasi* of the Jewish people *(Pesachim 66b)*. For this unusual display of modesty and dedication to the best interests of the Jewish people, the Sages gave high praise to the sons of Beseira.

With Hillel's appointment as *Nasi*, there began a new era in the annals of the Jewish people. Previously, the *Nasi* had been elected only by the members of the Sanhedrin. The new conditions of life in *Eretz Yisrael*, however, forced a change in this procedure. No longer could the Sanhedrin be given sole authority over the choice of a *Nasi*, because the Romans appointed and removed the membership of the Sanhedrin at will, according to their own political considerations. The Sages decided, therefore, that Hillel should be chosen not by the Sanhedrin alone, but by all the scholars of the great House of Study in Jerusalem.

As a result of this new procedure, Hillel and all the *Nesi'im* who followed him were not only the heads of the Sanhedrin, but also the recognized leaders of the people. True, they had neither police nor army to impose their will upon the people, but the people responded to them voluntarily, because they knew that the voice of the Torah spoke through them and that their decisions were based upon broad agreement among the Sages of Israel.

Out of concern for the stability of the spiritual leadership in times to come it was decided that this leadership should remain in the House of Hillel and be passed on from father to son. Hillel was succeeded by his son, Shimon, and then his grandson, Rabban Gamliel the Elder. Following him, in the time of the Destruction of the Temple, the *Nasi* was Rabban Shimon ben Gamliel; and so on.

Hillel's election as *Nasi* founded a long line of descendants to the high office, spanning some four hundred years. During that period of time the existence of our people was threatened: the Holy Temple was destroyed, the land was ruined, and the people were banished to the lands of the Diaspora. The continuity of Hillel's lineage became one of the means by which Divine Providence saved the Jews from extinction at the outset of their long and bitter exile.

The House of Hillel and the House of Shammai

Most of the scholars gathered around Hillel, and together they established a new *yeshivah* in Jerusalem, known as *Beis Hillel,* the Academy of Hillel. The *yeshivah* of Shammai continued to exist parallel to Hillel's House of Study; it was known as *Beis Shammai,* the Academy of Shammai. The outstanding scholars of both academies sought to understand and clarify the Halachah. One could have expected that these two *yeshivos* would be combined into one large and central House of Study, but the Sages chose otherwise for two reasons: first, because of the respect due to Shammai, and second, in order not to arouse the suspicion of Herod. Had a united academy been formed, the suspicious king would have accused the Jews of setting up a challenge to his authority.

On the fundamentals of the Oral Law there was no difference of opinion between the two great schools. Indeed, during the lifetimes of Hillel and Shammai, there were only three halachic disputes between the two. After their deaths, there were disagreements centered around the details of the Halachah, and the regulations which the Sages throughout the previous generations had enacted as a "fence" to safeguard the main body of a law. These differences of opinion are recorded in hundreds of places throughout the pages of the Talmud, both in the Mishnah and *Gemara.* For example, in the law of *eruv tavshilin,* the question of how many dishes one has to prepare before a festival that occurs on Friday in order to be allowed to prepare food for *Shabbos* on the festival itself:

> *Beis Shammai require two dishes while Beis Hillel hold that one dish is adequate. Both agree that fish and the egg that covers it are considered two dishes (Beitzah 2:1).*

Since the great Sanhedrin was abolished, there was no single authority competent to decide the many halachic disputes between the nation's outstanding Torah scholars. Many such questions remained unresolved until one generation after the Destruction of the Temple. At that time Rabban Yochanan ben Zakkai established a central *yeshivah* at Yavneh, where the rule was adopted that in most cases the Halachah follows the view of *Beis Hillel.* Until then, some followed the decisions of one academy while some followed the views of the other. Although the two academies disagreed in many halachic questions, there was always friendship and unity between them. They battled over the truth, but their disagreements were never personal.

Hillel — Teacher and Shaper of the Future

Hillel has been described in these words:

> His great and wondrous serenity; the purity of his personal traits, which reach the highest possible level; his terse statements which penetrate into the heart of the listener, filling him with strength and inspiration; his clear views in matters of Torah and his broad understanding of the world — all these made the hearts of his generation rally around him. The people found in him the pillar upon which they could lean, and the spirit which gave them life (Doros Ha-Rishonim).

Hillel lived one hundred and twenty years, during forty of which he served as *Nasi.* He was leader of the nation during the terrible reigns of Herod and Archelaus. In that era of unbearable suffering, he was a spiritual giant, who gave his stricken generation the strength to weather the worst conditions. The entire nation relied on him and he was its spirit of life.

One of the enactments for which Hillel is most famous is that of the *prozbul,* the means he devised to make it easier for people to borrow money. The Torah provides that all private loans are canceled at the conclusion of *Shemittah,* the Sabbatical Year, that comes every seven years. Although this precept was not in effect on a Scriptural level during the Second Temple era, a rabbinic decree had been enacted to keep its provisions in force. Hillel observed that as the seventh year came closer, people would refuse to lend money to those in need because lenders feared that the borrowers would not be able to pay them in time — with the result that *Shemittah* would cancel the loans forever. Such a refusal was a violation of the Torah's commandment that Jews should not let fear of such cancellation prevent them from making loans. No doubt Hillel also realized that loans were more important than ever during the period of Herod's confiscatory taxation.

In order to help borrowers get funds and to prevent lenders from violating the Torah, Hillel utilized the Torah itself. Only loans to *private* borrowers are canceled, but not loans to a public institution such as the court. Accordingly, Hillel devised a declaration called *prozbul.* It provided that lenders would transfer their loans to the court; in turn, the court would make them its "agents" to collect the loans. The *prozbul* is still used to make it easier for people to do business through loans.

Later Sages of the Talmud said of Hillel that the Divine Spirit would have rested on Hillel, if his generation had been worthy of it. The greatness of his disciples also testifies to the greatness of their master. Thus the Talmud states:

> They said, Hillel the Elder had eighty disciples. Thirty of them were worthy that the Divine Spirit should rest

upon them, as it did upon Moses our Teacher. Thirty of them were worthy that the sun should stand still for their sake, as it did for Yehoshua. Twenty were in between. The greatest of them all was Yonasan ben Uziel and the least of them all was Rabban Yochanan ben Zakkai (Sukkah 28a).

During the latter part of Hillel and Shammai's leadership begins the period of the *Tannaim,* or teachers of the Mishnah. During that time, which lasted 250 years, our Sages dealt with the clarification of the vast body of the Oral Law. The clear and accurate text of each law was crystallized, and placed in its proper location within the framework of the Six Divisions (or *Sedarim*) of the Mishnah. Collating and editing the work of the *Tannaim* was the monumental lifework of the last of these Sages — R' Yehudah *HaNasi* [the Prince], who died in the city of Tiberias about 150 years after the destruction of the Holy Temple.

It was G-d's will that during this turbulent era, Hillel, Shammai, and those who came after them discussed, taught, and clarified the Oral Torah. G-d prepared the antidote of Torah for the malady of exile. Thanks to the work of the *Tannaim,* wherever Israel would be in the many lands of their dispersion, they would not be lost. Now, wherever he went, every Jew could take with him both the Written and the Oral Law as an unfailing guide to direct his life and the life of his people. Though he had temporarily lost his geographical territory, he was always at home in his spiritual territory — the Torah.

View of Tiberias, photographed half a century ago. In the foreground, overlooking the Sea of Galilee, the tomb of R' Meir Baal HaNess. The city was the last home of R' Yehudah HaNasi, Hillel's descendant who compiled the Mishnah.

22

The First Roman Procurators

The New Rulers of Judea

About sixty years before the Destruction of the Second Temple, the Romans abolished the last vestiges of Jewish independence in Judea. This occurred after Augustus Caesar banished Archelaus son of Herod, ruler of Judea, because of his abominable treatment of the inhabitants of the land. Since the time of Pompey, Syria had been ruled by a Roman procurator, or governor, who was appointed by the Roman Senate and was responsible for the military, judicial and civil administration of his province. Judea was incorporated into Greater Syria.

The headquarters of the proconsul was in Damascus. As a rule the proconsul intervened in the local affairs of the Jews only in cases of internal crisis or general war, which required the use of military force on a large scale. The administration of everyday governmental business was handled by a Roman official of lower rank. He was called a procurator, or high commissioner, and had his headquarters in the city of Caesarea.

Until the procurators arrived on the scene Judea had a significant degree of autonomy and was not treated by the Romans as a colony. True, Herod and Archelaus were appointed as rulers by the Romans, but they carried the title of king and they felt free to act in the land as they pleased. This illusory independence was of little value to the Jews, however, for the Edomite kings favored the non-Jewish elements in the Land of Israel at the expense of its Jewish inhabitants.

This state of affairs changed only slightly for the better when the Roman procurators became the rulers of the land. Though they were just as selfish and unsavory as the Edomite kings, they had different desires. The procurators had no hope of ever becoming independent rulers. They were Roman officials sent by the Senate of Rome to govern a foreign province, and their main ambition was to enrich themselves as much and as quickly as possible. Whenever the Jewish leaders could satisfy their appetite for money, the Romans would somewhat ease the burden of their rule.

Generally, they suppressed the Jews out of hatred and wickedness. They did not flinch from outright acts of robbery, and in order to cover the evidence of their crimes they crudely provoked the people into open resistance, which in turn gave them a pretext to stamp out the "local Jewish revolt." However, they could not go too far — as far as did Herod and Archelaus — because they knew that their conduct was known to those above them, their overlords in Rome. Thus, fear that they might suffer reprisals from above if they went too far sometimes helped restrain them.

As a rule, the Romans did not intervene in the internal affairs of the native populations in their foreign provinces. Because their interest was in political control and personal enrichment, they found it convenient to allow the Jewish leaders to regulate the internal matters of their people. So it happened, paradoxically, that when the political independence of the people in Judea came to an end, they were granted a significant degree of local self-government. The Great Sanhedrin was restored to its rightful place in the Chamber of Hewn Stone alongside the Temple; there they could once more lead the nation according to the laws of the Torah and regulate everyday life for the common good. The leaders of the Sanhedrin supervised the Temple service and disbursements from its treasury. The sense of order and tranquility, that had so long been absent, returned to Judea.

The time of relative calm did not last long. The Sadducees could not tolerate the raising of the Sages from the Pharisee camp to positions of power and control and sought ways to regain their lost power and influence. The Sadducees quickly realized that the office of the High Priest held the best promise to achieve this aim. The Roman rulers followed Herod's example of bestowing this sacred office upon the highest bidder. As the Sadducees had no lack of money, they offered huge personal bribes to the procurators, and a candidate of their choice became High Priest.

The Roman officials soon realized that the office of the High Priest was an infallible source of income. At frequent intervals, they would dismiss the current *Kohen Gadol* and auction off the position to the highest bidder. From the beginning of the era of the Roman procurators until the Destruction of the Temple, a period of only sixty years, this exalted office had thirty occupants. For this reason the High Priest's chamber on the Temple Mount was called *Lishkas Palhedrin,* which means "the chamber of the king's officials." The prestige of the office thus suffered during this period as the *Kohen Gadol* came to be regarded as a petty politician who was appointed by the secular government and cared only about his own glory and enrichment.

Even after being dismissed from their office, the former High Priests would continue to exploit their connections for selfish ends. In the course of time, with their number growing, they became a domineering aristocracy and together with their relatives and friends, they abused the people and brought about the Destruction of the Temple.

Our Sages in the Talmud give us an idea of their influence:

> Said Abba Shaul ben Botnis, quoting Abba Yosef ben Chanin [with regard to four of these former High Priests]: "Woe to me because of the House of Baysos; woe to me because of their staffs. Woe to me because of the House of Chanin, woe to me because of their whispering [i.e., their slanderous whispering to the Roman officials against the people]. Woe to

me because of the House of Kasros; woe to me because of their pens [with which they write hateful things about the people]. Woe to me because of the House of Yishmael ben Piabi, woe to me because of their fists. For they are High Priests, and their sons are Temple treasurers, and their sons-in-law are Temple supervisors, and their servants strike the people with rods" (Pesachim 57a).

Deterioration after the Death of Augustus Caesar, 14 CE (3774)

Many changes affecting the position of the Jews took place during the rule of the Roman procurators. The period began in the reign of Augustus, who insisted upon law and order throughout his empire. Then, the procurators refrained from interfering excessively in the internal affairs of the people. Only two things reminded them that Rome was their master:

(a) The Roman procurator kept the sacred garments of the High Priest in a special stone chamber, and only with his approval were these clothes given to the High Priest a few days before a festival.

(b) During the festivals many Roman soldiers were stationed on the Temple Mount. The masses of people who came from all over the land to Jerusalem were thus shamefully reminded of their loss of national independence and their disgrace at being dependent on the whim of foreign tyrants, backed by the swords of the Roman legions.

Nevertheless, as noted above, the high commissioners tried not to antagonize the people unnecessarily. For example, Roman legions customarily carried ensigns consisting of floral designs around statuettes of the emperor. Knowing that this was a serious offense to Jewish sensitivity, the procurators did not allow their soldiers to display these ensigns. They realized that such displays could provoke a general uprising, for which Augustus would hold his procurators responsible.

Things grew worse after the death of Augustus Caesar. He was followed by Tiberius Caesar, whose first procurator in Judea, Valerius Gratus, changed the High Priests in such rapid succession that many of them did not even remain in office one whole year.

The procurator who followed him, Pontius Pilate, was even worse. He ruled in Judea for ten years, 25 [or 26]-35 [or 36] BCE (3785-3795). Two Jews — Agrippa and Philo — who were close to Rome said of him: "He is cruel by nature and so stubborn that nothing changes his mind." In his time Judea was overrun by "bribery, robbery, exploitation, insults, frequent executions without trial, and cruelty without end or limit."

This procurator wanted to show the Jews that he held their laws in contempt. He ordered his soldiers to enter Jerusalem during the night with their ensigns bearing the image of the emperor. In the morning, when the Jews saw the ensigns openly displayed, they were aghast. In their masses they traveled to Caesarea, where Pilate resided, to plead with him to remove the ensigns from the Holy City. He turned a deaf ear to their request. The petitioners thereupon prostrated themselves around his palace and remained there for five days and nights. The Roman soldiers, drawn swords in their hands, threatened to kill them, but to no avail; they would not budge unless they were promised that the ensigns would be removed from their city. "They stretched out their throats to the swords and cried that they were ready to die rather than transgress the laws of their faith" (Josephus, *Antiquities* 2:18,3).

Such a demonstration of moral courage impressed even Pontius Pilate — and he gave orders to have the offending ensigns removed from Jerusalem.

Another disturbance was caused by Pilate when it became known that he planned to loot the Temple treasury in order to built an aqueduct. The people protested loudly when Pilate came to Jerusalem. This time, however, he did not want to be taken by surprise. He had ordered his soldiers to disguise themselves as civilians and circulate among the people. As soon as the people protested his plan, the disguised soldiers fell upon them and struck them down brutally with their hidden weapons. Many were killed and others were trampled to death in the ensuing panic.

This bloody incident could easily have served as a signal for popular uprisings throughout the country. But the wisdom of the Sages and the Sanhedrin prevailed, and order was maintained. It appears from a Mishnah *(Eduyos* 7:7) that Rabban Gamliel the Elder (son of Hillel's son Rabban Shimon), as *Nasi* of the Sanhedrin, went to Damascus to talk to the proconsul Vitellius

Among the ruins of Roman Caesarea was found a stone bearing a dedicatory inscription in Latin by Pontius Pilate, procurator of Judea, in honor of Tiberius Caesar.

about various current problems and impressed upon him the savagery of his representative in Judea. As a result of this protest and the complaints of the Samaritans, who were also oppressed, Pontius Pilate was finally removed from his office and recalled to Rome.

When Vitellius visited Jerusalem he was received with great honor by the people. At their request he canceled the special tax that was imposed on the fruits of the market, and he had the garments of the High Priest returned from Roman custody in Caesarea to the *Kohanim* in Jerusalem.

Separatist Sects

The many hardships that befell our people towards the end of the Second Temple era produced sects that withdrew from normal life. Disheartened by life's harshness, they chose isolation, settling in small groups in the Judean wilderness near the Dead Sea, in villages around Jerusalem, and in the Galilee.

The Essenes were one such sect. In recent years fragments of scrolls, discovered by Bedouin shepherds and subsequent explorers in the Qumran Caves near the Dead Sea, have revealed the existence of another group, which is known as the Dead Sea Sect. The sealed earthen jugs and the dry climate preserved their scrolls throughout the centuries. The way of life they describe indicates a withdrawal from the pleasures of the world and a style of self-purification.

The members of these sects departed from the way of the Torah in many regards; they even rejected some principles of Jewish belief. The oppression of the people throughout this period stimulated expectations on the part of some people that the coming of the Messiah must be near. Many people were drawn after impostors who claimed they were the Messiah, or dreamers who may have believed their own fantasies. During the years when the Sanhedrin was permitted to function, it fought strenuously to prevent the propagation of such heresies. Then and later, the Roman authorities ruthlessly put to death such "messiahs," since their claims weakened the power of the central government.

From this ferment of sects and factionalism, Christianity [the Greek word *christos* is a translation of the Hebrew word *mashiach;* both mean "anointed"] was the only movement to achieve long-lasting success. It satisfied the longing for a "messiah" and it offered spirituality without the rigorous performance of the commandments. Especially in a period when Jews loyal to the Torah suffered intense persecution, Christianity offered a relatively easy way to gain the satisfaction offered by a religion without the demands of adherence to the Torah.

Yeshu of Nazareth, the founder of Christianity, was one of the many leaders of messianic sects. The Talmud contains no discussions of this sect's origins, yet medieval Christian censors removed a story from the Talmud on the grounds that it disparages Yeshu. According to Christian versions of Yeshu's life, however, that supposition is an impossibility. The Talmudic account speaks of an incident with Rabbi Yehoshua ben Perachiah and an apostate student of his named Yeshu, in which the student was guilty of deplorable behavior. But the incident under discussion occurred under the oppressive reign of King Yannai or, according to some, under the even earlier reign of Yochanan Hyrkanus. Thus it took place between 120 and 140 years before the time of the Roman consul Pontius Pilate, whom Christianity identifies as Yeshu's executioner.

The early Christian and similar sects caused great suffering to the loyal Jewish masses by slandering them to the Roman government. It was they whom the *Tanna* Shmuel *HaKattan* [the Humble] had in mind when he composed and appended a nineteenth blessing for the *Shemoneh Esrei,* the prayer against slanderers and blasphemers.

The new religion grew as the years went by and drew kings and rulers into its orbit. Because of their rejection of the Christian messiah, the Jews became a particular and permanent target of severe persecution. Christian leaders taught the masses of their followers to hate Jews with a violence that has been — and still is — responsible for untold Jewish suffering and loss of life.

23

Agrippa I — Last King in Israel

During the last forty years before the Destruction of the Temple the lot (for the Yom Kippur sacrifice) did not come up in the right hand (of the High Priest), the ribbon did not turn white (as a sign of forgiveness), the western candle (on the Menorah) did not burn (all day), and the doors of the Sanctuary opened by themselves (indicating that the enemy would enter easily). Then Rabban Yochanan ben Zakkai rebuked them and said: "Temple, O Temple, why are you so frightened? I know that you will finally be destroyed, because Zechariah ben Ido has prophesied about you (Zechariah 11:1): 'Open your doors, O Lebanon, that the fire may devour your cedars'" (Yoma 39b).

The Noose Tightens — Chaos and Gaius Caligula

The last forty years before the Holy Temple was destroyed were hard times for our people in the Land of Israel. Two things occurred early in that period that should have made people realize that catastrophe was impending and that only repentance and good deeds could avert the evil decree:

First, Rabbi Tzadok began to fast and pray that the Temple should not be destroyed. This continued until shortly before the Destruction, when Rabban Yochanan ben Zakkai removed him from the besieged city and asked the Roman emperor Vespasian for a doctor to help him regain his health. Second, the Great Sanhedrin left the Chamber of Hewn Stone and exiled itself to a place on the Temple Mount called Chanuyos, outside the Temple area. The move meant that lower courts of twenty-three judges no longer had the authority to impose the death penalty. Only when the Sanhedrin sat in the Temple area did other courts have the right to try capital cases.

The Sanhedrin took this drastic step in response to a general drift into lawlessness. Forty years before the Destruction of the Temple, the rich, the aggressive, and even some High Priests began to engage gangs of robbers and murderers to tyrannize the people and enrich themselves with the loot of the weak and poor. These evildoers had acquired Roman citizenship and enjoyed the support of the procurators. Consequently, the Jewish courts were powerless to prosecute them. Faced with a situation in which they could not enforce the law, the Sanhedrin said: "It is better not to try them at all, rather than to sentence them according to the law, without being able to carry out the law."

The two events mentioned above occurred during the rule of Pontius Pilate, at the end of the period of the earlier high commissioners. Later on, during the rule of the last high commissioners, the corrupt and exploitative practices of the rich and mighty assumed even more alarming proportions.

The relationship between Rome and Judea reached its lowest point during the reign of Emperor Gaius Caligula, 37-41 CE (3797-3801). The beginning of his reign gave no suggestion of evil, and, with all the peoples of the far-flung empire, the Jews rejoiced. They were particularly happy because he released from prison Agrippa, the grandson of Herod and Miriam. Agrippa had been orphaned at the age of three when his father, Aristobulus, was killed by King Herod. In one of his insane suspicions, Herod — who had Queen Miriam executed — accused his son Aristobulus and his brother of planning to avenge her death by poisoning him, Herod. Aristobulus was executed for this imaginary crime. When he was six Agrippa was sent to Rome to be educated with the sons of the Roman aristocracy. There he grew up and became friendly with two future emperors, Caligula and Claudius. These two friendships were to advance the fortunes of both Agrippa himself and the Jewish people to whom he remained loyal despite his Roman upbringing.

Not only did Caligula free Agrippa, he appointed him king over the realm of Agrippa's uncle, Philip, which included northern Transjordan. Later, Caligula added Galilee to Agrippa's realm.

Although Agrippa's lineage was flawed — his mother was a niece of Herod, whose family had the halachic status of slaves — the people of Israel were ecstatic because his paternal grandmother was the beloved Miriam, one of the last Hasmoneans.

Later in Caligula's rule, however, the Jews were rudely jolted from their calm. Like other Roman emperors after him, Caligula ordered that he be honored as a god with full pagan rites. When he was informed that the Jews of Alexandria and Ashdod refused to erect an altar in his honor, he ordered that a statue of himself be placed in the Temple of Jerusalem. The execution of this decree was assigned to Petronius, the Roman proconsul in Damascus.

Knowing that the Jews would never willingly allow such a thing to be done, Caligula ordered Petronius to march on Jerusalem with a large army and force the Jews to accept his imperial decree.

Petronius commissioned skilled artisans in Sidon to fashion the statue. Then at the head of two legions of soldiers he marched from Damascus to Acre, north of present day Haifa, to await the delivery of the statue. The terrible news spread like wildfire among the Jews of the country and they came in masses to Acre. They begged Petronius to withdraw from his intention of putting up a statue in the Holy Temple. When Petronius asked them: "Do you intend to fight the emperor?" They replied: "Heaven forbid! But we would rather die than transgress our holy Torah" (Josephus, *Antiquities* 18:8). With this, tens of thousands of Jews cast themselves to the ground and cried out that they were ready to die forthwith.

Petronius well knew Caligula's blood-thirsty cruelty. Caligula would never forgive him if he failed to carry out the order. But the sight of masses of people ready to die for their faith touched his very soul, and he said that it would be preferable that he lose his high office, and even his life, rather than allow these people, who are ready to give their lives for their laws, to perish. "It is fit for virtuous persons to die for the sake of such a multitude" (Josephus, *ibid.*). He promised that he would try to have the decree annulled.

Since Petronius wanted to gain time, he instructed the artisans in Sidon not to hurry with their work. To the emperor he wrote that since the inhabitants of the country would resist the placing of the statue in the Temple, it would be advisable to delay the matter and thus prevent a popular uprising which would bring about the destruction of the crops that were necessary for the emperor's forthcoming campaign in Syria.

Caligula was incensed at Petronius' daring, and sent word that the order must be carried out immediately. It seemed that all was lost, but unexpected "relief and deliverance" came to the Jews from another source.

At the time Agrippa was living in Rome, where his youthful friendship with Caligula continued to develop. Upon hearing of the impending disaster in Judea, Agrippa was greatly distressed and resolved to help the Jews. He invited Caligula to a banquet so lavish that the emperor was astonished and felt compelled to show his gratitude.

The more wine Caligula drank, the more he resolved to make a magnificent gesture to Agrippa. Finally he said that everything he had ever done for Agrippa was not enough. He begged his friend to choose any reward, convinced that Agrippa would ask for territory or new taxing authority. Agrippa refused, saying that Caligula had already given him more than he deserved. This spurred on Caligula even more and he insisted on being allowed to demonstrate his affection for Agrippa.

Agrippa replied, "I will ask nothing for myself. I want something that will increase your glory and reputation for piety and which will cause G-d to help you. I ask that you cancel your order that Petronius erect your statue in the Jewish Temple."

Agrippa's appeal succeeded. Caligula wrote Petronius instructing him not to place the statue in the Temple. But in a second letter he accused Petronius of postponing the deed because he had accepted a bribe from the Jews. Therefore, Caligula ordered Petronius to commit suicide.

But Divine Providence willed otherwise. In 41 CE (3801), Caligula was assassinated by soldiers of his guard, and the news of his death reached Petronius just before the fateful second letter arrived. So it was that G-d saved the life of Israel's benefactor. Caligula's death was greeted with joy not only by the Jews of Judea, but by those of Alexandria, all of whom had been under orders to worship Caligula's statue.

Agrippa — a Ray of Hope

After Caligula's death, Agrippa made use of his many friendships in Rome to help influence the Senate to elect Claudius as the next emperor. In gratitude, Claudius rewarded his friend by abolishing the procuratorship of Judea and appointing Agrippa as king. Thus, in addition to northern *Eretz Yisrael*, over which Caligula had made him ruler, Agrippa assumed authority over Jerusalem and its surroundings. This gave him a realm even larger than that of his grandfather, Herod.

Agrippa's rule was a lone ray of light in the period before the Destruction. Unfortunately, it lasted only three years, from 41-44 CE (3801-3804).

While growing up in Rome, Agrippa had lived like a Roman autocrat, indulging in life's pleasures and ignoring his Jewish ancestry. Once he became king of northern *Eretz Yisrael* under Caligula, however, he drew closer to the Jewish people, a loyalty that he climaxed by risking his career — and probably his life — to dissuade Caligula from setting up his statue in the Temple.

When he became king of all Judea he wanted to be a Jewish king. For advice in matters of Jewish law and conduct he would turn to Rabban Gamliel the Elder, the head of the Sanhedrin, and Agrippa's piety is praised a number of times in the Mishnah for his careful observance of *mitzvos*.

Upon his arrival in Jerusalem he offered a thanksgiving sacrifice. On Shavuos he brought the gift of First Fruits to the Temple together with the Jewish Pilgrims. Upon arriving at the Temple Mount, he took the basket of produce from his servants and lifted it onto his own shoulder to carry to the Temple court. In accordance with the Halachah, during the festival of Succos in 41 CE (3802), immediately following the *Shemittah* [Sabbatical] Year, he was handed a scroll of the Torah from which to read the Book of Deuteronomy to the gathered people. Although a king is allowed to sit while he reads, Agrippa put his own honor aside in favor of the Torah's honor: he read while standing. When he came to the verse concerning the king: "You must not put a foreigner over you, who is not your brother" *(Deuteronomy* 17:15), he wept. Seeing this, the people called to him: "Do not fear, Agrippa; you are our brother, you are our brother!" (Mishnah *Sotah* 7:8).

The Sages, however, did not approve of this reaction of the people. Though Agrippa's grandmother was a Hasmonean, his mother was from the family of Herod. Thus he was not qualified to be king and their flattery was not proper.

In response to the people's consoling exclamation, the Sages went so far as to say:

> It was taught in the name of R' Nassan: At that moment the Jewish people became liable to destruction because they flattered Agrippa (Sotah 41b).

Though dependent on Rome, Agrippa's rule was characterized by honor for Israel. During his reign, the land was at peace and foreign rulers were not seen. He befriended the Sages and assigned them the important administrative offices. He also advanced the country economically and built many buildings throughout the land.

To protect Jerusalem from future enemies he fortified its northern side with strong walls. He also began to erect the "Third Wall," enlarging the size of the city and encompassing Bizitiya, a northern neighborhood whose houses were outside the previous wall. The proconsul in Damascus reported Agrippa's activities to Rome. The Emperor Claudius, suspecting that the Jews were preparing a rebellion against Rome, immediately ordered them to stop building the wall.

The Greek inhabitants of the Holy Land

took a hostile view of the revival of the Jewish community, and they decided to kill Agrippa. When he visited Caesarea to participate in a local festivity, they poisoned his cup. After five days of terrible agony, Agrippa died. Rome then renewed the rule of the high commissioners, and their rule now proved to be much more oppressive than that of their predecessors. It drove the people into open revolt, the outcome of which was the Destruction of the Holy Temple and the exile of the people from its homeland.

Roman aqueduct leading from the Carmel range to Caesarea. The section at right is still covered by sand dunes.

24

The Last High Commissioners

Florus planned to provoke the people into open warfare in order to cover his intolerable crimes. He realized that in times of peace the Jews would eventually send a delegation to Rome to lay before the emperor the record of his misdeeds. But if he could drive them into open rebellion, then this "great evil" would overshadow his "small" evils. And so he increased the sufferings of the people day by day (Josephus, The Jewish Wars, 2:14).

The Roman High Commissioners and Agrippa II

The emperor Claudius was grieved over the death of his friend Agrippa. He wanted to name the dead king's seventeen-year old son, also named Agrippa, to replace his slain father. His advisors argued that the son was too young for the task, however. Instead, they influenced him to restore the rule of the high commissioners over the land. The new order, which lasted for twenty-two years, 44-66 CE (3804-3826) — from the death of Agrippa until the outbreak of the Jewish revolt against Rome — was much worse than the first period of procuratorship. No fewer than seven Romans occupied the office of high commissioner: Fadus, Tiberius Alexander, Cumanus, Felix, Festus, Albinus, and Florus. Knowing that their terms of office would be brief, the procurators concentrated on a single goal: enriching themselves, no matter how much injustice

they had to inflict on the people in order to do so.

In the light of the lawlessness of their superiors, the lower officials, soldiers, and non-Jewish residents also adopted an attitude of disdain and oppression toward the Jews. The Jews, in turn, would not always swallow these insults and acts of injustice. Frequently they resisted their tormentors with force. In this unending chain of action and counteraction the end could only be a climactic explosion — a war of the Jews against the Romans.

Tormented by enemies from without and within, the Jews found their situation plummeting to an unbearable level. Finally, they saw no alternative but to revolt against Rome, thus setting the stage for the Destruction of the Temple and the exile of the nation. It is this plunge toward tragedy that we are about to study.

In the eighth year of his reign (48 CE),

Bronze coin minted by Agrippa II. Obverse: Head of Nero, encircled by Greek inscription, "Neron Kaisar Sebastos." Reverse: five-line inscription surrounded by wreath.

Claudius felt that Agrippa was mature enough for responsibility and appointed him to succeed King Herod (a brother of Agrippa I) as ruler of Chalcis. Four years later, Claudius removed Chalcis from him and gave him a different territory east of the Jordan. Claudius also entrusted the young ruler with the supervision of the Temple and the right to appoint the High Priests, but withheld from him the rule over Judea.

Agrippa II was popular with Claudius and with the Roman officials in Judea. He could have intervened to help his people from the excesses of the high commissioners and other enemies, but he did so only twice. In all other cases he remained aloof and did nothing to help his persecuted brethren. He did not intercede, for example, on the festival of Pesach some twenty years before the Destruction of the Temple, when the procurator provoked an incident that ended in a tragic loss of life.

On the eve of that Pesach, the high commissioner Cumanus ordered his soldiers to occupy the halls and courts of the Holy Temple and remain there until the end of the festival. The very presence of the gentile soldiers on the hallowed grounds of their Sanctuary greatly angered the Jews. When one of the soldiers publicly displayed his contempt for the Jews and their Temple in a very disgusting manner, the people could not contain themselves and hurled insults at Cumanus.

This was exactly the excuse that Cumanus wanted. He commanded his soldiers to encircle the Temple Mount on its northern side, where the Antonia Fortress was located. Assuming that the enemy would now storm the Temple Mount, the Jews panicked and fled the area. Then tragedy struck. As they ran through the narrow alleyways of the city, many people were trampled to death.

Since Claudius had put Agrippa in charge of the Temple area, he had the power to prevent the Roman provocation, but he did not do so.

The first of the two occasions on which Agrippa did help the Jews came when the high commissioner Fadus arrived in Jerusalem. He convened the priests and leaders of the people and, on behalf of Claudius, demanded that the garments of the High Priest be placed in the Antonia Fortress under Roman control from one festival to the next. The Jews sent two emissaries to Rome to prevent this foreign control over the sacred garments. Agrippa was in Rome at the time and influenced the emperor to cancel the decree.

The second instance happened in the time of the high commissioner Cumanus. A group of Jews on their pilgrimage from Galilee to Jerusalem were murdered by Samaritans in the hills of Samaria, resulting in a battle between Jews and Samaritans. Cumanus sent four units of soldiers to help the Samaritans. Many Jews were killed by the Roman legions and others were taken captive.

Both the Jews and the Samaritans sent delegates to Rome. It was expected that Claudius would side with the Samaritans, because Roman soldiers and their commander were involved. But Agrippa interceded and convinced the emperor to condemn the Samaritans for provoking the war and the damage it caused. Three Samaritan leaders were sentenced to death and the procurator Cumanus was banished into exile.

These two incidents point up Agrippa's ultimate failure. He had the power and influence to be a great benefactor of the Jewish people, but he preferred to maintain his close relationship with his Roman and Saducean friends.

Felix, Nero, and Internal Conflict

At the request of the High Priest, Claudius now appointed Felix as high commissioner. He ruled for eight years (52-60 CE) and during this time matters got worse. Many Jews rallied to the party of the Zealots who called for a general rebellion against Rome.

Bloodshed increased in the land, and there were daily scuffles between Jews and their foreign oppressors. Felix cruelly persecuted the young men whom he suspected of being members of the Zealot party.

About one year after appointing Felix, the emperor Claudius died and Nero succeeded him to the throne, 54 CE (3814). This was about fifteen years before the Temple was destroyed. The ears of the new

Antonia Fortress (left) in the northwestern corner of the Temple Mount, and the Beis HaMikdash (center), in the Holyland model (see caption, p. 137).

emperor were deaf to the complaints of the Jews and there was no way they could even bring their plight to his attention.

Nero was a corrupt and cruel despot. He paid little attention to the affairs of his empire and devoted himself to the pursuit of his pleasures and outright madness. He loved art exhibitions, and the bloody sports that provided entertainment for the masses in the Coliseum. He was jealous of the Greek singers who entertained the crowds and competed with them on stage. He craved honor, but reaped scorn. In such contempt was he held that the story spread that when a great fire broke out in Rome he forbade having it extinguished because he enjoyed the spectacle of the city going up in flames.

The lack of imperial authority affected all the provinces of the empire. High officials, including the high commissioner Felix, did as they pleased. To make matters worse, Felix had a brother in Rome, like himself a former slave, who was close to Nero as an influential advisor.

During the period of the last procurators, there were three Jewish factions in Jerusalem. They were not organized parties in the modern sense; rather they represented three general viewpoints about how to deal with the Romans. The three were: those who were ready for open warfare to overthrow Roman domination (Zealots); moderates who supported the goals of the Zealots but hoped to avoid violent confrontation if at all possible; and those loyal to Rome (Friends of Rome).

The groups had vastly different goals and the cleavage between the extremes continued to widen until it resulted in civil war. The actions of various factions were responsible for harming Jewish interests and hastening the Destruction.

The Friends of Rome became numerous and strong after the death of Agrippa I, when Claudius removed control of the Temple and its treasury from loyal Jews and gave it first to Herod, Agrippa's brother, and then to Agrippa II, who was a sympathizer of the Sadducees. His appointees used their position in the Temple to gain control over the people and dislodge the Sages whom Agrippa I had placed in most positions of power. The Friends of Rome attracted Sadducees — particularly those who were so assimilated that they were barely recognizable as Jews, and corrupt High Priests, whose lust for money and power blinded them to any other consideration.

Unsurprisingly, most Jews tended to be moderates, hoping to remain loyal to the Torah without provoking war with the powerful and murderous Roman army. The Zealots grew in numbers and influence as the years went by and more Jews came to the conclusion that there was no choice but to fight. They came to this decision reluctantly, because of the increasing oppression of the greedy Roman procurators and their Sadducean allies. As usually happens in the case of aggressive groups like the Zealots, hotheads and criminals tend to join their ranks. The violent members of the Zealots were called *Biryonim* and the criminals were called *Sicarii*. These criminal elements were utilized by the procurator Felix, who was appointed due to the intervention of the *Kohen Gadol* Yonasan. When the new high commissioner disappointed Yonasan by showing himself to be a greedy and heartless oppressor of the Jews, the High Priest demanded that Felix change his policies toward the Jews.

Anxious to rid himself of the meddling High Priest, Felix hired two criminals, hangers-on of the Zealots, to murder Yonasan.

The killing opened the way for other lawless people to take the law into their own hands, killing and plundering innocent people at will. The *Biryonim* and *Sicarii* hoodlums would excuse their crimes by inventing political reasons and making it seem as though they were resisting Rome, but their true motive was greed.

"The foreigner in your midst will rise higher and higher"
(Deuteronomy 28:43)

Lawlessness and violence stalked the streets of Jerusalem. In the so-called Greek cities along the coast the non-Jewish residents looked down at the hapless Jews. In Caesarea the Greeks even tried to strip the Jews of the city's citizenship and claimed that they were aliens. This conflict went on for a few years and ultimately the case was brought before the Emperor Nero.

Section of the Roman theater at Caesarea, before its restoration.

The decision of Nero, who was a great admirer of the Greeks and their culture, was predictable enough. He declared that the Syrian-Greek inhabitants of Caesarea were its rulers and the Jews living there had the status of aliens. Nero's answer was one of the last causes that kindled the flames of revolt against Roman oppression.

Nero's decision regarding Caesarea was rendered during the tenure of Gessius Florus, the last procurator, who was appointed by Nero in 64 CE (3824). About Florus, Josephus Flavius, the contemporary historian of the period, says:

> Though Albinus (the previous high commissioner and successor to Felix) was a corrupt man, his successor Florus made him seem a model of righteousness by comparison. For Albinus attempted to hide his misdeeds as much as possible, while Florus boasted publicly about his abominations, acting like a hangman. He did not recoil from any robbery or murder, any evil or corruption. No one could match him as a liar and manipulator. It was beneath his dignity to rob individual persons; he plundered cities and destroyed entire communities. It was as if he had officially declared that robbery was legal, provided he was given a goodly share of the loot. To satisfy his greed, he devastated entire districts; there were many who left their homesteads and fled to other countries.

Florus outdid all his predecessors in criminal greed and cruelty. When he went to extremes he thought of ways to cover up the traces of his crimes. In this he found no more effective method than to force the Jews into desperate acts of open defiance and revolt. He knew that whenever the Jews resisted — no matter how great the provocation — they would always be judged by the Romans as the guilty party. Under the pretext of "suppressing the uprisings," Florus felt free to do whatever he pleased, even when there was no disturbance.

Once the Jews of Caesarea had been denied citizenship, the impertinence of the non-Jewish inhabitants reached new heights. For example, they set up workshops near the synagogue in order to disturb the worshipers. In their distress the Jews turned to Florus and pleaded with him to have the workshops removed, with a promise that they would make him a personal gift of eight talents of silver in return for his kindness. Florus took the money, but did not keep his promise to the Jews. When the tension between Jews and gentiles reached the boiling point, he simply left the city.

One Sabbath, as the Jews were gathered for prayers, a Greek citizen approached the synagogue and contemptuously slaughtered a bird. The Jews knew what he meant: he was symbolizing the Greek taunt that the Jews had been driven out of ancient Egypt like lepers, and, like cleansed lepers, should bring a bird offering to their Temple. The Jewish congregants charged the Greek and his friends and drove them off, but Roman soldiers quickly came to the rescue. The Jews were forced to flee the city, taking their Torah scrolls with them. When a Jewish delegation appeared before Florus, asking for his help, he threw them into prison, charging them with illegally removing the Torah scrolls from the city of Caesarea without his permission.

The First Resistance

Florus' insolence knew no bounds. After the incidents in Caesarea he came to Jerusalem and demanded a great sum of money from the Temple treasury. This was oil upon the fire. The people were outraged, and a group of youths demonstrated their feelings by taking charity boxes and walking through the streets, calling: "Charity for poor Florus!"

To Florus this was a good enough reason to proceed from robbery to mass murder. He summoned a large body of troops to Jerusalem and then demanded that the elders of the city hand over the youngsters who had mocked him. When the elders refused, he ordered his soldiers to attack the Jews in the streets of Jerusalem.

Here is Josephus' account of the merciless slaughter:

> Greedy for loot, the soldiers rejoiced at the procurator's order. They plundered the upper market and broke into many houses, robbing and killing the residents. Jews were running into the streets, trying to save their lives. Those who were caught were cruelly cut down. There was no type of robbery and murder that the Romans did not commit on that day. They also took a number of peaceful Jews as prisoners and hauled them before Florus. He had them whipped and then nailed to the cross. The number of slain on that day — men, women and children — was 3,600 (The Jewish Wars, 2:14).

Florus anticipated that, after so much bloodshed, the Jews would no longer remain passive, but rise up in open revolt against their overlords. This would give him an excuse to declare Jerusalem a conquered city and to treat it according to Roman law. He would have the right to plunder the entire city and confiscate the Temple treasury. But he was wrong. The people did not rise up. On the next day, when they gathered to mourn for the slain, and many angry, grieving Jews wanted to retaliate, the sages and elders prevailed upon them to remain calm. On the contrary, the sages convinced the people to greet the marching Roman soldiers peacefully — in order to pacify the bloodthirsty tyrant and prevent a new slaughter.

Led by the priests and the elders, the people went in a procession to meet the soldiers and greet them. Contemptuously, the Romans did not return their greeting. Some of the people could not contain themselves at this insult of their leaders and protested loudly. This was what the Romans wanted. The horse-borne soldiers knew what to do. At a pre-arranged signal they burst into the ranks of the people.

The Jews retreated in panic — but when they noticed that the Romans were advancing toward the Temple Mount they stood their ground. Many youths who had watched from the rooftops hurried to the scene and together they battled the hated enemy. They tore down the halls that connected the Antonia Fortress with the Temple and thus prevented the Romans from occupying the Temple. When Florus saw that the Jews had foiled his plans, he left the city with his soldiers. This incident took place in 66 CE (3826) and marks the beginning of the Jewish revolt against Rome.

25

From War Against Florus to War Against Rome

On account of Kamtza and Bar Kamtza, Jerusalem was destroyed. A man whose friend was Kamtza and whose enemy was Bar Kamtza made a feast. He said to his servant: "Go bring me Kamtza." He went and brought him Bar Kamtza. The host came and saw that Bar Kamtza was seated. He said to him: "That man is the enemy of this man — What is he doing here? Get up and leave!" He replied: "Since I have already come here, let me stay, and I will pay for whatever I eat and drink." Said the host: "No!" Said the other: "I will pay for half of your banquet." Said he: "No!" Said the other: "I will pay for your whole banquet!" He said: "No!" — and took him by the arm, stood him up, and led him out. He [Bar Kamtza] said to himself: "Since the Rabbis were present and did not protest against it, obviously they agreed to it. I will slander them to the emperor!" He went and said to the emperor: "The Jews are rebelling against you!" He replied: "Who says this?" Said he: "Send them a sacrifice and see if they offer it." He sent with him a choice calf. On the way he made a cut in its upper lip [rendering it unfit as a sacrifice]; some say [that the animal had] a membrane over its eye — a place that we regard as a disqualification, but they [the Romans] do not regard as a disqualification (Gittin 55b-56a).

The Slanders of Florus and Agrippa

After his slaughter and his unsuccessful assault on the Temple Mount, Florus returned to his headquarters in Caesarea. He was afraid that Cestius Gallus, the Roman proconsul in Damascus, would put him on trial because his treatment of the Jews endangered Rome's hold on the Middle East. To forestall this, he hurriedly dispatched a letter to Gallus in which he described the Jews as rebels against Rome and justified his use of force as necessary to quell the revolt.

The Sages and leaders of the people also sent a letter to Gallus in which they made it clear that their resistance was directed against Florus alone, and not against Rome. They asked him to send a personal representative to Jerusalem who would see for himself that the Jews desired peace and not war. At the same time they promised that if only he would remove Florus, there would be law and order in Judea.

The emissary of Cestius Gallus duly arrived in Jerusalem and became convinced that it was true, as their leaders had said, that the people were not seeking war. But unfortunately he was not the only one who came; Agrippa II came with him. Instead of helping his brethren during the upheaval and the riots, Agrippa had gone to Egypt to congratulate his relative Tiberius Alexander on his appointment as governor of Egypt. Now he came back, and — instead of at least now supporting the Jews — he conveyed the impression that the Jews really wanted to revolt against Rome.

It is noteworthy that Alexander, to whom Agrippa was so loyal, was a Jew who converted to Roman idolatry. In Egypt, he supported the Greeks against the Jews and even ordered two Roman legions there to attack and massacre the Jews who were fighting the Greeks. Later, when Vespasian was besieging Jerusalem, Alexander supported Vespasian as the next emperor of the Roman empire. As his reward, Alexander was named a general in the attack against Jerusalem.

Assembling the people at the Temple Mount, Agrippa held a long speech in which he played the role of a peacemaker whose only desire was to prevent a rebellion. With subtle falsehood he begged of them: "Do not rise up against Rome" — thus giving the impression that this was their intention. His listeners were silent. At the end they undertook to show by their actions how sincere they were in wanting to restore peaceful co-existence with Rome. They now began to rebuild the

A relic from the period of the revolt against Rome (66-70 CE) — a shekel inscribed "Jerusalem the Holy."

halls near the Temple that were destroyed during the disturbances, and collect the taxes that were due to Rome.

After the Jews proved their desire for peace, Agrippa took another daring step. He urged them to accept Florus again as their high commissioner. The demand was rejected outright. The people pleaded with Agrippa to allow them to send a delegation to Rome and lay their grievances before the emperor, asking him to replace Florus with someone else. However, Agrippa, who was a friend of Florus, refused to do so. Agrippa's decision may have been influenced by the fact that Florus' brother, Pallas, was a close confidant of Emperor Nero. The people therefore turned their bitterness against Agrippa — and drove him out of Jerusalem in shame.

The Temple becomes Involved in the Conflict

With Florus and Agrippa gone from Jerusalem, the people wanted more than ever to be able to govern themselves.

They now wanted to remove the Sadducees and other assimilationists from their positions of influence in public life and particularly from the Temple service. Officially, Agrippa was still in charge of Temple matters. In order to remove Agrippa and his non-Jewish friends from contact with the Temple, a group of zealous *Kohanim*, who were then on duty in the Temple, decided no longer to accept sacrifices sent by gentiles. This was directed primarily against Agrippa whose ties with the gentiles were closer than those with the Jews.

The Sages opposed this decision, since according to the law voluntary sacrifices of gentiles could be offered on the altar, but the *Kohanim* were determined not to allow it. They were sincere in their desire to remove foreign and Sadducean influence from the Temple; in their zeal, however, they failed to realize how far they should go and where to limit themselves. Their refusal to obey the Sages caused unnecessary bitterness that aggravated an already difficult situation.

The Friends of Rome realized that their position was in danger now that the people of Jerusalem and the zealous priests had turned actively against Florus, Agrippa, and all who wished to appease Rome. The party schemed to find some way to make the higher Roman authorities angry enough to put down the angry Jews so that they, the Friends of Rome, could return to power in the city, and especially regain their control of the Temple and its large treasury.

In the passage quoted at the beginning of this chapter, the Talmud tells how Bar Kamtza was insulted publicly and how he went to the Roman emperor with a false charge in order to avenge himself against the Sages. Bar Kamtza's act makes plain that he was a Sadducee, and his method of retaliating shows how low the Friends of Rome and their Sadducee partners would stoop to have their way. Bar Kamtza told Nero that the Jews were rebelling against him personally and that their refusal to offer his sacrifice in the Temple would be proof that they no longer were loyal to him. In order to make sure that the emperor's animal could not be offered, Bar Kamtza made a small blemish on its lip (or, according to some, chose an animal with a disqualifying blemish in its eye) — a blemish so minor that the Romans considered it insignificant, even though it would disqualify the animal under Jewish law. The Romans would never believe that the Jews would refuse the sacrifice because of the small blemish — unless they were truly ready to revolt against Rome.

It is clear from the Talmudic account that even the zealous *Kohanim* would have performed the service on the emperor's offering — had it not had a blemish — even though they refused to offer the sacrifices of other non-Jews. Most of the Sages felt that for the sake of peace, even the blemished offering should be accepted in order not to anger the emperor and risk the terrible danger that he might order an attack on Jerusalem. However, R' Zechariah ben Avkulas convinced his colleagues that they should not make an exception, despite the possible danger. Many of the Sages then felt that if Bar Kamtza were permitted to go back to Nero with a new slander, many Jewish lives would be lost; therefore he should be put to death. Again, R' Zechariah ben Avkulas convinced them not to do so.

The great Talmudic Sage R' Yochanan said that R' Zechariah's willingness to tolerate Bar Kamtza's outrages was responsible for the future Destruction of the Temple.

Civil War in Jerusalem

Calm returned to Jerusalem. Florus and Agrippa had left the city and there was no special reason to fear further upheavals. But the Sadducees were still active. Though only a minority party, they would not give up their attempts to regain power, even though at this time such attempts carried the seeds of civil war and national disaster.

They turned to Florus and Agrippa for help. Florus did not respond; apparently he was afraid that he would have to stand trial before Cestius Gallus if he were responsible for new disturbances. Not so Agrippa. He dispatched an army of 3,000 soldiers from his northern kingdom to aid his Sadducee friends and supporters in Jerusalem.

With the help of these soldiers, the Sadducees and the Friends of Rome were able to occupy the Upper City. The Zealots and many of the people who joined them entrenched themselves in the Lower City and on the Temple Mount.

The fighting between Agrippa's forces and the Zealots began on the eighth day of Av, and continued for seven days with neither side gaining an advantage. On the fifteenth day of Av many people came to Jerusalem for the Festival of the Wood

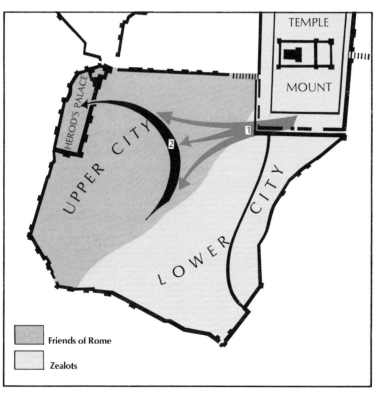

**First Civil War
(8 Av-7 Elul 66 CE)**
1. Zealots attack.
2. Friends of Rome retreat to Herod's palace.

TEMPLE

MOUNT

HEROD'S PALACE

UPPER CITY

LOWER CITY

Friends of Rome

Zealots

Offering (for the altar). Among them there was a number of *Sicarii* (the violent hangers-on of the Zealots), led by Menachem the Galilean, who was staying in Masada, the fortress overlooking the Dead Sea.

With the help of Menachem's men, the Zealots captured the Upper City, which was occupied by Agrippa's Jewish allies, who surrendered and were allowed to leave unharmed. The victorious revolutionaries were followed by an excited mass of people who set fire to the palace of the High Priest and the tax office of the Roman authorities.

Head of Titus on bronze coin struck by Agrippa II, with Greek inscription, "Autokr[ator] Titos Kaisar Sebastos." Reverse: pagan figure, and the date, "year 26 of Agrippa's reign."

The Roman soldiers continued to fight from their fortified positions in the three northern towers of Herod's palace. In the beginning of the month of Elul, some two weeks later, they too surrendered. The Zealots promised them a free withdrawal, provided they would lay down their arms. But when the mob, led by Menachem and his *Sicarii*, saw the hated soldiers walk by unarmed and undefended, they fell upon them and killed them. Only one soldier was saved, because he promised to become a convert.

Menachem boasted about his achievements. The more moderate Zealots, who were led by Elazar, the son of the former High Priest Chananiah [Ananias], killed him in the fight that followed, and Elazar remained the sole leader of the freedom fighters in Jerusalem. Many of Menachem's men under the leadership of Elazar ben Yair, a relative of Menachem, now returned to the fortress of Masada.

The Romans feared that the success of Jewish resistance in Jerusalem would inspire Jews throughout the land to follow their example and take up arms against the occupation forces, or to reinforce their Jewish brethren in Jerusalem. To forestall this they used their tried method — "divide and conquer" — and incited the non-Jews in the cities of the mixed population throughout the land to start pogroms against their Jewish neighbors and kill them.

The Greek residents were long time enemies of the Jews and welcomed this invitation to the slaughter. In Caesarea they attacked the Jews cruelly and killed almost all of them. The few who survived fell into the hands of Florus and his soldiers and were sold as slaves in foreign lands. Terrible pogroms occurred also in other cities, including Alexandria, the capital of

Egypt, and Damascus, the capital of Syria.

The Jews realized that there was no alternative but to organize themselves for self defense. Nor did they always wait until they were attacked. Their fighting units not only avenged the murder of their fellow Jews, but sometimes struck first, before their Greek neighbors were able to attack them.

The pogroms and riots lasted for several months, and the number of men, women and children who were murdered and tortured to death rose into the tens of thousands. But all this did not break the spirit of the Jews, especially those in Jerusalem. On the contrary, they now closed ranks behind their leaders to fight for their lives and their country.

Agrippa's Treachery

During these frightful months Agrippa left his kingdom in the northern part of the land and went to Cestius Gallus in Antioch. In Agrippa's absence from his kingdom, his governor, Noarus, murdered seventy of the most prominent Jews in the district of Batanea — but this did not concern Agrippa. He pleaded for protection of his own interests. He saw the weakening of the hold of the Romans on the country and with it the loss of power of his Sadducean friends. He therefore tried to persuade Gallus to send an army to suppress the Jewish revolt.

At first, Gallus was not interested in military intervention. He knew that the resistance of the Jews was not directed as much against Rome, as against Florus, Agrippa and the Greek residents of the mixed cities. Only when the riots reached proportions that threatened to undermine Roman control over the country, did Gallus listen to Agrippa. At the head of his legions, which were reinforced by 3,000 soldiers provided by Agrippa, Gallus marched toward Jerusalem. On the way he decimated a number of Jewish communities which happened to be located on his route. Many Jews who escaped the Greek slaughter now died at the hands of Gallus and Agrippa. Thus, the descendant

of the Hasmoneans and guardian of the Temple became a partner in the destruction of the Jewish people.

Before the gates of Jerusalem Agrippa sent word to the defenders, demanding their surrender. But they knew that if they submitted now, Agrippa would be reinstated as supervisor over the Temple and possibly ruler of the city. They refused.

Gallus and his army entered Jerusalem, but they did not succeed in dislodging the Jewish defenders from their fortified positions within the city. Realizing that his army was not powerful enough to conquer such an extensive and fortified area, Gallus withdrew. While he was retreating through the valley of Beis Choron, Jewish soldiers attacked from the two hills overlooking the valley and killed close to 6,000 of his men.

Gallus waited till sundown. Then under cover of night he fled with his remaining soldiers to the coastal plain, leaving behind great quantities of arms and equipment. The Jews of Jerusalem excitedly brought the spoils of war into the city and distributed them among the defenders. They well knew that the Romans would return with a much bigger army to avenge the embarrassing defeat and to reestablish their rule over Judea and all of the land.

On the eighth day of Cheshvan, 66 CE

The exact date is given by the inscription surrounding the amphora on the obverse of this bronze perutah: "shnas shtayim" (year two — i.e., of the Jewish revolt against Rome). Reverse (not shown here): vine leaf with stem and tendril, surrounded by Hebrew inscription, "cheirus Tziyon" (freedom of Zion).

(3827), the victors, laden with their spoils, returned triumphantly to Jerusalem. Now nothing stood in the way of establishing a Jewish government. With the removal of Florus and the defeat of Cestius Gallus, Roman authority over Judea had been removed and a Jewish goverment took its place. The *Nasi* of the Sanhedrin, Rabban Shimon ben Gamliel, was one of its leaders.

So great was the joy over the restoration of political independence after such long and bitter years of foreign oppression that new coins were minted which bore the inscription: "Freedom of Jerusalem."

These days of independence were not destined to last. The divine decree of Jerusalem's destruction still stood. The city had become filled with groundless hatred of Jew against Jew. Because of that hatred, the destruction had been decreed, and the guilty people had not repented their sin. A very few years later the fearful end came — the Temple was burned to the ground; the land was ruined; and its population was decimated and sent into the exile that has not yet ended.

26

The War in Galilee

Josephus was convinced that the city of Yodefat [Jotapata] could not hold out much longer, and that it would be exceedingly difficult for him to save his life if he were to stay in the city. He therefore consulted with the notables on escaping from it. But the matter became known to the townspeople, who came to him in a panic, surrounded him in great numbers, and implored him not to desert them. Josephus concealed from them that he meant to leave only to save his life. He told them that his intention was only for their benefit ... because if he could get away from the siege successfully he would be in a position to achieve great salvation for them (The Jewish Wars, 3:7).

Preparations for War — The Wrong Man

The victory over Cestius Gallus brought about unity in Jerusalem, although opinions differed as to the chances of peace and the necessary steps to be taken to meet an uncertain future. The excitement over the victory and the fear of what was in store bridged the various opposing views. The new government concentrated on military preparation for the inevitable Roman counterattack. Military commanders were appointed over the various areas of the country to prepare for war, train soldiers, store weapons, and build and strengthen walls and fortresses.

When the Sadducees and neutralists saw the determination of the people to defend themselves and that a Jewish government had taken charge, they too wanted to participate in the joint struggle. Because many of them came from distinguished families, the populace felt that they would make good military leaders and that this time the Sadducees had the national interest at heart. Many of them were appointed as the military commanders and administrators of the districts.

Yosef ben Mattisyahu, who later became famous under the name of Josephus Flavius as the author of *Jewish Antiquities* and *The Jewish Wars,* was sent to organize and command Galilee. It was clear that the Romans would begin the war of conquest by marching southward from there, hence it was of vital importance that a qualified strategist and a loyal Jew lead the fight to prevent the Roman advance.

But he was the wrong man in the wrong place. Josephus came from a priestly family that traced itself to the Hasmoneans, and he was highly gifted, but he was young and inexperienced in military matters. Like many other members of aristocratic families in those days, he was more interested in his own advancement than in the welfare of his people. He was an opportunist — one who utilized any situation to his own advantage, regardless of its morality. He changed sides regularly, depending on which one seemed to be the eventual winner.

One of his instructions from the central government was to gain the cooperation of the extreme nationalistic elements in the Galilee — the patriots and the *Sicarii* — and integrate them into the overall plan of military preparedness. Recognizing that many of the extremists were very poor people who hoped to better their economic situation by overthrowing Rome, Josephus gained their support by paying them. He succeeded in unifying the northern Jews that way — but in the process weakened their fighting spirit.

Having demonstrated his ability to administer Galilee, Josephus became sure of himself and began acting independently of the Jerusalem government. Instead of unifying the population for the war against Rome, he utilized local conflicts to increase his own power.

Many Galileans accused Josephus of really being a supporter of Agrippa II and of the Friends of Rome. One of his main opponents was Yochanan of Gush Chalav (near Meron). Realizing that he could not overpower Josephus, Yochanan sent his complaint to the government in Jerusalem. He also asked Rabban Shimon ben Gamliel to prevail upon the members of the government to put Josephus on trial. Rabban Shimon sent a delegation of influential Jews to remove Josephus from power by turning the local people against him. Josephus foiled the attempt and forced the delegation to return home. The government sent agents to summon Josephus to Jerusalem to answer the charges, but he simply drove away the messengers.

Rome Flexes its Muscles

While Josephus and his opponents were feuding with each other, the news came that a Roman army, sent by the Emperor Nero, was landing in Acre. The defeat of Cestius Gallus and his legionnaires had alarmed Rome. Losing no time, Nero dispatched a vast army, led by his best general, Vespasian [Aspasyanus], who had distinguished himself in battles against Germanic and British tribes.

In the spring of the year 67 CE (3827) Vespasian arrived with an army of more than 60,000 troops, equipped with the latest weapons of war. His son Titus brought additional forces from Alexandria. Agrippa also furnished soldiers to help the Romans fight his own people.

The Jews of Galilee hastily prepared themselves for the inevitable. Nine months had passed since the defeat of Gallus, during which they fortified a number of cities, among them Tiberias, Gush Chalav, Gamla and Yodefat. In his biography Josephus claims to have had 65,000 men under his command, but this seems to be a great exaggeration. In any event, he was not wholeheartedly devoted to his task, and it is doubtful whether he really wanted to make a strong stand against the Romans.

Even before Vespasian arrived, the city of Sepphoris [Tzippori] sent a delegation of notables to Acre to inform Cestius Gallus of their city's surrender. They also asked to be given a Roman garrison to protect them from the revenge of their fellow Jews, whom they had betrayed.

Sepphoris was the biggest city in Galilee and its fortifications formed a vital link in the chain of fortified cities that stood in the way of the foreign invaders. Its surrender thus opened a serious gap in the line of defense of the Galileans.

The Roman army units that advanced towards Sepphoris established their camp in the Valley of Jezreel, from which they attacked the surrounding villages. They applied the "scorched earth" policy of destroying fields and farms by day, and by night looting the inhabitants of city and farm, killing the able-bodied men capable

VESPASIAN'S CAMPAIGN IN GALILEE (67 CE)

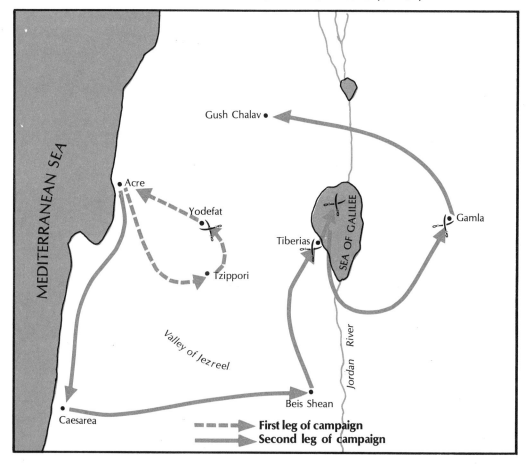

of fighting, and selling the weaker citizens as slaves. The Galilee was filled with fire and blood.

This Roman tactic was designed to terrify the defenders, to impress upon them the fate that was in store for them if they did not surrender. Only once did Josephus' soldiers meet the Roman army in open battle, not far from Sepphoris. They were defeated; Josephus and some of his men escaped and fled to Tiberias, and from there they fled to Yodefat.

After this experience the Jews no longer dared to face the well-trained and mightily armed Roman legions in open battle. Instead they entrenched themselves behind the walls of the cities, preferring a war of defense rather than offense. One of the more strongly fortified points was the city of Yodefat. It soon became filled with refugees from the countryside, and Josephus and his men organized its defense against the imminent onslaught of the Roman army.

Yodefat Falls

Yodefat was located on the slope of Mount Atzmon, some six miles north of Sepphoris. On three sides it was defended by steep valleys; only on its northern side was it vulnerable to attack. They then built a strong wall to block the advance of the enemy. This wall was the scene of a bitter and heroic fight that lasted forty-seven days.

Citadel at Sepphoris, in the Galilee. To this town the conquered Jews brought their Sanhedrin, and the victorious Romans — their hippodrome ... This citadel was apparently built during the Crusader period, and its stones tell its story, which starts in Maccabean and Roman times, proceeds (according to its construction) through the Crusader occupation, and is concluded (according to the roof, and the stones at upper left) in the Arab period.

Stone benches and fallen pillars in the ruins of the synagogue in Gamla. At left, heap of stone missiles catapulted into Gamla during the Roman siege; at center, view of the Golan plateau.

The attack on Yodefat began in Iyar, 3827 (67 CE). The Roman onslaught was powerful and furious. Josephus and his men joined the defenders and for many days they fought vigorously in defense of the city and beat back the Romans. The invaders changed their strategy. Facing the city wall, the Romans put up high earthen ramps upon which they placed catapults — the "artillery" of ancient warfare. With the catapults, they hurled boulders, spears, and burning torches over the wall into the city, but the defenders bravely coped with these fearsome machines of destruction, until Vespasian gave up his plan to take the city by force. He decided to tighten the siege around Yodefat and force the city to surrender through hunger and thirst.

Just before Rosh Chodesh Tammuz, the Romans learned that starvation had weakened the inhabitants to the point that the defenders were falling asleep during guard duty. Silently, the enemy scaled the wall, killed the guards, captured the fortress, and penetrated into the city. They perpetrated an awful slaughter on the inhabitants, killing some 40,000, old and young alike, and selling 12,000 of the survivors into slavery.

When the final battle began, Josephus saved his life at the last moment. Together with forty of the more prominent townsmen he hid in a cave, hoping to stay alive until the worst was over. In response to the townspeople who pleaded with him to stay, Josephus falsely promised that he was going for reinforcements. In reality, he was interested only in saving his own life.

When Vespasian learned about the hideout he sent word to them to leave the cave and surrender. Josephus was ready to do so, but the others prevented him from doing so. Instead, they decided to kill each other and not fall into the hands of the cruel enemy.

Cleverly, Josephus persuaded his comrades to cast lots as to the order of the killing. He himself organized the casting of the lots in such a way that he and a friend would be the last survivors. Then he persuaded his friend to join him in surrendering.

At first Josephus was put into prison, but it did not take long before he found ways of impressing Vespasian. He was freed and attached to the army to chronicle the Roman victories over the Jews. Twice he tried to persuade his fellow Jews in Jerusalem to come to terms with the Romans because of their hopeless situation, but the Jews contemptuously rejected his approaches.

VESPASIAN'S CAMPAIGN IN JUDEA (68 CE)

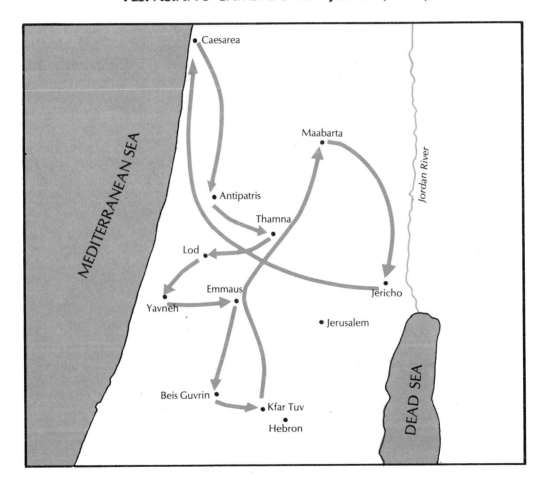

From the Fall of Yodefat Until the Death of Nero

After the fall of Yodefat it took the Romans four more months — Tammuz, Av, Elul and Tishrei — to conquer the other cities of the Galilee. Tiberias surrendered without a fight, but Meged near the sea of Galilee, Gamla in the Golan Heights, and Gush Chalav in the Upper Galilee put up a heroic resistance before they too were conquered.

The commander in the defense of Gush Chalav was its native son, Yochanan, the opponent of Josephus. When he saw that there was no chance to hold out against the mighty Roman army, he and his comrades secretly left the city and succeeded in reaching Jerusalem, where they continued in their struggle against the Romans.

While the Galileans waged a desperate war against the foreign enemy, the Jews of Jerusalem were locked in internal strife and military confrontation. Questions as to the overall leadership and the methods of resistance set one group against the other. The Romans took full advantage of the situation and advanced southward, meeting practically no resistance. Vespasian first made sure of the port cities — Jaffa, Yavneh, Ashdod — so as to provide safe anchorage for the ships that brought provisions and reinforcements for his army. Then he turned eastward and reoccupied Transjordan, returning it to Roman sovereignty. His strategy was to isolate Jerusalem and sever it completely from the surrounding countryside. In doing so he captured the Judean cities of Antipatris, Lydda, Emmaus, Beis Guvrin, Kfar Tuv, Nablus [Shechem] and Jericho. He was now ready to move on Jerusalem.

At that time Nero died (68 CE) and a desperate struggle for the succession broke out in Rome. When this news reached Vespasian, he was in Caesarea preparing for an assault on Jerusalem after having conquered and fortified all the strategic points surrounding the city. Hearing about the turmoil in Rome, Vespasian called a temporary halt in his campaign against Jerusalem pending resolution of the governmental crisis in Rome.

27

Civil War in Besieged Jerusalem

What was the origin of R' Eliezer ben Hyrkanus? He was twenty-two years old and had not studied Torah. Once he said, "I will go and learn Torah from Rabban Yochanan ben Zakkai" ... His father Hyrkanus heard that he was learning Torah from Rabban Yochanan ben Zakkai. Said he, "I will go to Jerusalem and disinherit my son Eliezer." They told him, "Today Rabban Yochanan ben Zakkai is lecturing in Jerusalem and all the prominent men of Israel are sitting before him ..." Hyrkanus came and wanted to sit among them, but they did not let him. He maneuvered his way forward until he came near Ben Tzitzis HaKsas, Nakdimon ben Gurion, and Ben Kalba Savua. He sat down among them and trembled ... R' Eliezer rose and shared with them thoughts that no ear had ever before heard ... Rabban Yochanan ben Zakkai rose and kissed his head ... Hyrkanus his father then stood up and called out, "My teachers, I came here to disinherit my son Eliezer, but now all my property shall be given to him" (Avos of R' Nassan 6:3).

Uncontrolled Factionalism

We have seen how the spirit of unity prevailed in Jerusalem after its defenders defeated Cestius Gallus. After the fall of Galilee, however, differences of opinion as to how to meet the impending danger sharpened, leading to conflict and outright hatred. This evil gnawed at the very soul of the people, destroying all that was good and promising among them.

In the camp of the Zealots the extremists gained the upper hand. Instead of blaming the loss of the Galilee on Josephus and his Sadducean friends, the extremists put the responsibility on the rich and prominent Jews and called for a war against all privileged Jews to prevent them from further mischief and render them harmless. In the camp of the moderates, the Sadducees and the Friends of Rome gained fresh influence. Seeing how powerful the Romans now were, they insisted on making peace with them and reestablishing the old order.

Thus it was that in beleaguered Jerusalem, instead of combining all forces and resources to fight the common enemy, the various parties spent their strength in cruel civil wars.

When Yochanan of Gush Chalav arrived in Jerusalem he described the heroic stand of the Galileans and proclaimed that the Romans would never conquer the strongly fortified city of Jerusalem, "even if they made themselves eagles' wings." He thus stirred the Jerusalemites with new hope in their ultimate victory.

There were other elements whose political views were mixed with criminal tendencies, including the *Sicarii* who, under the pretext of fighting the influence of the rich Friends of Rome, robbed them of their property. Rabban Shimon ben Gamliel and other friends of the defenders of Jerusalem pleaded with the Zealots to curb the extremists and stop the robberies of the *Sicarii* in order to avoid a civil war between the moderate and the extreme nationalists. But things had gone too far already; Rabban Shimon and his colleagues pleaded in vain.

The weakening of the revolutionary government gave the Friends of Rome their chance. Led by Chanan ben Chanan they drove the Zealots from the inner city, though not from the fortified halls of the Temple Mount. Seeing that the Friends of Rome were in control of the city, Yochanan of Gush Chalav joined and became leader of the Zealots in the Temple area. Rabban Shimon ben Gamliel, realizing that the civil war had gotten completely out of control, thus precluding victory in the battle against the Romans, withdrew altogether from the political scene.

Ruins of the 3rd-century CE synagogue at Gush Chalav, a village whose name was made famous by its son Yochanan.

An Invitation to Foreigners

The forces of Chanan ben Chanan and the moderates who controlled the city laid siege to the Temple Mount where the Zealots were isolated. The beleaguered Zealots now did an incredible thing: they invited the Edomites, whose forefathers had forcibly been converted to Judaism by Yochanan Hyrkanus, to come to their aid. They lived in the south of the land and were known to be marauders who lived by the sword. They gladly accepted the invitation to come into the big city with their weapons, anticipating rich plunder. But Chanan ben Chanan closed the city gates and they could not enter. The Edomites therefore encamped in their thousands outside the city and awaited their opportunity.

One stormy night the Zealots surprised the unsuspecting guards and overcame them. They broke open the heavy bars that secured the gates and admitted their Edomite allies into the city. The soldiers of the moderate party were now trapped from both sides: from the direction of the Temple Mount they were confronted by the Zealots, and from the rear the Edomites attacked them.

The outcome was inevitable. The moderates lost and many of them were

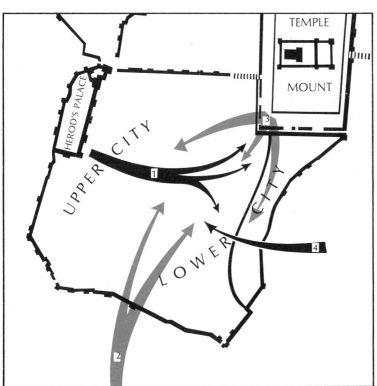

Second Civil War (68 CE-69 CE)
1. Moderates attack Zealots on Temple Mount.
2. Edomites enter the city at Zealots behest.
3. Zealots, aided by the Edomites, gain control of the city.
4. Shimon ben Giora comes to the aid of the moderates.

killed in the fighting. The Zealots and Edomites killed their leaders and cruelly murdered peaceful citizens whom they merely suspected of loyalty to the Romans. Jerusalem was filled with fear and horror at the terrible things perpetrated that day by the fanatic elements of the Zealots and their Edomite allies.

Finally, sated with plunder and murder, the Edomites left the city, and Jerusalem came under the control of the Zealots and their leaders, Yochanan of Gush Chalav and Elazar ben Shimon.

The Sadducean High Priests and leaders and their allies, the Friends of Rome, did not reconcile themselves to the rule of the Zealots. Looking for an ally to help them defeat the Zealots, they turned to Shimon bar Giora, who was known for his personal hatred of Yochanan of Gush Chalav, to come to their aid.

This invitation turned out to be the last act in the drama that led to the destruction of Jerusalem. Shimon bar Giora led a band of violent people who had been uprooted from their normal way of life by the years of war and lawlessness. For a time he and his men were headquartered in Masada where they often cooperated with the Zealots led by Elazar ben Yair. Later, Shimon left Masada and made his camp elsewhere. From his new headquarters his men fought the Edomites, and attacked helpless towns and villages in order to plunder whatever they wanted. Their devotion was only to their leader, who held sway over them through the power of his tongue and the promise of loot.

The arrival of Shimon bar Giora and his men was the signal for the outbreak of civil strife that in intensity and cruelty surpassed all that had gone on before in the bleeding city. Ruthless battles were fought in the streets of Jerusalem between the forces of Yochanan of Gush Chalav, who had taken up positions on the Temple Mount, and the forces of Shimon bar Giora, who were entrenched in the Lower City.

The residents of Jerusalem, led by three wealthy citizens — Ben Tzitzis HaKsas, Nakdimon ben Gurion, Ben Kalba Savua — who were disciples of Rabban Yochanan ben Zakkai, had for months stored provisions in anticipation of the Roman siege. The three men had filled vast warehouses with enough flour, oil, and wood to help their fellow Jews survive an extended siege. Now these storehouses were set on fire by Shimon bar Giora's men, in order to force the people into an immediate armed confrontation with the Romans.

Vespasian, after conquering the entire country around Jerusalem, had interrupted his campaign to capture the city upon learning that Nero had died. He awaited news of the struggle for succession to Nero's throne, but he could afford to be patient because he knew of the internal strife in Jerusalem, by which the Jews were weakening themselves.

Unlike the situation in earlier times, the Roman Senate no longer had the power to enforce its choice of new emperor. Instead, the throne was seized by whichever aspirant had the most raw power. During the period of Vespasian's siege, the various Roman legions held the decisive influence. If an army was large enough and sufficiently loyal to its general, it simply proclaimed him emperor — and anyone choosing to contest the choice had to be ready for war.

During the pause in Vespasian's siege, three emperors were chosen in quick succession: Galba ruled from June 9, 68 to

January 15, 69, when Otho had him murdered and proclaimed himself emperor. However, Vitellius' armies had declared for him and civil war broke out. Otho's forces were defeated and he committed suicide on April 15, 69. On July, 69, Vespasian's troops in Judea declared for him, and they were joined by all the legions in the East. Vespasian expected that with the help of his powerful army, he would prevail in the end. To further this ambition, he planned to take his troops to fight Vitellius' legions stationed in Germany. He succeeded and Vitellius was killed on December 22, 69 CE (3829).

This was an opportune moment for the Jews to come to an understanding with Vespasian under relatively easy terms, but it was not done. Due to the bloody warfare in Jerusalem, there were no men of stature and authority who were willing to listen to the advice of the Sages and make peace with the Romans. The evil of groundless hatred had blinded the people to wise counsel.

A dramatic find at Masada — this ostracon inscribed בן יאיר, presumably referring to Elazar Ben Yair, the commander of the Sicarii there.

Rabban Yochanan ben Zakkai — The Leading Sage

The two leading Torah personalities at the end of the Second Temple period were Rabban Yochanan ben Zakkai, dean of the Sanhedrin, and Rabban Shimon ben Gamliel, of the family of Hillel, the *Nasi*. Of the two, the undisputed leader was Rabban Yochanan ben Zakkai. He counteracted every attempt of the Sadducees to tamper with the Halachah. The importance of his success in this defense of the Torah is highlighted by the fact that the Sages proclaimed as minor holidays the occasions when Rabban Yochanan defeated his Saducean opponents. The Sages forbade fasting on those days.

Rabban Shimon ben Gamliel, in his capacity as president or *Nasi* of the Sanhedrin, participated in the central government, and led the political opposition to the treacherous conduct of Josephus in the Galilee. The Sages, led by Rabban Yochanan and Rabban Shimon, generally supported the political line of the more moderate Zealots in their resistance to Rome. However, when they realized that because of the internal conflicts and wars there was no chance of withstanding the Romans, they chose to take the initiative in a daring action to save

Jerusalem and the Holy Temple from total destruction.

The situation in strife-torn Jerusalem was becoming more intolerable day by day. The extremists and bar Giora's violent camp imposed their will upon the population. In their irrational desire for open and hopeless war against Vespasian's huge army, they had set fire to the storehouses which the wealthy followers of Rabban Yochanan ben Zakkai had prepared to feed the people. The Sage decided to do something daring and drastic at the risk of his life. He would leave

Entrance to the courtyard of the synagogue in the Old City of Jerusalem built on the site where, according to tradition, Rabbi Yochanan ben Zakkai prayed on the eve of the Destruction of the Second Temple. Following its desecration in the years before the Six-Day War, this historic synagogue has been reconstructed according to pre-1948 photographs and recollections, and restored to its former grandeur.

Jerusalem and proceed to Vespasian's headquarters in Gofna, north of Jerusalem. The Talmud *(Gittin* 56a,b) relates this fateful event in detail:

Abba Sikra, a leader of the bandits who attached themselves to the Zealots, was a nephew of Rabban Yochanan ben Zakkai, who requested him to come secretly. When Abba Sikra came, Rabban Yochanan said to him, "How much longer will you starve the people to death?" Abba Sikra answered, "What can I do? As soon as I will complain my cohorts will kill me." Said he, "Help me get out of the city; perhaps some small salvation will result from it." Abba Sikra advised his uncle to act as if he were deathly ill, and a few days later to make it known that he had died. (Only for the burial of the dead did the extremists open the city gates; thus, by feigning death Rabban Yochanan could be carried out of the city.) Rabban Yochanan ben Zakkai accepted his nephew's advice. After he "died," two of his disciples, R' Eliezer and R' Yehoshua, carried the casket with their teacher in it to the outskirts of the city ...

When Rabban Yochanan ben Zakkai appeared before Vespasian he greeted him, saying, "Peace upon you, O Emperor!" Vespasian replied, "You have forfeited your life for two reasons; one, because you called me Emperor, which I am not; and two, if I am the Emperor, why did you not come before?" Rabban Yochanan ben Zakkai answered him, "As for what you said, that you are not an emperor — you will be one in the future, because if you were not a king, Jerusalem could not fall into your hands, as it is written: 'And the Lebanon will fall through a mighty one' *(Isaiah* 10:34); 'mighty one' refers to a king, and 'Lebanon' refers to the Holy Temple. As to your second question, I could not come sooner because the *Biryonim* [bandits] would not permit me to leave Jerusalem."

As they spoke, messengers arrived and announced to Vespasian that he had been proclaimed Emperor.

Upon hearing the wonderful news, Vespasian decided to depart at once, and appointed another general to complete the conquest of Jerusalem.

First, however, Vespasian showed his respect for, and gratitude to, Rabban Yochanan by asking him to request whatever he wished. He made three requests:

(a) תֵּן לִי יַבְנֶה וַחֲכָמֶיהָ, "Give me Yavneh and its Sages!" The study of the Torah must be maintained; without it the future of Jewish life and of the Jews themselves would be doomed.

(b) He asked that the family and dynasty of Rabban Shimon ben Gamliel should not come to harm. This would insure the continued proper leadership of the nation.

(c) He asked Vespasian to provide a physician for the *tzaddik* of the generation, R' Tzadok, who for the past forty years had been fasting and praying that Jerusalem and the Temple should be spared from destruction. His saintliness was needed for the period following the Destruction.

Vespasian kept his promise, leaving the necessary instructions. He then turned the command of his army over to his son, Titus, in order to assume the role of Emperor over the mightiest empire on earth in its capital city, Rome, while Rabban Yochanan ben Zakkai assumed the crown of leadership over the mightiest spiritual empire on earth in its capital city — henceforth Yavneh. There he and his disciples prayed and studied, and waited in trepidation for news from Jerusalem.

Rabban Yochanan ben Zakkai's three requests must have seemed foolish in the eyes of the gentile general who probably expected to be asked for wealth and power. But in truth, their value was of vital importance for the future of the Jewish people whose land would be taken from them and whose central sanctuary would soon be destroyed. Rabban Yochanan knew that Israel's physical power was doomed, therefore he looked ahead to the spiritual well-being of the people and what was necessary to preserve it.

There were some among the Sages who felt that Rabban Yochanan should have asked that Jerusalem be spared completely. He felt, however, that if he had requested so much, Vespasian would have given him nothing.

28

Siege and Destruction

*Hashem will bring against you a nation from afar, from the end of the earth,
as the eagle swoops down, a nation whose tongue you will not understand; a
nation of fierce countenance that will not respect the old, nor show favor to
the young ... And he shall besiege you in all your gates, until your high and
fortified walls come down, those in which you put your trust, throughout all
your land ... (Deuteronomy 28:49-52).*

The Last Pesach in the Second Temple

Before going to Rome to accept his new crown, Vespasian named his son, Titus, to succeed him as commander of the siege against Jerusalem. Before Pesach of the year 70 CE* (3830), Titus marched on Jerusalem with an army of some 80,000 soldiers. Even now, with the Roman army in full view, the defenders of the city did not bury their differences and make a common front against the outside enemy.

The division of the warring camps was as follows: The Sadducees, aided by Shimon bar Giora and his band, held the Lower City, while the Zealots were entrenched on the Temple Mount. However, there was no peace even within the Zealot camp, for a moderate faction, led by Elazar ben Shimon, opposed the stand of the extreme patriots, who were led by Yochanan of

Gush Chalav. There were open clashes between the two factions, with the result that the moderates concentrated their forces within the Temple itself, and the extremists surrounded them outside, on the Temple Mount. Yochanan, who led the extreme Zealots, thus found himself and his men in the middle, between Elazar within the Temple grounds and the Sadducees in the city.

In honor of Pesach, many Jews ignored the danger and made their pilgrimage to Jerusalem, some of them arriving just ahead of the marching Roman army. In an act of great generosity and dedication to the Temple service, the men of Elazar ben Shimon opened the gates of the Temple so that the visitors could offer their Pesach sacrifice. The men of Yochanan of Gush

* It should be noted that there is disagreement regarding the year of the Destruction. According to *Rashi* (*Avodah Zarah* 9b) it took place in 68 CE; according to *Tosafos* (ibid.) it took place in 69 CE; according to others it took place in 70 CE. See Appendix, 'The Year of the Destruction'.

Chalav also entered, seemingly for the same sacred purpose, but as soon as they were inside they drew their swords which they had hidden inside their garments and threatened their opponents.

Elazar and his men wanted to avoid panic and bloodshed among the masses of Jews assembled in the Temple courts and offered no resistance. As a result of their shameful exploitation of the Pesach commandment and Elazar's benevolence, Yochanan and his followers now had control over the entire Temple area, but the two groups remained in fierce opposition to one another.

The Romans did not open their attack during the festival. They feared that despite their overwhelming numbers they would not conquer the city and they hoped that the peace party of the Sadducees would gain the upper hand over the Zealots and hand over the city.

The bombardment of the walls began one day after the festival. Now that the writing was on the wall and the sound of war was heard throughout the city, the parties at last drew together in a common defense of the beloved city. Yochanan and his men defended the eastern part of the wall and Shimon bar Giora's party was in charge of its northern, southern, and western parts.

This belated unity joined some 20,000 men — moderates and extremists, residents and pilgrims — into one army of brothers, whose battle for Jerusalem and the Holy Temple constitutes one of the most heroic and tragic chapters in the long history of our people.

The Battle for the City

The Romans now launched a massive assault on the northern wall. Their battering rams pounded against it incessantly, and the impact of the rocks hurled by their catapults shook the city.

The defenders fought heroically and furiously. From atop the city's walls, they sprayed the Romans with a rain of stones and burning torches. From time to time they made surprise attacks beyond the city walls and fought the enemy face to face, setting his war machines on fire. This phase of the war lasted fifteen days. On the seventh day of Iyar the enemy breached the third outer wall and after fierce fighting succeeded in breaching the second wall as well. The new city of Jerusalem was in the hands of the Romans. All the houses and stones were burned to the ground and preparations were made for the attack on the Old City, the heart of Jerusalem.

Following the fall of the new city, Yochanan of Gush Chalav withdrew and entrenched himself and his army in the Temple area, while Shimon bar Giora took over the defense of the Upper City. When Titus saw that it would not be easy to overcome the resistance of Jews who were well fortified in their positions and who fought like lions, he tried to achieve his aim by peaceful, but treacherous, means.

At his request, Josephus approached the wall with a group of soldiers and called on the Jews to surrender, since they had no chance of winning. The reply was a shower of stones and shouts of contempt. Josephus was forced to make a humiliating dash for his life.

Now the battle for the Old City began in earnest. The Roman army had three objectives: the Temple Mount in the east, the Upper City in the west, and the Lower City in the south. The Old City was protected on its north by two powerful fortifications, the Antonia Fortress that flanked the Temple Mount, and Herod's palace with its three towers that flanked the Upper City to its northwest. The Temple Mount was separated from the Upper City by a deep valley.

Titus' strategy was first to conquer the Antonia Fortress in order to occupy the Temple area, and from there to conquer the Upper City. At the end of the month of Iyar, after piling up a huge ramp of earth close to the wall and placing his war machines on it, he gave the signal for attack. But Yochanan of Gush Chalav and his men had anticipated Titus' battle plan. Under the ramp whose upper slope supported the tall wooden tower with its battering ram, Yochanan's men dug a tunnel and filled it with wood and tar which they ignited. The flames broke through to the surface causing the ramp to collapse. The catapults and battering rams fell into the flames and were totally destroyed.

Victory Through Famine

When Titus saw that he could not subdue the defenders by force he decided to conquer them through

In time of siege Jerusalem used to receive its water supply through the Siloam [Shilo'ach] Tunnel, dug by King Chizkiyahu through the solid rock from the Gichon stream outside the city walls to the Pool of Siloam, which in Biblical times was within the city (see II Kings 20:20, and II Chronicles 32:30). Today the Shilo'ach is Jerusalem's favorite site for the Tashlich ceremony on Rosh HaShanah.

starvation. He commanded his soldiers to erect a stone fence and seal all the city's exits. Guards watched the fence day and night. Now it became impossible for anyone to leave the city secretly to bring in food. Jews who tried to smuggle their way out were caught and nailed to the cross in full view of those on the inside.

A terrible hunger spread throughout the beleaguered city. All the dire prophecies of the Torah became fulfilled among the people of Jerusalem. Josephus writes:

> The roofs were filled with women and small children expiring from hunger, and the corpses of old men were piled in the streets. Youths swollen with hunger wandered like shadows in the market place until they collapsed. No one mourned the dead, because hunger had deadened all feeling. Those who fell to the ground turned their eyes for the last time to the Temple and beheld the defenders still fighting and holding out (The Jewish Wars, 5:10).

Titus saw that even famine could not

break the spirit of the defenders. He decided therefore to take the Antonia Fortress by direct assault. In order to build the framework for four earthen ramps he cut down all the trees around Jerusalem, and the mountain slopes became bare and desolate. The ramps were built in the month of Sivan; by then hunger had so weakened the defenders that they no longer had the strength to attack the enemy and his machines as they had done in the past.

The Seventeenth of Tammuz

At the end of Sivan the Romans began to batter the walls of Antonia and in the beginning of the month of Tammuz they breached them and conquered the fortress. The approach to the Temple Mount was open. The remaining defenders withdrew behind their last line of defense — the high walls of the Temple itself.

The next Roman objective was to take the entire Temple Mount, but Yochanan and his men were not yet defeated. With unparalleled courage they beat back the Roman assault for ten days, until they forced the enemy to retreat into the Antonia stronghold.

Titus anxiously followed the progress of his offensive. His hopes for a quick conquest of the Jewish Temple had crumbled, and — fearing that the Jews might even retake Antonia — he ordered that the fortress which adjoined the wall of

For over two-and-a-half thousand years this inscription was hidden from view — until its discovery in 1880. It records the excitement of the great moment when the two teams of workers quarrying from opposite ends of the Siloam Tunnel met underground — a remarkable engineering feat. Under Ottoman rule the slab was cut out of the rock wall and taken of to a museum in Istanbul (then Constantinople); a plaster cast of it may be seen in the Israel Museum, Jerusalem.

the Temple Mount be razed to the ground. With Antonia out of the way there would be a wide approach for his forces to make a direct assault on the Temple.

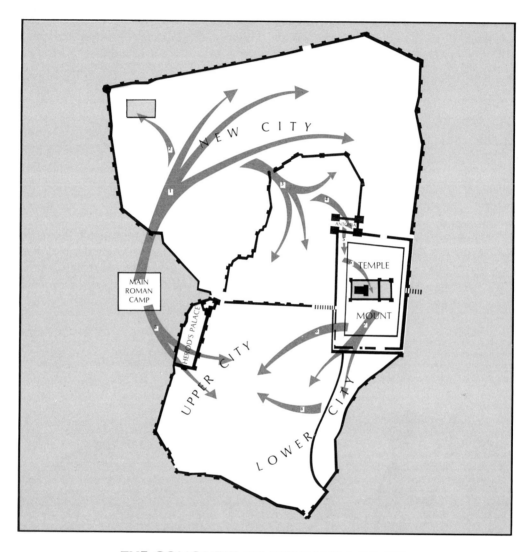

THE CONQUEST OF JERUSALEM (70 CE)

1. Romans penetrate the New City (7 Iyar).
2. Romans establish a new camp within the city.
3. Romans breach the second wall (15 Iyar).
4. The enemy takes the fortress of Antonia (5 Tamuz).
5. Antonia is raged; the enemy penetrates the Temple Mount (17 Tamuz).
6. The attack against the Temple itself is mounted (8 Av).
7. The legions take the lower city (11 Av).
8. Titus attacks the upper city from two sides (7 Elul); Jerusalem is totally conquered (8 Elul).

The assault began. On the seventeenth of Tammuz, the wall of the Temple Mount was breached and the fate of the Temple was sealed.

During the many weeks of fighting and siege, the *Kohanim* in the Temple had persevered in their service. Even the stones and arrows that were hurled into the very courts of the Sanctuary did not deter them from carrying out their appointed task. But on the seventeenth of Tammuz there was no longer a single lamb left for the daily sacrifice. The Altar of G-d was idle.

During those days the famine took a terrible toll in Jerusalem. People died in droves. Those who were alive fought each other tooth and nail for anything, even leather and straw, that for a moment could still the unbearable pangs of hunger. "The tongue of the suckling cleaves to its palate for thirst; young children begged for bread, no one extended it to them" (*Lamentations* 4:4).

How true now was the prediction which Moshe *Rabbeinu* had prophesied in the name of G-d: "The man who is tender among you and very delicate, his eye will be evil against his brother and the wife of his heart and against his children who are still left to him" (*Deuteronomy* 28:54). The Talmud and Josephus tell about a mother who ate the flesh of her dead son, even as it is foretold in the Torah: "And you will eat the flesh of your sons, and the flesh of your daughters will you eat" (*Leviticus* 26:29).

Titus, who knew the situation in the beleaguered city, considered the time ripe for another attempt at persuasion. Once again he sent his spokesman, Josephus, hoping that his eloquence would influence his fellow Jews. Josephus presented his case as if his main concern was to save the Temple from certain destruction and pleaded with them to end their resistance. The reaction of the defenders was the same as before: they drove off the traitor in contempt. They were resolved not to surrender the Holy Temple into the hands of aliens, still believing that G-d would come to their aid.

The Destruction

For three weeks, from the seventeenth of Tammuz to the ninth of Av, fierce battles were waged in the Temple area. Trying to prevent the penetration of the enemy into the courts of the Temple at all costs, the defenders took a desperate step — they set fire to the halls that had connected the Antonia Fortress and the Temple. Many Roman soldiers were trapped and killed, for they were advancing through the halls to attack the Temple.

On the eighth day of Av the Romans approached the very walls and gates of the Temple and attempted to break through. They had finished building their ramps and towers, their battering ram was now in position, and with it they hammered day and night against the wall, but not a single stone moved from its place. They then tried to undermine one of the Temple gates by digging and removing its foundation stones — but the gate stood firm as before. They next put up ladders against the wall and climbed to the top. But the moment they reached the highest

The Kosel Maaravi (Western Wall) as it looked in 1934. In 1967 the area available for worshipers was broadened from a strip a couple of yards wide to the present plaza which holds many thousands of people. At the same time the ground level was lowered, laying bare another two layers of Herodian stone, and thereby clearing the entrance to the vast underground tunnels at the left (which had been filled with the debris of succeeding civilizations), including the place of worship near and under Wilson's Arch.

rung the defenders pushed the ladders back, and the invaders fell to their death.

It seemed as if the Temple itself was fighting the Romans. Even the stones and arrows which they now catapulted over the wall did not made its defenders surrender. They therefore set fire to the chambers adjoining the Temple. When the defenders saw to their horror that flames were licking the walls of the Temple "their strength and their heart failed them and they stood in panic and no one tried to extinguish the flames." The Romans tried to exploit the momentary dread of the Jews and rushed to the Temple. But the defenders rallied and fought them off.

The last battle took place on the ninth day of the month of Av in the morning hours. The adjoining halls had been burned, but the Sanctuary itself and its courts were still intact. The defenders were starved and exhausted from weeks of heavy fighting and severely outnumbered. But their love for the Temple poured new strength into their weary bodies and tired hearts, and again and again they lifted their weapons and beat the Romans back, performing deeds of incredible heroism until the last moment.

Even the most heroic resistance could not prevail when G-d withdrew His Presence from the Temple. One Roman

Jews from all backgrounds join in prayer in the vast underground synagogue vault near Wilson's Arch, which juts out from the Western Wall. The visitors at left are looking down the shaft dug last century by Warren, which bares over a dozen layers of stone extending down to the Roman street level, and to the solid bedrock underlying it. This Arch was the first span in a mighty bridge crossing the Tyropeon Valley, which enabled residents of the Upper City to pass directly to the Temple Mount without risk of contact with any source of tumah (ritual impurity) in the busy marketplace below.

soldier rushed to the northern chambers of the Temple. Hoisted on the shoulders of another, he reached a window and threw a firebrand into the Temple. The fire spread rapidly in all directions and before long the Temple was engulfed in flames. A piercing cry of woe came from the lips of the Jews. They tried desperately to extinguish the flames, even running into them. But it was as if the fire had come down from Heaven; nothing could put it out.

The rest of that day and into the next, the tenth day of Av, the flames rose into the very heavens, accompanied by the cries of the people of Jerusalem who saw in the loss of the Temple the loss of the spiritual content of their lives. Many could not endure the sight and cast themselves into the fire, preferring to die together with the House of G-d than to live without it.

When the Romans finally saw the Temple burning they rushed into it like madmen, plundering whatever they could put their hands on. The Jews whom they met they slew mercilessly, sparing neither young nor old. The number of those slain was enormous, until the very earth of the Temple Mount was covered with their bodies. The shrieks and groans of the wounded and dying, the roar of the hungry flames, the thunder of the lofty walls and turrets as they crashed to the ground, reached the ears of the starved survivors in the Upper City as they watched the spectacle in horror.

Before the fire consumed the interior of the Temple, Titus and his men entered the Holy of Holies. To show his contempt for the Jewish people and their G-d he committed the most disgraceful acts of desecration. After they robbed the holy golden vessels they saw to it that the fire would consume whatever was still standing. Only one wall remained — the Western Wall of the Temple Mount, the *Kosel Maaravi* — and from there the Presence of G-d has never departed.

29

After the Destruction of the Temple

"Give me Yavneh and its Sages!"Nearly 2,000 years have passed since Rabban Yochanan ben Zakkai stood before the Roman emperor and asked of him, not the preservation of the state, because it was no longer a state of the Torah, and not the preservation of the Holy Temple, because Herod's name was associated with it — but the preservation of the Oral Law of the Torah, which depended on Yavneh and its Sages. He knew that if there was the Oral law of the Torah, there would be a people of the Torah; and if there was a people of the Torah, there would be a land of the Torah; and in the future — a state of the Torah. With "Yavneh and its Sages" he saved everything.

Now this emperor, his people, his empire — Rome, the world power: where are they now? But the people of the Torah, the people of Yavneh and its Sages are alive and vigorous, every day awaiting the coming of the righteous Mashiach and the establishment of the state of the Torah in the land of the Torah. The towering personality of Rabban Yochanan ben Zakkai is likewise kept vigorously alive in the hearts of the people of the Torah, and every new generation learns to love and revere him, just as they do "Moshe and Aharon among His Kohanim, and Shmuel among those who call upon His name ..." (Psalms 99:6).

"Give me Yavneh and its Sages!" There is no people on earth that has a phrase expressing this kind of pride — "And who is like Your people, Israel, one nation on earth?" (from Iyunim, "Studies," by R' Eliyahu Dessler).

The Rest of the City Destroyed

After the Destruction of the Temple, the Upper City under the command of Shimon bar Giora was still holding its own. Yochanan of Gush Chalav, the defeated commander of the Lower City and the Temple area, succeeded in escaping from the hands of the Roman soldiers through one of the tunnels of the Temple Mount and joined the defense forces of the Upper City. With the Temple lost, they had not much reason to continue the fight with the Romans. They announced their readiness to surrender, provided they would be allowed to leave the city with their weapons. But Titus would not agree. Standing on the Temple Mount near the bridge that led to the Upper City he addressed them as follows:

> You have come today to speak to me. What do you have left to save, after your Temple is lost to you? In whom do you still trust? Your people — slain by the sword. Your Temple — ruin and desolation. Your city — trodden under my feet. Even your very lives and souls are in my hands. If you will lay down your arms and surrender to me, I will let you stay alive (The Jewish Wars, 6:6).

The defenders chose not to fall into the merciless hands of Titus and his army and rejected his offer. Instead, they continued their preparations for defense, despite their sufferings from hunger. Yochanan and Shimon and their followers took up positions in Herod's palace, and the other defenders in other parts of the Upper City.

Before their impending assault on the Upper City the Roman soldiers went through the streets of the Lower City on a rampage of sword, fire, and destruction. No house was spared. They burned the Acra Fortress and the part of the city called the Ophel on the southeastern slopes of the Temple Mount. The houses filled with dead victims of starvation were set afire.

The Upper City was well-fortified and Titus was again forced to build ramps, bulwarks and towers to bring his war machines into effective range. On the seventh day of Elul, the battering rams and catapults began to pound at the walls. A few days later the walls were breached; the Romans stormed the city, and another bloodbath began. Many Zealots tried to avoid capture by hiding in subterranean caves and tunnels. But their fate was no better. Some of them died of hunger, others committed suicide, and a few who emerged to the surface were captured by the Romans. When Yochanan of Gush Chalav left his hideout, sick and broken by famine, he was taken alive. Shimon bar Giora tried to escape through one of Jerusalem's underground passages leading to the outside. But he was also taken alive. Both commanders were put in chains and brought to Rome, there to be displayed before the jeering masses at the triumphal procession in honor of Titus. Shimon died soon after, and Yochanan was imprisoned for life.

Ruthless Victors

The war was over. Jerusalem was almost totally destroyed. Hundreds of thousands of corpses, victims of the sword and of hunger, filled the desolate city which in the past had been known as the "Crown of Beauty" and the "Joy of the Earth." But even worse was the fate of the tens of thousands of its surviving sons and daughters. They moved like gaunt shadows in the squalor of the alleys or in the gloom of the underground tunnels until they collapsed or were captured by the Romans.

At Titus' orders all surviving fighters and those suspected of belonging to the Zealots were killed. The old and sick were next to be murdered. Young boys and girls were gathered on the Temple Mount and subjected to another selection. Those suspected of having in some way participated in the revolt against Rome were put to the sword. Those remaining were divided according to their physical appearance and strength: those over seventeen were sent as slave laborers to the copper mines of Egypt; younger ones were sold as slaves; the largest group was sent to the Greek cities on the coast, there to provide entertainment as the victims of gladiators and beasts in the bloodthirsty sports of the circus; and the last contingent, some 700 of the tallest, handsomest of Jerusalem's youths, was taken to Rome to be marched in Titus' victory parade.

During the days of the selection of the survivors, some 11,000 more perished of hunger.

According to Josephus, 1,100,000 Jews perished during the entire period of the siege and 97,000 were taken captive.

Thousands of captives from all over the land were taken by boat to Rome and other cities of the empire to be sold on the slave markets. Knowing that what awaited them as slaves was a life of forced immorality and other sins in violation of the Torah, many chose to die rather than live in sin.

The Talmud relates the story of one such group:

> Four hundred boys and girls were taken captive for a life of shame. When they realized what was in store for them they asked: "If we drown in the sea, do we have a share in the Resurrection of the Dead?" The oldest among them answered: "It is written, 'Hashem said: I will bring back from Bashan, I will bring back from the depths of the sea' (Psalms 68:23). 'I will bring back from Bashan' — this means from the teeth of the lion; 'from the depths of the sea' — this speaks of those who drown in the sea." As soon as the girls heard this they leaped into the sea. The boys reasoned that they should surely do so ... and they too leaped into the sea. Concerning such as these Scripture (Psalms 44:23) says: "For Your sake we are killed all day, we are accounted as sheep for the slaughter" (Gittin 57b).

Only very few fighters managed to escape from Jerusalem. They fled to the desert and took refuge mainly in three fortified places: Michvar in Transjordan, Herodium in the Judean desert, and Masada, overlooking the Dead Sea.

Titus departed from the land with the bulk of his army, leaving one legion behind him under Flavius Silva, with orders to liquidate the remaining nests of the rebels. In Herodium, the Jews were quickly forced to surrender. In Michvar, the Romans had to fight longer before they overcame the resistance. It was the conquest of Masada, however, for which they had to pay the highest price.

Masada, built by Herod, was a fortress of spectacular location. On top of a huge rock that was surrounded on all sides by steep slopes and deep valleys, it was protected by a wall which prevented rocks and arrows that were hurled from a distance to reach the interior. Here a few hundred fighters and their families — a total of 960 people — had found refuge.

The siege went on for years with the defenders holding out and beating off all Roman attempts to breach the fortress. The Romans surrounded Masada with a siege wall and towers to prevent anyone from escaping. The defenders had large stores of food and water. Their fortress included scrolls of the Torah and other books of the Tanach, a synagogue and *mikva'os* [ritual baths]. It seemed almost as if they could hold out forever.

The Romans saw no alternative but to build a ramp as high as the mountain itself, from which they could storm the fortress. The effort would require the movement of hundreds of tons of sand and rock, but the Romans were determined to wipe out all resistance. They built a ramp, signs of which are still clearly visible today, on the western side of the mountain. According to Josephus, the fortress was 300 cubits above the nearest Roman camp. The Romans built a 200-cubit ramp, upon which they built a fifty-cubit platform. Atop that they erected a sixty-cubit siege tower, its top standing approximately twenty feet above the walls of Masada.

During the siege the defenders of Masada built a wall of wood and earth within the existing stone wall, but the Romans managed to destroy it by hitting it with firebrands.

The invaders now had only to set the date for the attack to begin. But the option was snatched from them by the

Inside the thickness of the casemate wall — a fortified double wall housing within it scores of rooms — the defenders of Masada built themselves a mikveh. The archaelogist who discovered it immediately helicoptered two veteran Talmudic scholars from Jerusalem to the site to confirm the mikveh's halachic dimensions. Clearly seen here are the water conduit (1) through which rainwater collected from the roof reached the plastered storage pool (2); this was connected by a narrow hole with the smaller pool (3) used for ritual immersion. Near it is another small pool (4) used for washing oneself before entering the mikveh for purification. The arched opening (5) in the inner wall leads from the interior of the fortress to the mikveh.

decision that was made by the defenders. Under no circumstances would they fall into the cruel hands of the Romans; the enemy would have his victory over dead bodies. Every man would first kill his family and then by lot they would kill each other. On the next day the Romans entered Masada. They beheld a scene that was as ghastly as it was heroic: hundreds of men, women, and children lay in their blood — free Jews to the end. The only survivors were two old women and five children, who avoided the mass suicide by hiding in a cave. This happened on the first day of Pesach in the third year after the destruction of Jerusalem.

The Triumphal March in Rome

The Romans celebrated the victory over Judea with great pomp and ceremony. After attending some bestial festivities in Middle Eastern cities, during which thousands of Jewish captives were tortured and murdered savagely, Titus made his triumphal entry into Rome in the year 71 CE (3831). The Senate had decided to hold a special victory parade in his honor. Hundreds of the most beautiful young prisoners of war were made to march in the streets of Rome, while bearing on their shoulders the holy vessels of gold that had been robbed from the Temple in Jerusalem. The vessels were kept in the Temple of Jupiter in Rome, until the year 455 CE (4215), when the mighty capital was invaded and sacked by the Vandals. They plundered the city of all its treasures, including the Temple vessels, which they took with them to their capital, probably Carthage, in North Africa. Since then the whereabouts of the Temple vessels have been unknown.

A reminder of the victory parade may still be seen on the Arch of Titus, which was built in Rome in honor of the great victory. It depicts in stone relief the scene of Jewish captives carrying the holy *Menorah* on their backs. Also displayed in the victory parade were the two heroes of the resistance, Shimon ben Giora and

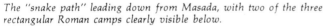

The "snake path" leading down from Masada, with two of the three rectangular Roman camps clearly visible below.

One of a series of bronze coins in which Vespasian celebrated his victory over Judea. Obverse: head of Vespasian, with long Latin inscription giving all his flamboyant titles, some in abbreviated form. Reverse: veiled figure of Judea seated in mourning under a palm tree, with Roman soldier standing proudly to the left, resting his foot on his helmet. This inscription can be read clearly: IUDEA CAPTA.

Yochanan of Gush Chalav. The climax of the celebration was held at the temple of Rome's idols, but by the time the celebrants arrived there, Shimon was dead. Yochanan spent the rest of his life in prison.

The importance that the Romans attached to their victory over the Jews may still be seen today in another way. They minted a special coin, one side of which shows the likeness of Emperor Vespasian's head, while the other side shows a woman whose hands are bound and who sits weeping under a palm tree. Behind her stands an armed Roman soldier. The inscription reads: "Iudea Capta" (Judea is Captured).

True, Judea was defeated by Rome, but the Jewish people were not. Just as the words of the prophecy, "And I will scatter you among the nations" (Leviticus 26:33), came true against the Jews, so did the words of consolation: "And I will remember My covenant with Jacob, and also My covenant with Isaac, and also My covenant with Abraham will I remember; and I will remember the Land" (ibid. v. 42). The Roman empire was destroyed by wild and primitive tribes and disappeared from the stage of human affairs. Only history books and ancient ruins remind us of her former existence and power. But the Jewish people lives on.

From Jerusalem to Yavneh

Before the destruction of Jerusalem, Rabban Yochanan ben Zakkai and his disciples were able to leave the doomed city and settle in Yavneh. Rabban Yochanan had asked of the Roman emperor: "Give me Yavneh and its Sages," a request that was granted.

Yavneh became the spiritual center of the people, and the secret of its survival. Rabban Yochanan ben Zakkai re-

That the mighty Roman Empire's conquest of Judea was hardwon achievement is proved by Rome's massive Arch of Titus, one panel of which represents the Menorah borne aloft in the Emperor's triumphal procession.

organized the Sanhedrin, which fixed the date of each new month and the time of each leap year. From Yavneh he sent instructions to the scattered Jewish communities in matters of law and observance, and Jews from all over the Diaspora turned to Yavneh for answers and advice. Without any formal declaration, Yavneh became the new center of the Jewish people.

G-d had caused the sun of Yavneh to rise before the sun of Jerusalem had set — it became a new national center and a new heart for all the scattered remnants of the Jewish people. Yavneh was the seat of the great *yeshivah* for the study and teaching of Torah, and for prayer, which now took the place of the sacrifices in the Temple, as the Prophet wrote: "Instead of oxen, we will offer the prayer of our lips" *(Hosea 14:3)*.

Thus Yavneh embodied the means by which G-d preserves His people even during the darkest and most dangerous times of our long exile, until the time comes when He, in His mercy, will redeem His people and restore us to our land, and our Holy Temple to Jerusalem — "speedily, in our days."

If a visitor to Damascus Gate in the walls of the Old City of Jerusalem looks down to his left before entering, he will see the northern entrance to Aelia Capitolina, the city which the Romans built on the ruins of destroyed Jerusalem. An inscription above the arched gate identifies it.

30

Babylonian Jewry

Originally they used to light torches (to announce the time of the New Moon to distant Jewish communities) ...

How did they light the torches? They would bring long poles of cedar wood, reeds, balsam wood, and fiberchips of flax. Someone would tie them together with rope, climb to the mountaintop, set fire to them, and wave it back and forth and up and down until he saw his colleague doing likewise on top of the second mountain, and so too, on top of the third mountain ... until he saw the entire Diaspora before him like a mass of fire (Mishnah Rosh HaShanah 2:2-4).

Babylonia — a Torah Center

In the previous chapters we have read about the stormy events that befell our forefathers during most of the Second Temple period. The external and internal wars severely interfered with the spiritual life of the people. The study of Torah suffered until at times it was nearly forgotten, and it was only due to the arrival of some outstanding Sages from Babylonia that the spiritual level in the Land was raised to its previous heights.

Looking back, we can observe the hand of G-d, for even before the Destruction of the First Temple, a group of Sages were exiled from Judea to Babylonia, together with King Yehoyachin, in 434 BCE (3327). These men established houses of learning and prayer which continued to flourish throughout all the years of the Second Temple and beyond — during the period of the *Tannaim* and *Amoraim* of the Talmud, and during the period of the *Geonim*. The pre-eminence of Babylonia lasted for nearly 1500 years, until the death of R' Hai Gaon in 1038 (4798).

It is true that with the arrival of Ezra and his followers Jerusalem had returned to its place of pre-eminence in Jewish life, and it was from there, and especially the Sanhedrin, that authoritative instructions went forth to Jews everywhere. Nevertheless, the study of Torah continued in Babylonia uninterrupted.

A close tie existed between the Jews of the two centers. All enactments of the Men of the Great Assembly and the decisions of the Sanhedrin were accepted without question by the Babylonian Jews, and every new explanation and interpretation of the Babylonian scholars in the field of Torah quickly came to the attention of their colleagues in the Land of Israel.

When the Sanhedrin proclaimed the beginning of a new month, messengers were sent out to the more remote communities, and fire signals were used to communicate the news to the Jews in Babylonia. In deliberating on whether to add a month to the year, the Sanhedrin considered whether bad weather would prevent the far-flung exiles from arriving in Jerusalem in time for the Pesach pilgrimage.

Every year the Babylonian Jews, like all their brethren, contributed half a shekel for the needs of the Temple. This amounted to large sums of money, and it was kept in well-fortified cities like Nehardea and Netzivin [Nisibis]. When the money was delivered to Jerusalem, it was accompanied by an armed escort of thousands to protect it against robbers on the way.

A number of Babylonian cities entered Jewish history because of their flourishing Jewish communities. Nehardea to the north was the closest to *Eretz Yisrael* and was the site of one of the world's great *yeshivos*. Sura and Masa Mechasya were major Jewish centers in the south of the country. Sura and its environs attracted many Jews when the government put two Jewish brothers — Chasinai and Chanilai — in control over the entire area — about 30-40 CE (3790-3800).

But this state of affairs was not to last very long. The two Jewish rulers and the prosperous Jewish community aroused the jealousy of the surrounding non-Jewish population. They banded together and attacked the Jewish communities of Sura and Masa Mechasya. Many Jews were killed, some escaped to the safety of Nehardea and Netzivin, and only few remained around Sura. Because they feared for their safety they endeavored to hide their religious observances from the suspicious eyes of their gentile neighbors and practiced their Jewishness secretly. This isolation and fear led to a situation in which even some of the laws of the Torah were forgotten. Only with the arrival of Rav, first and foremost of the Babylonian *Amoraim* [Talmudic teachers] approximately 120-150 years after the Destruction of the Holy Temple, did a new era of spiritual awakening come to the Jews of Sura.

Famous Personalities

Chasinai and Chanilai began their careers as workers for a weaver in Nehardea. When their employer grew angry with them and wanted to punish them they fled to the outskirts of the town. Soon they gathered around them a band of strong and embittered young men who began to impose terror upon the local residents.

The king of the Parthians heard about the two brothers and was impressed with their courage and ability. In order to enforce his own authority, he appointed them as governors of the Sura district, where they ruled for fifteen years, during which the gentiles did not dare to harm the Jews.

But power often corrupts. Chasinai took a non-Jewish wife, and when Chanilai rebuked him for it, the angry new wife poisoned him. From then the star of Chasinai began to fade. The surrounding tribes waged war against him and defeated him. Then the local residents attacked the Jewish community. Many refugees fled to the capital city, but there too they were persecuted, and escaped again. They finally came to Nehardea and Netzivin, both of which were fortified cities with large and powerful Jewish populations. There the fleeing Jews found a safe haven.

The Jews of Babylonia enjoyed considerable prestige and their influence extended even to the royal families. One such royal house was that of Adiabene, a vassal state of the Parthian kingdom of which Babylonia was a major part. Adiabene's rulers accepted the Jewish faith and later helped their coreligionists, in particular the Jews of the Holy Land.

The kingdom of Adiabene was situated in what was formerly known as Assyria, along the border between the Parthian kingdom and the Roman sphere of influence. Toward the end of the Second Temple period it was ruled by King Monobaz and his wife Helena. Their son, the crown prince Izates, was educated in a neighboring kingdom, where he met a Jewish merchant by the name of Chananiah, with the result that he converted to Judaism. His mother Queen Helena also became Jewish. When his father Monobaz died and Izates ascended the throne, the fact of his and his mother's conversion to Judaism became known. But this did not weaken his position; on the contrary, he even strengthened his rule.

Queen Helena left her homeland and lived out her life in *Eretz Yisrael*. A number of times our Sages mention the many deeds of lovingkindness that she and her elder son Monobaz II, successor and brother of Izates, did for the people in the Holy Land. Monobaz made the handles for the golden vessels used on Yom Kippur, and Helena made a gold chandelier for the entrance to the Temple. About twenty-five years before the Destruction, there was hunger in the land. Helena and Monobaz spent great sums of money to buy grain from Egypt and fruit from Cyprus to feed the hungry.

The Sages expressed extravagant praise for their generosity:

> The Sages taught: King Monobaz spent his fortunes and the fortunes of his forebears to feed the hungry in the years of drought. His brothers and his father's family rebuked him, "Your fathers saved, and added to the treasures of their fathers, while you squander them." He replied, "My fathers saved up for this World Below; I save up for the World Above ... My fathers preserved for this life, and I preserve for the life in the hereafter" (Bava Basra 11a).

After Helena's death and the death of her son, Izates, Monobaz II was king in Adiabene. He had his mother and his brother buried in the gravesite which she had prepared in Jerusalem. These graves have been discovered; they are not far from the Damascus Gate in the northern wall of the Old City, and are called "The Tombs of the Kings," or "The Cave of Kalba Savua." When Titus conquered Jerusalem, the children and relatives of Izates were in the city. They asked Titus for safe-conduct, but Titus had them bound and taken to Rome as hostages.

31

The Jewry of Egypt

Mishnah: The priests who served in the Temple of Chonyo [Onias] may not serve in the Temple of Jerusalem, and certainly not, if they had served something else [i.e., idolatry] ...

Gemara: Since the Mishnah adds, "if they had served idolatry," it is clear that in the Temple of Chonyo there was no idolatrous worship (Menachos 109a,b).

The Jewish Exiles in Egypt

In the latter days of the First Temple, Pharoah Nechoh invaded Judea. He conquered Jerusalem and exiled King Yehoachaz to Egypt. The unfortunate king certainly did not meet any Jews in Egypt, for the Torah had forbidden the return to that land: "You shall henceforth no more return that way" *(Deuteronomy* 17:16). Thus Yehoachaz lived and died there in isolation.

After Yehoachaz's exile, Babylonia became the dominant power. Its ruler, King Nebuchadnezzar, conquered *Eretz Yisrael* and exiled a Jewish king — Yehoyachin — but he did not go to Babylonia alone. With him went a large group of leading Jews and scholars, who laid the foundations for the long-lasting and flourishing Jewish community of Babylonia.

Later, in the Second Temple period, many Jews left their homeland and settled in Egypt. But, as we shall see, they did not develop a meaningful Jewish life there, as a result of which many of them assimilated in the course of time and became lost to their people.

After the First Temple was destroyed and after the assassination of Gedaliah ben Achikam, the governor of Judea, the prophet Yirmeyahu brought G-d's message to the remnant of Jews in the Holy Land:

If you are determined to go to Egypt and to settle there, then it shall come to pass that the sword which you fear shall overtake you in the land of Egypt, and the famine about which you worry shall pursue you in Egypt, and there you will die (Jeremiah 42:15-16).

But the voice of stubborn and short-sighted men proved to be stronger. They influenced and forced the entire people, including even Yirmeyahu and his disciple Baruch ben Neriah, to go down to Egypt. There they settled in Migdol,

Tachpanches, Noph, and Pasros. The exiled people continued to ignore Yirmeyahu, who spoke to them in the name of G-d. Instead of recognizing their misfortunes as a divine punishment for their past misdeeds they turned to the local idols, believing that their salvation would come from them.

Now the predictions of Yirmeyahu came true. Nebuchadnezzar and his army conquered Egypt, and most of the Jews who had settled there perished. Among the few who escaped the sword were Yirmeyahu and Baruch ben Neriah, who made their way to Babylonia and joined their brethren there.

It is likely that some of the Jews who survived the war and who felt unsafe in their own communities moved to the southern part of Egypt, where they joined military colonies that were stationed there to guard the border. Relics of such a Jewish military colony were discovered in the beginning of this century in the town of Elephantine [Yev] in Upper Egypt, not far from the present Aswan Dam. In those days documents were written on the tough leaves of the papyrus plant. For two-and-a-half thousand years the hot and dry climate of Egypt preserved a rich variety of documents, which include a letter of the Jewish community of Elephantine asking the governor of the province of Judea to allow them to rebuild their local temple that had been destroyed by gentiles.

Community and Temple of Alexandria

When he founded Alexandria, Alexander of Macedonia encouraged Jews to settle in the city, together with members of other nations and sects, as part of his vision of unifying the population of his mighty empire.

Some time later, when Ptolemy I conquered Jerusalem, he took many Jews captive and settled them in Alexandria. Ptolemy II freed them and showed them a friendly attitude. It was he who commissioned the Septuagint, the first Greek translation of the *Chumash*.

The Jewish community kept growing until, by the end of the Second Temple era, it constituted a third of Alexandria's population. But its influence on the economic, administrative, and cultural life of the general community was felt far out of proportion to their numbers. Among the Jewish residents were wealthy businessmen and even high-ranking military officers. Their artisans were famous for their crafts, and they even produced items for the Temple in Jerusalem. When a wealthy Jew named Nikanor wanted to contribute two ornate gates for the Temple in Jerusalem, he had them made in Alexandria.

In the Ptolemaic period Alexandria was the center of Hellenism in the Middle East. It was not the classical Hellenism of Greece, but rather a mixture of Greek learning with the spirit and culture of the various peoples of the East. This Hellenism was well developed in science, the arts and technology, but its morality was on a low level and it had a bad effect on the nations of the East.

The civil rights that the Jews enjoyed brought them into open contact with their non-Jewish environment, and opportunities for assimilation increased. First, they learned Greek, until gradually it replaced Hebrew as their own mother tongue. Indeed, they even began studying the Torah from the Greek translation. With many Jews one step led to the next on the road to assimilation among the Egyptian idolaters. A large part of them remained loyal to the traditions of their people, as is proved by the number of their synagogues, particularly the main synagogue, which was renowned for its size and beauty.

The leading Hellenists of *Eretz Yisrael* studied in Alexandria, especially in the court of Ptolemy, where they learned the ways of the Greeks, and later attempted to impose them on the inhabitants of Judea with the help of Antiochus.

During the oppressive rule of Antiochus Epiphanes in the period before the Chanukah miracle, Chonyo [Onias] IV, left Jerusalem and went to Alexandria. His father, Chonyo III, was the last High Priest of the House of Tzadok who lived up to his high position faithfully.

Chonyo left Jerusalem because he could no longer tolerate the desecration of the High Priesthood and of the Holy Temple itself. He built a temple in Heliopolis, near Alexandria. In this he was supported by King Ptolemy VI, who wanted to weaken the bonds unifying the Jews of Egypt with their fellow Jews in the Land of Israel.

Chonyo's motivation in building this temple is not quite clear. Perhaps he thought that the desecration of the Temple in Jerusalem removed its holiness; hence it would be permissible to erect a "high place" [*bamah*] for sacrificial service in another place. Or perhaps he did it to satisfy his ambition to be a *Kohen Gadol*. At any rate the Sages, as we have seen in the introductory passage to this chapter, did not approve of it. Their attitude to the synagogue in Alexandria was entirely different.

Many Egyptian Jews filled important positions in the public life of their host country, and from time to time they used their influence to help their fellow Jews in Judea. When Queen Cleopatra of Egypt planned to go to war against Alexander Yannai in order to bring Judea under her control, her army was headed by Chilkiyah and Chananiah, the sons of Onias IV, who built the Temple in Heliopolis. Chananiah succeeded in dissuading the queen from her intention by telling her: "You should realize that such a wrong will turn all the Jews into your enemies."

Anti-Semitic Outbursts against Jews of Alexandria

The wealth and influence of the Alexandrian Jews was a thorn in the eyes of the non-Jewish inhabitants. Jealousy and religious intolerance combined to create a climate of hatred against the Jews. All that was lacking was a spark to make the hatred burst into the open. When it came, the hatred exploded with frightening fury and cruelty.

The first occasion was when Agrippa I passed through Alexandria on his way from Rome to Jerusalem to assume the kingship over the northern part of the land of Israel. The Jews of Alexandria received him with great joy and honor. The happiness of the Jews aroused jealousy among the anti-Semites, who publicly ridiculed the Jews and "their king." They incited the masses, who promptly broke into the synagogues and set up statues of their idols. Responding to the mood of the mob, the government decreed that the Jews were no longer full and equal citizens.

This was a signal to the anti-Semites that they had the approval of the government. They expelled the Jews from their living quarters and concentrated them in one neighborhood — the first ghetto in Jewish history. Then they ransacked their former residences and stores, and Jews whom they met on the way were stoned and beaten to death. This was the first pogrom, and it was not the last.

Following the pogrom — the year was 40 CE (3800) — the Alexandrian Jews sent a delegation to Rome to beg the Emperor Caligula to cancel the decrees of the head authorities and to restore their rights and privileges. The delegation was headed by Philo, the universally famous Jewish philosopher.

To counter the plea of the Jewish delegation, the gentiles of Alexandria also sent a delegation to Rome. Caligula listened to Philo's delegation with contempt and gave the gentiles a sympathetic hearing. The emperor disdainfully rejected Philo and sided with his enemies, but relief came to the Jews from another source. Caligula died a year later, and his successor Claudius restored to the Jews of Alexandria their former civil status.

Philo and other Jewish scholars wrote many books in defense of the Jewish people and its religion. They tried to prove that the basic beliefs and concepts of the Jewish religion can be reconciled and harmonized with the fundamentals of Greek philosophy and Hellenistic culture. But to do this, they distorted facts of Jewish history and articles of belief. Moreover, their efforts proved to be fruitless; the gentiles were not impressed with the Jewish philosophers, and even if they were, they did not change their age-old hostile attitude toward the Jews and their religion.

The Destruction of the Temple in Jerusalem had tragic aftereffects on Egyptian Jewry. Perhaps influenced by Jerusalem's revolt against Rome, the Alexandrian Jews rioted. The riot was precipitated by constant attacks on the Jews by the city's Greek citizens. The Roman governor at the time was Tiberius Alexander — a nephew of Philo — who renounced Judaism and became a bitter enemy of his former people. He ordered two Roman legions to storm and plunder the Delta, as the Jewish quarter of Alexandria was called. Fifty thousand Jews were killed in the battle. After the Destruction of the Temple in Jerusalem, Chonyo's temple at Heliopolis was destroyed, in 73 CE (3833).

The decimation of Jewish Alexandria was completed between 115 and 117 CE (3875-3877), when there was widespread unrest among Jews in the Roman empire. The Emperor Trajan took advantage of the situation to launch a murderous attack on the embattled Jewish community of Alexandria.

Babylonia and Alexandria — Lessons for the Future

The last two chapters gave us a picture of the two largest Jewish centers outside the Holy Land: Babylonia and Egypt. There were dramatic differences in the lifestyle of these two communities. The Jews of Egypt, particularly of Alexandria, strove to master the culture of the surrounding non-Jews and nourish themselves with it. They used their civil rights as a stepping-stone to their integration with Hellenistic culture, whether in commerce, culture, administration, or military life. And they did indeed reach high positions in society. But ironically, their very success turned into a stumbling block and brought repeated disaster upon them.

Like a magnet, their rising power attracted the jealousy of their gentile neighbors; anti-Semitic rabble-rousers exploited these feelings; there were violent attacks on Jews, sometimes with the hope of plunder. The final result was the reduction of flourishing Jewish communities in Alexandria and in other cities of Egypt to small surviving groups of impoverished Jews. Their efforts in philosophy and literature, designed to find favor in the eyes of the gentiles, turned out to be an illusion. Neither did the Jewish people derive any real value from these writings.

The Jews of Babylonia present an entirely different picture. They did not assimilate with their surrounding non-Jewish environment, but rather maintained and cultivated their own unique way of life, for: "Behold, this is a people that shall dwell alone, and shall not be reckoned among the nations" (Numbers 23:9). Whatever civil rights they were given by non-Jewish rulers they utilized to better develop their own communal life.

And thus, except for occasional periods of political upheaval and persecution, for some 1500 years they succeeded in persevering and maintaining, even in exile, a major center of Torah learning and observance. Even after the decline of the Babylonian gaonate with the death of R' Hai Gaon, the Babylonian Jewish community remained strong and loyal, until very recent times.

The Traditional Jewish Chronology

by Rabbi Hersh Goldwurm

The dates in this volume are based primarily on the traditional chronology given in the *Seder Olam,* an authoritative work dating back to Talmudic times, and, of course, on the Talmud itself. Based on Scriptural and Rabbinic sources, *Seder Olam* is founded on an uninterrupted tradition and forms the basis for such halachic determinations as the dating of *Shemittah.* Secular historians, however, have adopted a sharply divergent chronological system for the period covered in this book. They date the destruction of the First Temple and the construction of the Second Temple 167 years earlier than does *Seder Olam* and all other traditional Jewish sources.

Secular history identifies 538 BCE (3223) as the year Cyrus conquered the Babylonian Empire, while our tradition puts this event at 371 BCE (3390). As Scripture states clearly *(Ezra* 1:1ff and *II Chronicles* 23:22-3), it was in the first year of Cyrus' reign that the Jewish exiles were permitted to return to Jerusalem. Cyrus'

reign began a year after he and Darius the Mede conquered Babylon (see *Daniel* 9:2 with *Rashi, Megillah* 12a, and *Seder Olam* ch. 28-29). Eighteen years after that, the Second Temple was built (see *Seder Olam* ch. 30, *Megillah* 11b). Jewish tradition also states frequently and unequivocally that the Second Temple stood for 420 years (see *Seder Olam* ch. 30); *Arachin* 12b et. al). According to the secular dating of Cyrus' victory, the Second Temple era would have had to be far, far longer than that ascribed to it by every Talmudic source.

Another discrepancy involves the duration of Persian domination of the near East. In the Rabbinic tradition, Persian rule spanned the relatively brief period of fifty-two years, from 370-318 BCE (3391-3443),[1] thirty-four of these years being after the construction of the Second Temple (see *Seder Olam* ch. 30, *Avodah Zarah* 9a). Secular history assigns 208 years to Persia, from 538-330 BCE (3223-3431).[2] According to this latter version, ten Persian kings reigned during those years: Cyrus the

---

1. The year 371 BCE (3390), when Cyrus conquered Babylonia, is counted by the Rabbinic tradition as the last year of the Babylonian dynasty. In other words, the first *full* year of Persian domination was 370 BCE (3391). It is important to note that the dates given in this appendix follow the current Hebrew calendar, which adds one year to those found in the Talmud and *Seder Olam.* The reason for this is explained in the appendix: "Year of the Destruction."

2. According to the Talmudic account *(Avodah Zarah* 10a), the year 318 BCE (3443) is the year of Alexander's conquest of Elam, which is the Kuzistan of modern Iran and the province that contained the Shushan of the *Book of Esther.* This victory marked the end of the Persian Empire. Thus, its fifty-two years lasted from 370-318 BCE (3391-3443). We may assume that the "conquest of Elam" corresponds to what secular history describes as the defeat and death of Darius III in Persia, which modern historians date at 330 BCE. Thus, since secular historians use 538 BCE for the year Cyrus conquered Babylonia, they arrive at 208 years for the Persian Empire, from 538-330 BCE (3223-3431).

Great, Cambyses II, Darius I, Xerxes I, Artaxerxes I, Xerxes II, Darius II, Artaxerxes II, Artaxerxes III and Darius III. Jewish tradition, however, recognizes no more than four Persians as rulers of the entire known civilized world: Cyrus, Achashvairosh [Ahasuerus], Darius, and possibly Cambyses. Such discrepancies make it most difficult to assign events recorded only in secular history (such as the Persian and Pelloponnesian wars) to their proper time slot in the framework of traditional Jewish chronology.

This discrepancy has been noted by numerous Jewish scholars throughout the centuries, who have insisted that the traditional chronology is incontrovertibly supported by Scripture.[3]

Don Isaac Abarbanel (in his comm. to Daniel, Mayenei HaYeshuah, maayan 2, tamar 3) suggests that some of the Persian kings mentioned in the ancient sources may have ruled Persia prior to its conquest of Babylonia. The Talmudic reference to a fifty-two year Persian hegemony, however, refers only to the years when Persia ruled the former Babylonian Empire.

As in all such cloudy areas, it is essential — but difficult — for modern people to understand that the everyday historical tools we take for granted simply did not exist in ancient times. We, who know that World War II broke out in 1939 (5699) or that the Six Day War took place in 1967 (5727) find it hard to understand how there could be such gaping discrepancies regarding the years of such major epochs as the Second Temple and Persian Empire eras. However, in ancient times, events were dated from the year a king assumed the throne. When a new man became king, it was as if the world had been created anew, and all documents were dated from the year 1 again. Furthermore, people did not think of their own countries as part of a large world; to a Persian, his country was the only one that mattered, whether Persia was a province or the globe's mightiest empire. As country after country assumed center stage as the most powerful, each tended to impose its own version of events upon its victims. The result has been a scarcity of historical material and the dilemma of choosing between conflicting versions. If modern scholars disagree sharply on lavishly documented events that occurred within memory, how much more so must we realize that events of two thousand years ago and more are far from clear. On the other hand, none of the ancient documents have the authority or were as scrupulously preserved by so many multitudes as the Tanach, Seder Olam, and the Talmud.

---

3. R' Saadiah Gaon (Emunos V'Deos, near end of maamar 8); R' Yaakov Emden, in his glosses to Seder Olam, comments: "Those who assume that the Second Temple stood longer than 420 years are forced to contradict the simple meaning of Scripture." See also Tzemach David, part I, year 3448 s.v. אמר המחבר; Maharal MiPrague, Be'er HaGolah, end of be'er 6; Igros Chazon Ish part I §206.

Year of the Destruction

by Rabbi Hersh Goldwurm

In this book we identify 70 CE (3830 from creation) as the year in which the Second Temple was destroyed. This designation is based on the Talmudic statement in *Taanis* 29a and *Arachin* 11b (see also *Seder Olam Rabbah* ch. 30) that seems to describe the Destruction as occurring the year after *Shemittah* [the Sabbatical year]. This is the interpretation followed by *Rashi, Tosafos* (*Avodah Zarah* 9b, s.v. האי), and most other commentators. The halachically accepted calculation of *Shemittah* that has been in use since Talmudic times — and must therefore be regarded as accurate — is given by *Rambam (Hil. Shemittah V'Yovel* 10:5-6). According to this calculation, *Shemittah* occurs in every year in the Jewish calendar that is divisible by seven. Consequently, the year 69 CE (3829) was a *Shemittah* and, since the Destruction occurred the next year, it took place in the year 70.[1] This dating of the Destruction is supported by Josephus, who was an eyewitness to the event.

Although *Rashi* and *Tosafos* agree that the Destruction took place a year after *Shemittah,* they do not agree that it took place in the year 70. *Rashi (Avodah Zarah* 9b and *Arachin* 12b) holds that the Destruction took place in 68 (3828) and *Tosafos* (loc. cit.) holds that it happened in 69 (3829).[2]

It should be noted, however, that although *Tosafos* uses the year 69, this probably does not contradict our thesis that it happened in 70. This is because the calendrical system used by the *Gemara* and *Seder Olam* varies by one year from the one in common use. As pointed out by R' Saadiah Gaon and R' Hai Gaon (cited in *Sefer HaIbbur* by *R' Avraham bar Chiya, Maamar* 6, ch. 7), the chronological computation of the *Gemara* and *Seder Olam* uses the creation of Adam as its starting date. However, the universally held Hebrew calendar begins a year earlier, from 1 Tishrei of the year preceding creation.[3] Accordingly, in our

1. Strangely, *Rambam's* figures (*Hil. Shemittah V'Yovel* 10:4) put the Destruction at 69 (3829) — in the *Shemittah* year. *Kessef Mishnah* notes that this view is contradicted by *Avodah Zarah* 9b. He concludes that *Rambam* must have had a different version of the Talmudic passage.

2. The dispute between *Rashi* and *Tosafos* is based on the following: All agree that the Second Temple was built in 3408 (in *Seder Olam's* chronology) and stood for 420 years. *Rashi* holds it was destroyed in the 420th year of its existence (i.e., in 3828); *Tosafos* holds it was destroyed after 420 *full* years — i.e. in the 421th year. However, according to the calendrical system we are about to describe, the Destruction may well have been in 3830, according to *Tosafos.*

3. The year before creation is known in halachic literature as שְׁנַת תֹּהוּ, *Year of the Void.* Although nothing had yet been created, that year is presumed to have existed for purposes of reckoning the *molad* (new moon). As students of the Hebrew calendar know, the very first *molad* of the calendar system in use today is calculated from the Year of the Void. Furthermore, Adam was created on Rosh Chodesh Tishrei, while the previous five days of creation took place at the end of the Year of the Void. Therefore, it is not surprising that that year is part of our calendar.

calendar we must add one year to the dates given by the Talmud and *Seder Olam;* for example, Adam was created in the year 1 according to the Talmudic calendar, but in the year 2 according to ours. Thus, the year 3829 adopted by *Tosafos* as the year of the Destruction would be translated as 3830 in our calendar, meaning that there is no discrepancy between the year as defined by *Tosafos* and the year we arrived at based on *Rambam. Rashi's* view, however, remains difficult: According to his chronology, the Destruction could not have taken place a year after the halachically accepted *Shemittah,* and the *Shemittah* of that period must be presumed to have occurred one year earlier than accepted by tradition (see *Tos. Avodah Zarah* 9b).

This thesis regarding the calendar is developed by R' Levi ibn Chaviv (a major fifteenth century halachic authority) in a lengthy responsum dealing with the determination of the *Shemittah* year *(She'elos u'Teshuvos Ralbach* §143, p. 50-1 in ed. Lemberg). His formulation is the basis for the *Shemittah* year accepted by universal tradition, which seems to be one year later than that indicated by the Talmud in the above cited passage. Thus, such events as the Exodus, Destruction of the First Temple and so on must be dated one year later than the traditionally accepted dates given in *Seder Olam.*

Chronology of Events

by Rabbi Hersh Goldwurm

	From creation	BCE
Battle of Gaza; Seleucus controls Syria and Babylonia	3449	312
End of wars among Alexander's successors	3460	301
Rule of Ptolemy II; the Torah translated (Septuagint)	3476-3515	285-246
Egyptian king appoints Yosef ben Toviah tax collector	c. 3536	225
Seleucid monarchy occupies *Eretz Yisrael*	3562	199
Pagan idol set up in Temple	*25 Kislev 3594	168
Miracle of Chanukah	*25 Kislev 3597	165
Death of Yehudah	3601	160
Yonasan becomes *Kohen Gadol;* pact with Alexander Balas	*3609	153
Death of Yonasan	3618	143
Shimon rules and gains Judean independence	3619	142
Expulsion of traitors from Acra fortress	3620	141
Shimon proclaimed *Nasi* and *Kohen Gadol*	3621	140
Death of Shimon	3626	135
Rule of Yochanan Hyrkanus	3626-3657	135-104
Rule of Yehudah Aristobulus	3657-3658	104-103
Rule of Alexander Yannai	3658-3685	103-76
Rule of Salome Alexandra	3685-3695	76-66
Civil War: Hyrkanus vs. Aristobulus	3698	63
Pompey intervenes; Judea becomes Roman Vassal	3698	63
Conquest of Jerusalem by Pompey	3698	63
The Triumvirate — Caesar, Pompey, Crassus	3701	60
Abolition of the Great *Sanhedrin* by Gabinius	3704	57
Crassus robs the Temple treasury	3707	54
Civil War: Caesar vs. Pompey	3712	49
Aristobulus dies during Caesar-Pompey war	3712	49
Death of Alexander, son of Aristobulus	3712	49
Caesar victor at Pharsalus	3713	48
Caesar appoints Antipater ruler of Judea	3714	47

*The events of the dates marked with an asterisk occurred after Rosh Hashanah but before January (Kislev in the cases of the idol and Chanukah, and Tishrei in the case of Yehudah). Therefore, although the new Hebrew year had already begun, the year BCE had not. This explains, for example, why a comparison of the dates given for the Seleucid monarchy occupation and the idol in the Temple shows that the idol was emplaced *nineteen* years later in the Hebrew chronology, but *twenty* years later in the years BCE. This is because the new Hebrew year had begun in Tishrei; but the secular year would not begin until January.

Antipater appoints Herod ruler of Galilee	3714	47
Caesar assassinated by Brutus and Cassius	3717	44
Antipater cooperates with Cassius after Caesar's death	3719	42
Death of Antipater	3719	42
Antony and Octavian defeat Brutus and Cassius at Philippi	3719	42
Antigonus and Parthians lose Jerusalem to Herod and Romans	3725	36
Antony renews war against Parthians	3725	36
Battle of Actium; Octavian defeats Antony	3730	31
Octavian confirms Herod's rule	3731	30
Attempted revolt against Herod	3737	24
Assassination of Miriam's sons	3753-3754	7-8
Death of Herod	3757	4
Rule of Archelaus	3757-3766	4-6 CE

	From creation	CE
Rule of the high commissioners begins	3766	6
Death of Augustus Caesar	3774	14
Agrippa rules over Bashan, Hauran and Argov	3797	37
Galilee and Transjordan annexed to Agrippa's domain	3798	38
Caligula's decree concerning the statue	3800	40
Caligula's death; Claudius crowns Agrippa king of Judea	3801	41
Death of Agrippa	3804	44
Nero denies citizen's rights to Jews of Caesarea	Iyar, 3826	66
Florus' soldiers riot in Jerusalem	Iyar, 3826	66
Florus and his soldiers banished from Jerusalem	Sivan, 3826	66
Battle in Jerusalem between Zealots and Agrippa's men	Av-Elul, 3826	66
Jewish victory over Cestius	Cheshvan, 3827	66
Siege of Yodefat	25 Iyar 3827	67
Yodefat falls	1 Tamuz 3827	67
Conquest of Gamala	23 Tishrei 3828	67
Internecine strife in Jerusalem	Winter of 3828	67-68
Vespasian takes Gadara	4 Adar 3828	68
Shimon bar Giora enters Jerusalem	3 Nissan 3829	69
Further internecine strife in Jerusalem	3829-3830	69-70
Vespasian declared emperor by his troops	3829	July 69
Vitellius killed	3830	Dec. 69
Vespasian departs for Rome	3830	Jan. 70
Titus takes up siege of Jerusalem	Nissan 3830	70
Romans penetrate the new city	Iyar 3830	70
Antonia is razed; Romans enter Temple Mount	17 Tamuz 3830	70
Temple set on fire	9 Av 3830	70
Romans enter lower city and set it on fire	11 Av 3830	70
Upper city falls	8 Elul 3830	70

A Note on Calculating Years

In determining dates of the period discussed in this book, it is usually necessary to compute the years from Creation to BCE and vice-versa. In doing so, the reader must bear in mind a mathematical quirk: there is no year 0 in the secular calendar. By way of illustration let us take the five years beginning 3762/2 CE.

From Creation		
3762	=	2 CE
3761	=	1 CE
3760	=	1 BCE
3759	=	2 BCE
3758	=	3 BCE

Notice that the year before 1 CE is not 0, but 1 BCE. In other words, if we were determining the dates in the above illustration by simple arithmetic, our answer would be off by one year. If we subtract 4 years from 2 CE, simple subtraction would yield 2 BCE [2−4=−2], but the true answer is 3 BCE, as the above table illustrates.

Therefore, whenever calculating from CE to BCE by means of simple subtraction, 1 year must be added to the BCE total. Likewise, when adding years from BCE to CE, 1 year must be added to the total.

Seleucid Dynasty*

		From creation	BCE
Seleucus I Nicator		3449-3480	312-281
Antiochus I Soter		3480-3499	281-262
Antiochus II Theos		3499-3515	262-246
Seleucus II Callinicus		3515-3535	246-226
Seleucus III Soter		3535-3538	226-223
Antiochus III the Great (son of Seleucus II)		3538-3574	223-187
Seleucus IV Philopater		3574-3586	187-175
Antiochus IV Epiphanes (son of Antiochus III)		3586-3598	175-163
Antiochus V Eupator		3598-3600	163-161
Demetrius I Soter (son of Seleucus IV)		3600-3609	161-152
Alexander Balas (impostor)		3609-3614	152-147
Demetrius II Nicator (son of Demetrius II)	throne	3614-c. 3621	147-140
Antiochus VI Dionysius (son of Alexander)	in	3615-3619	146-142
Diodotus-Tryphon (usurper)	contention	3619-3624	142-137
Antiochus VII Sidetes (son of Demetrius I)		3621-3632	147-129
Demetrius II Nicator (regained throne)		3632-3635	129-126
Antiochus VIII Gryphus		3636-3665	125-96
Antiochus IX Cyzicenus (son of Antiochus VII)		3648-3666	113-95
Demetrius III Eucerus (son of Antiochus VIII)		3685-3673	96-88

*Unless otherwise indicated, each king is the son of his predecessor.

Ptolemaic Dynasty*

	From creation	BCE
Ptolemy I Soter	3438-3476	323-285
Ptolemy II Philadelphus	3476-3515	285-246
Ptolemy III Euergetes	3515-3540	246-221
Ptolemy IV Philopator	3540-3556	221-205
Ptolemy V	3556-3581	205-180
Ptolemy VI Philometor	3581-3616	180-145
(Ptolemy VI and VII co-rulers)	(3591-3597)	(170-164)
Ptolemy VII Physcon	3616-3645	145-116
Ptolemy VIII Lathyrus	3645-3654	116-107
Ptolemy IX Alexander (brother of Ptolemy VIII)	3654-3673	107-88
Ptolemy VIII Lathyrus (regained throne)	3673-3680	88-81
Ptolemy X Alexander (son of Ptolemy IX)	3681	80
Ptolemy XI Auletes (son of Ptolemy VIII)	3681-3703; 3706-3710	80-58; 55-51
Ptolemy XII	3710-3714	51-47
Ptolemy XIII (brother of Ptolemy XII)	3714-3717	47-44

*Unless otherwise indicated, each king is the son of his predecessor.

Roman Emperors Until the Destruction of the Temple

	From creation	CE
Augustus	3731-3774	30 BCE-14 CE
Tiberius	3774-3797	14-37
Gaius Caligula	3797-3801	37-41
Claudius	3801-3814	41-54
Nero	3814-3828	54-68
Galba	3828-3829	June 68-Jan. 69
Otho	3829	Jan. 69-Apr. 69
Vitellius	3829-3830	Apr. 69-Dec. 69
Vespasian	3830-3839	Dec. 69-79

Roman High Commissioners

Coponius	3766-3769	6-9	Fadus	3804-3806	44-46
Ambivius	3769-3772	9-12	Alexander	3806-3808	46-48
Rufus	3772-3775	12-15	Cumanus	3808-3812	48-52
Gratus	3775-3786	15-26	Felix	3812-3820	52-60
Pilate	3786-3796	26-36	Festus	3820-3822	60-62
Marcellus	3796-3797	36-37	Albinus	3822-3824	62-64
Marullus	3797-3801	37-41	Florus	3824-3826	64-66

INDEX

Names of People: Names of Biblical personalities are usually given in three forms — Hebrew, English transliteration and the names commonly used in Bible translations. Examples are

Rechavam [Rehoboam] רְחַבְעָם 24, 89

Javan [Yavan] יָוָן 42

Please note that in most cases we have preferred the transliterated Hebrew name as the major entry for Jews, and the commonly used names for gentiles. This follows the style of the text.

Omitted Items: Certain items appear so often that it becomes ludicrous to enter them into the index. Thus, words like *Beis HaMikdash* (Holy Temple), *Eretz Yisrael* (Land of Israel), Jews, Jerusalem, Judea, are not in the index.

Glossary: Some Hebrew terms have been mentioned in the text without explanation. Definitions for the least common of them have been entered in this index.